IMAGES
of America

ALAMOGORDO

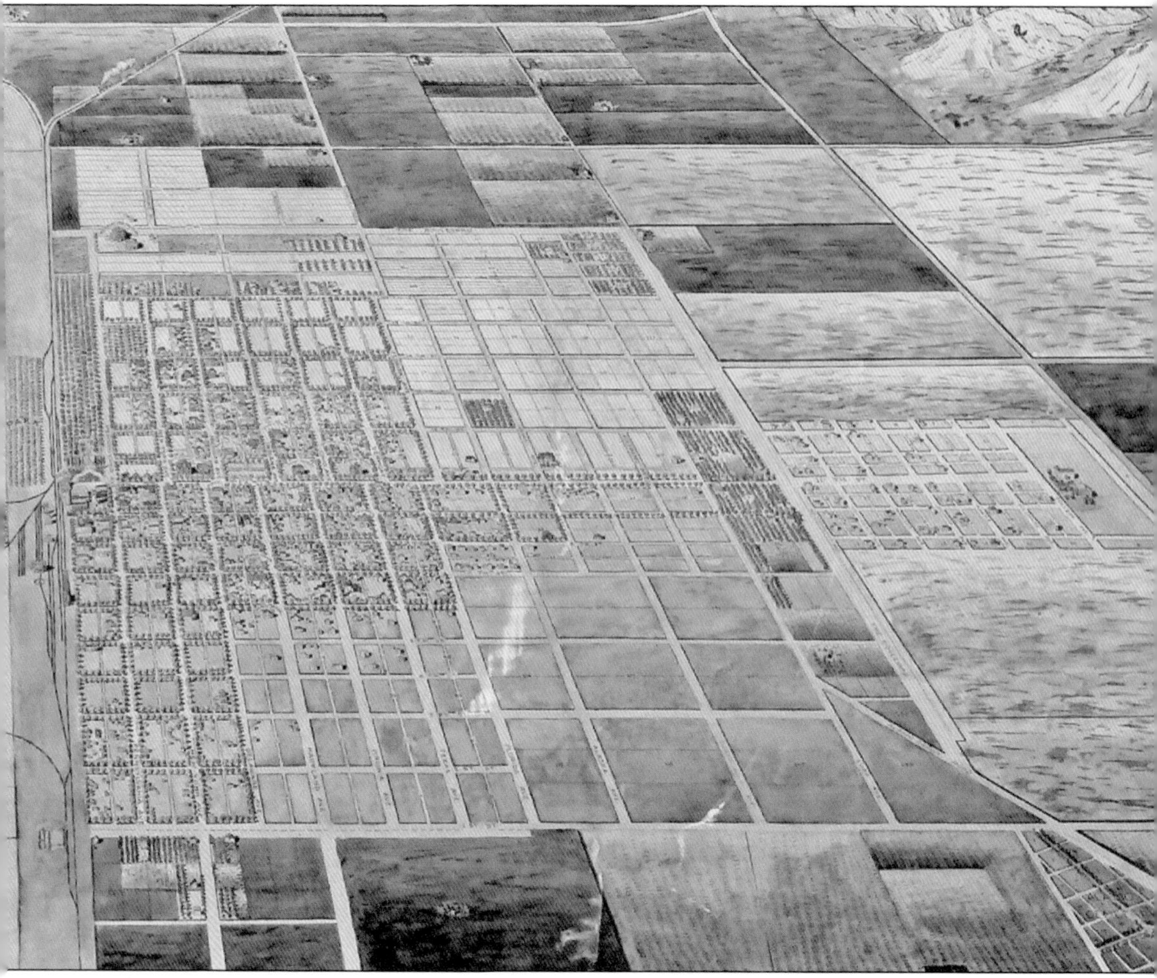

The city of Alamogordo, New Mexico, at "Sweet 16," looking north, is depicted in a 1914 original watercolor by Harry A. Chandler of Deming, New Mexico. This detailed map was donated to the Tularosa Basin Historical Society in 2009 by Bank 34. (Courtesy of the Tularosa Basin Historical Society.)

On the Cover: The first Alamogordo eighth grade graduating class of 1910 stands at the edge of the Alameda Park pond. The class included, from left to right, (first row) Herbert Shelton and Conway Pierce; (second row) Effie Dodgen, John Turner, Llewellyn Sutton, Lee Walker, Effie Latham, Virgie Wooten, Elmo Haynes, Celesta ?, Bill Woods, Ankie Oliver, Clair Fetzer, ?, and Louise Ben ?. (Courtesy of the Tularosa Basin Historical Society.)

IMAGES
of America

ALAMOGORDO

Peter Eidenbach

ARCADIA
PUBLISHING

ISBN 978-0-7385-8451-5

Published by Arcadia Publishing
Charleston, South Carolina

Printed in the United States of America

Library of Congress Control Number: 2009942098

For all general information contact Arcadia Publishing at:
Telephone 843-853-2070
Fax 843-853-0044
E-mail sales@arcadiapublishing.com
For customer service and orders:
Toll-Free 1-888-313-2665

Visit us on the Internet at www.arcadiapublishing.com

This volume is dedicated to the people of Alamogordo and Otero County who tamed this vast unknown wilderness in the late 19th century and who "climbed for water and dug for wood."

Contents

Acknowledgments

Many people provided inspiration and contributed family photographs to make this project possible. Eugene Manlove Rhodes, who first captured the essence of the city; W. H. Hutchinson, who helped us remember Rhodes; C. L. "Doc" Sonnichsen, the original "grassroots historian;" and members of the original pioneering families were the inspiration. Special thanks to my wife and partner, Sara, and the Wood, Potter, Baca, Gililland, Tucker, and Miller families.

Once again, the author was volunteered by his good friend and colleague David Townsend, professor emeritus, New Mexico State University Alamogordo, and Dave's partner in crime Clif McDonald. Thanks, Dave and Clif!

Thanks again to my home institution New Mexico State University Alamogordo, a true community of scholars, and to my institutional collaborators: the Tularosa Basin Historical Society (TBHS), The Sacramento Mountains Historical Society (SMHC), the TVHS (TVHS), the Historical Center of Southeastern New Mexico (HCSNM), and the Artesia Museum, who so generously shared their collections.

Special thanks to Sue Watkins, Jim Snyder, and the Van Winkle clan who got me started with the murals in the IGA Supermarket (now Lowe's) and all those who contributed images for this and the earlier Visual History Project. So many people shared their family photographs, and I'll undoubtedly forget to name a few—my deepest apologies. Many thanks to Davis Baca, Clif, June Harwell, Cynthia Prelo-Reidlinger, the Bellows family, the Mackinsons, Orpha Wingfield, Don and Ernie Lee Miller, Marjorie Curtis, Emily Watson, Beth Mahill, Michael and Millicent Shyne, Billie Pender, Harry and Virginia Wilcox, Zeke Castro, Bob Carr, Frances Evans, Rick Miller, and Goldie Posey.

INTRODUCTION

Eugene Manlove Rhodes nicknamed Alamogordo and its surroundings "Arcadia." The area's ancient past began 10,000 years ago. During that vast, silent stretch of time, an ancient landscape of forest and woodland faded to desert scrub under the relentless desert sun. Human interest shifted from hunting to agriculture, and finally to the conquest of the air and outer space.

At the end of the last ice age, Asian hunters gradually spread into this new, unpopulated continent pursuing herds of mammoth, camel, horse, bison, and other ancient species. As these large animals faded into extinction, local Native Americans shifted to hunting smaller game and gathering wild plants, finally adopting corn agriculture 3,000 years ago. These farmers built large adobe villages, made decorated pottery, and etched or painted religious art on cliffs and rock outcrops. Mysteriously, these villagers abandoned the region 500 years ago. Shortly thereafter, Apaches began to move into Arcadia. Spanish conquistadores began to explore the southwest in the 16th century, avoiding this region except for occasional punitive expeditions against the Apache. European colonization here was delayed by Apache resistance until 1862, when the Apache were forcibly relocated to Bosque Redondo on the Pecos River.

During the 1860s, Hispanic New Mexicans settled at the mouths of La Luz and Tularosa Canyons. After 1873, when the Mescalero Reservation was established, the expanding western frontier brought populations from the eastern United States and western Texas to the Tularosa Basin. Mining and timber industries, construction of railroads, and other communication and transportation systems followed after Alamogordo was established in 1898. In the late 1930s, the U.S. government began to set aside vast tracts of land in the Tularosa Basin and established the Alamogordo Bombing and Gunnery Range with the onset of World War II. By the end of the 1940s, these tracts were designated for defense systems testing as part of present-day White Sands Missile Range.

In 1898, the first preplanned development community of Alamogordo, New Mexico, burst from the dry desert sands of the eastern Tularosa Basin, a region almost as large as Connecticut. Alamogordo ("fat cottonwood" in Spanish) was conceived by John and Charles Eddy who built the El Paso and Northeastern Railroad (EP&NE) from El Paso, Texas, to the new town site, and northward.

Local cowboy author Eugene Manlove Rhodes, who dubbed the town "Arcadia" in his prototypical western romance *Bransford in Arcadia*, penned the best description of Alamogordo's inception:

> Arcadia's assets were the railroad, two large modern sawmills, the climate and printer's ink. The railroad found it a patch of bare ground, six miles from water; put in successively a whistling-post, a signboard, a depot, townsite papers and a water-main from the Alamo; and, when the townsite papers were confirmed, established machine

shops and made the new town the division headquarters and base for northward building.

The railroad then set up the sawmills, primarily to get out ties and timbers for its own lanky growth, and built a spur to bring the forest down from Rainbow [the Sacramento Mountains] to the mills. The word "down" is used advisedly. Arcadia nestled on the plain under the very eavespouts of Rainbow Range. The branch, following with slavish fidelity the lines of a twisted corkscrew, took twenty-seven miles, mostly tunnel and trestlework, to clamber to the logging camps, with a minimum grade that was purely prohibitive and a maximum that I dare not state; but there was a rise of six thousand feet in those twenty-seven miles. You can figure the average yourself. And if the engine should run off the track at the end of her climb, she would light on the very roundhouse where she took breakfast, and spoil the shingles.

Yes, that was some railroad. There was a summer hotel—Cloudland [Cloudcroft]—on the summit, largely occupied by slackwire performers. Others walked up or rode a horse. They used stem-winding engines, with eight vertical cylinders on the right side and a shaft like a steamboat, with beveled cogwheel transmission on the axles. And they haven't had a wreck on that branch to date. No matter how late a train is, when the engine sees the tail-lights of her caboose ahead of her she stops and sends out flagmen.

The railroad, under the pseudonym of the Arcadia Development Company [Alamogordo Improvement Company], also laid out streets and laid in a network of pipelines, and staked out lots until the sawmill protested for lack of tie-lumber. It put down miles of cement walks, fringed them with cottonwood saplings, telephone poles and electric lights. It built a hotel and a few streets of party-colored cottages—*directoire*, with lingerie tile roofs, organdy facades and peplum, intersecting panels and outside chimneys at the gable ends. It decreed a park, with nooks, lanes, mazes, lake, swans, ballground, grandstand, bandstand and the band appertaining thereunto—all of which apparently came into being over night. Then it employed a competent staff of word-artists and capitalized the climate.

The result was astonishing. The cottonwoods grew apace and a swift town grew with them—swift in every sense of the word. It took good money to buy good lots in Arcadia. People with money must be fed, served and amused by people wanting money. In three years the trees cast a pleasant shade and the company cast a balance with gratifying results. They discounted the unearned increment for a generation to come.

It was a beneficent scheme, selling ozone and novelty, sunshine and delight. The buyers got far more than the worth of their money, the company got their money—and everyone was happy. Health and good spirits are a bargain at any price. There were sandstorms and hot days; but sand promotes digestion and digestion promotes cheerfulness. Heat merely enhanced the luxury of shaded hammocks. As an adventurer thawed out, he sent for seven others worse than himself. Arcadia became the metropolis of the county and, by special election, the county-seat. Courthouse, college and jail followed in quick succession.

For the company, Arcadia life was one grand, sweet song, with thus far, but a single discord. As has been said, Arcadia was laid out on the plain. There was higher ground on three sides—Rainbow Mountain to the east, the deltas of La Luz Creek and the Alamo to the north and south. New Mexico was dry, as a rule. After the second exception, when enthusiastic citizens went about on stilts to forward a project for changing the town's name to Venice, the company acknowledged its error handsomely. When dry land prevailed once more above the face of the waters, it built a mighty moat by way of the *amende honorable*—a moat with its one embankment on the inner side of the five-mile horseshoe about the town. This, with its attendant bridges, gave Arcadia an aspect singularly medieval. It also furnished a convenient line of social demarcation. Chauffeurs, college professors, lawyers, gamblers, county officers, together with a few tradesmen and railroad officials, abode within "the Isle of Arcady," on more or less even terms with the Arcadians proper; millmen, railroaders, lumberjacks, and the underworld generally, dwelt without the pale.

The company rubbed its lamp again—and behold! an armory, a hospital and a library! It contributed liberally to churches and campaign funds; it exercised a general supervision over morals and manners. For example, in the deed to every lot sold was an ironclad, fire-tested, automatic and highly constitutional forfeiture clause, to the effect that sale or storage on the premises of any malt, vinous or spiritous liquors should immediately cause the title to revert to the company. The company's own vicarious saloon, on Lot Number One, was a sumptuous and magnificent affair. It was known as the Mint.

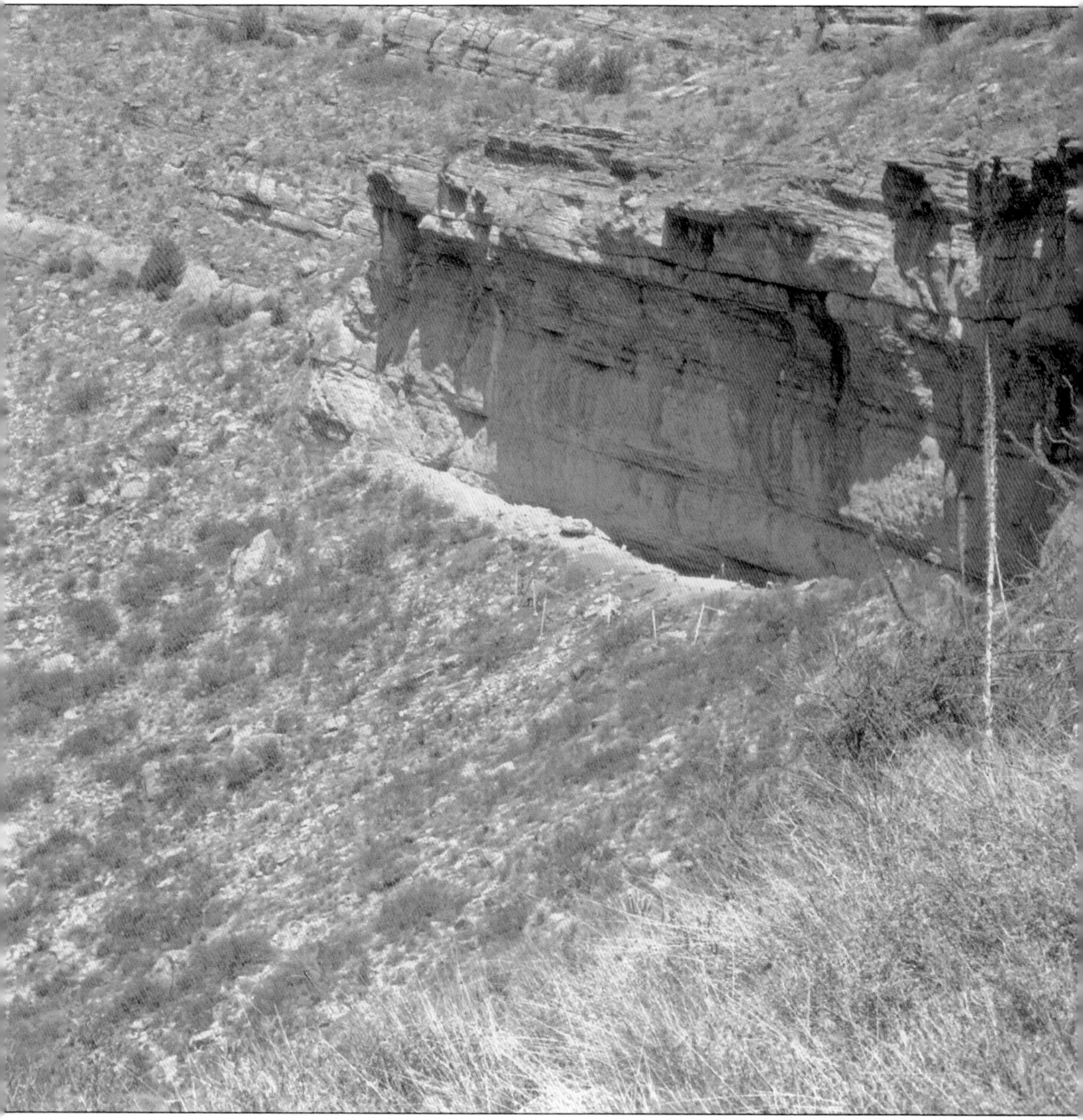

Fresnal Rockshelter, 10 miles northeast of Alamogordo, contained preserved maize and beans dating to the Archaic period 3,000 years ago. The Fresnal farmers were among the first to adopt agriculture north of Mexico. (Author's collection.)

One

The Railroad Creates Alamogordo

After the Treaty of Guadalupe Hidalgo concluded the Mexican War, Hispanic New Mexicans founded Tularosa and La Luz, and settlers began to filter into the Tularosa Basin. In 1871, James Hill, Tom Keeney, J. M. Aguayo, and Eugene Dow homesteaded the mouth of Alamo Canyon, developing its water sources until conflict with Apaches forced them to abandon their farms. West Texas rancher Oliver Milton Lee migrated to the basin in 1884 and purchased the Alamo Canyon property. In December 1897, John Eddy bought Lee's Alamo Springs property and water rights for $5,000.

Alamogordo was platted in 1898, followed by the Chihuahua addition ("Chihuahuita") in 1900. One of the first buildings in Alamogordo was an ice factory established by George Carl from Salida, Colorado, who drilled the first town water well. When the first El Paso and Northeastern Railway (EP&NE) train reached Alamogordo on June 15, 1898, most of its freight consisted of building materials. The Alamogordo Improvement Company immediately began town site development, building example homes, landscaping Alameda Park, planting street-side cottonwood trees, and constructing its own facilities.

The first structure within the town site was the D. S. Sears Confectionery. Sears and his wife had driven from Bland, Texas, arriving two days before the first train. The *Sacramento Chief*, renamed the *Alamogordo News*, was moved from La Luz, where it had been published since 1896. Tom Frazier's Meat Market and the A. D. "Pumpkin" Wallace Store was built next. The Jackson-Galbraith-Foxworth Lumber Company shipped its first load of lumber to Alamogordo on that first train and immediately began selling building materials for town construction.

The Alamogordo Improvement Company began erecting residential houses, beginning with the Prather house at 1101 Michigan Avenue, originally used as the county courthouse; the Ross house at 1109 Michigan Avenue; and a large two-and-a-half story, 13-room house at 1123 Michigan Avenue, rented to the Commercial Club, later occupied by Dr. E. D. McKinley. The Ackley house at 1115 Indiana Avenue was also built at that time. The Alamogordo Lumber Company erected 30 cottages on the south end of town. The EP&NE replaced its temporary depot with the "largest and most artistic depot along the road," surpassing the depot in El Paso, and began construction of Hotel Alamogordo. The Railroad and Improvement Company built company offices (later Hotel Southwestern) adjacent to the depot, south of Alameda Park.

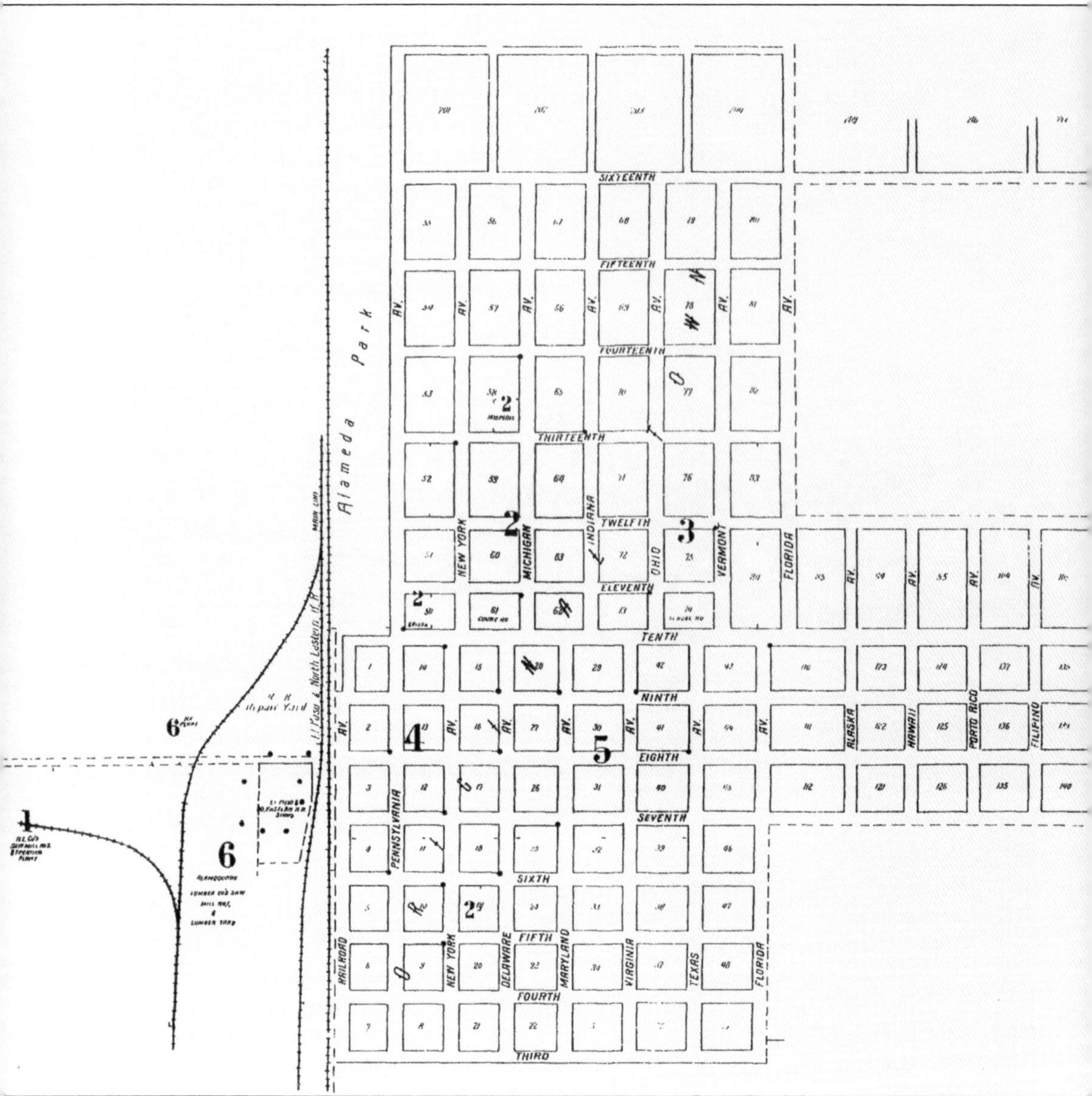

The original Alamogordo town site, portrayed on the 1905 Sanborn Fire Insurance maps, was divided into several quadrants with distinct land uses, roughly divided by Tenth Street and Maryland Avenue. The southwest quadrant was commercial, the southeast was mixed commercial/residential, and the north was residential. Larger blocks surrounded the town's core east of Florida Avenue and north of Sixteenth Street. (Courtesy of Library of Congress.)

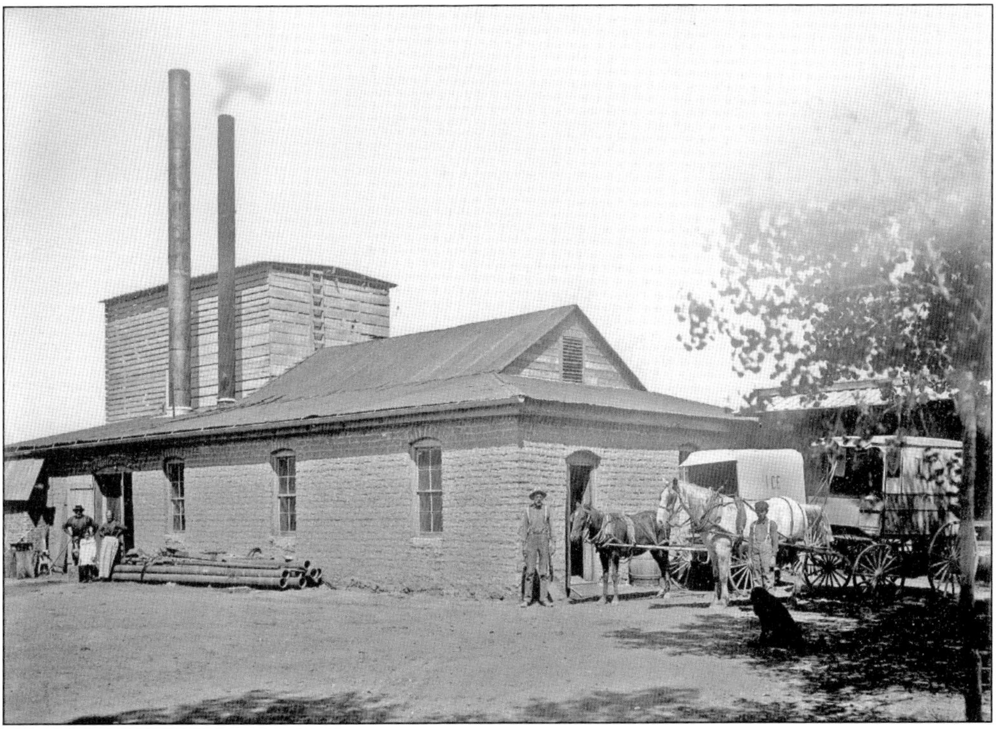

The George Carl ice factory was one of the first buildings in Alamogordo. Ice for refrigeration was probably the first urban amenity available in the new town. (Courtesy of TBHS.)

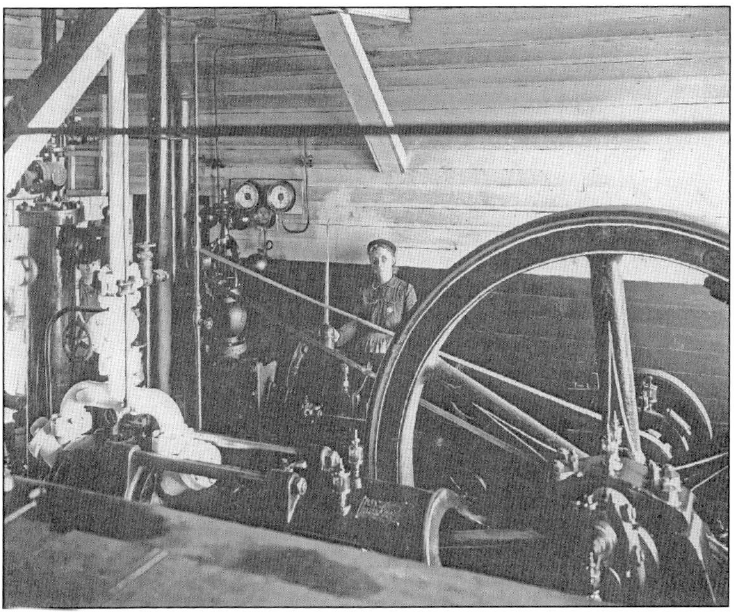

George Carl "freighted his machinery all the way up from El Paso in order to be the first on the ground, and when the first train of the El Paso and Northeastern pulled in, he had ice to melt." (*Alamogordo News*, August 24, 1899, courtesy of Zeke Castro.)

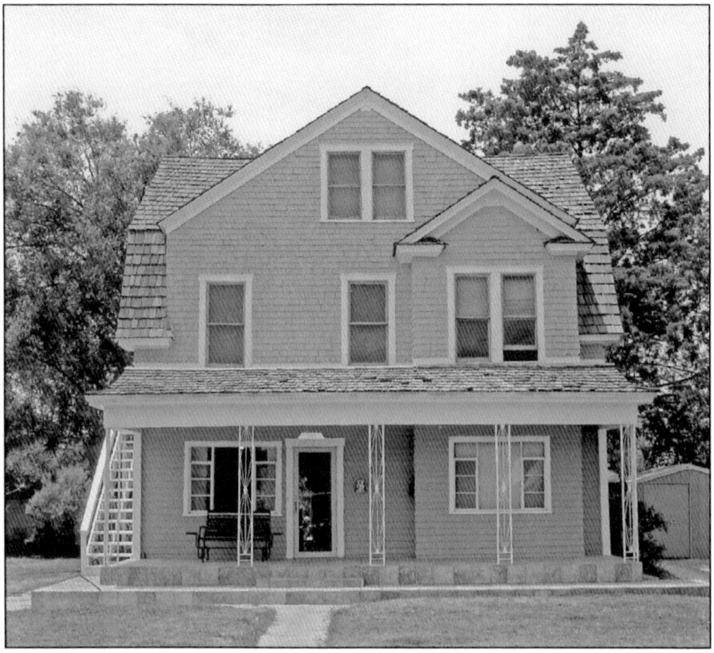

The Colonial Revival Ross house, 1109 Michigan Avenue, was the second house built in Alamogordo by the Alamogordo Improvement Company. P. A. Ross was the superintendent of the tie treatment plant. (Author's collection.)

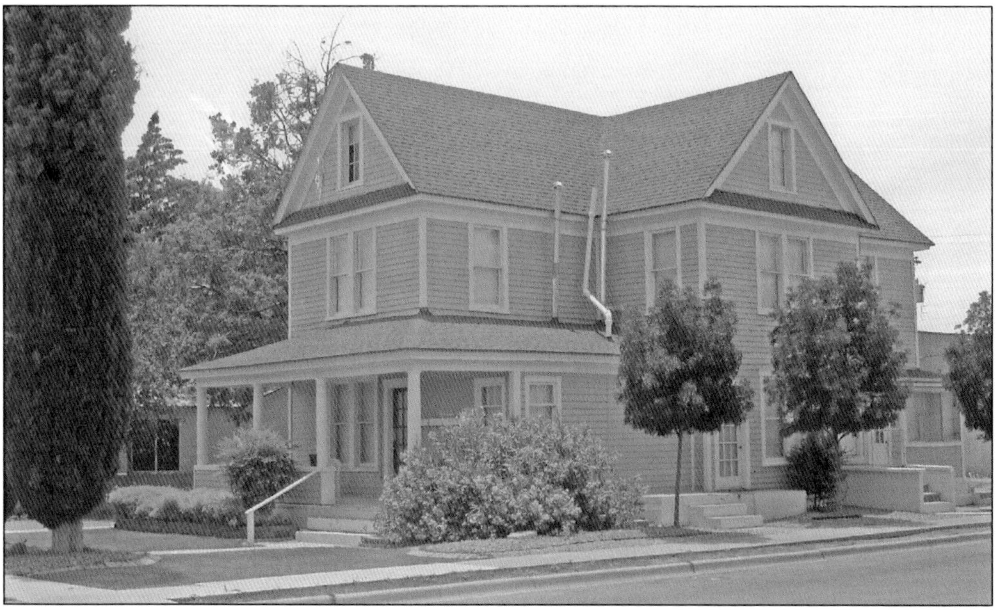

The third house built, 1123 Michigan Avenue, was the home of the original Commercial Club. Col. J. F. Harvey, who managed the Hotel Alamogordo, was the club's president. (Author's collection.)

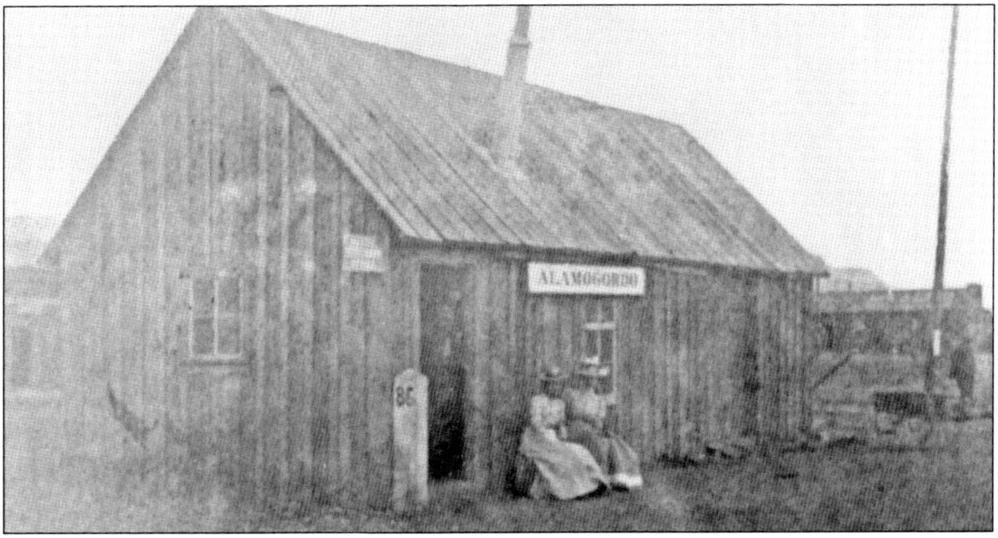

Nell Rolland, sister of Frank C. Rolland, the owner of Rolland Drugs on New York Avenue, and Minnie Rhomberg, sister of Frank. M. Rhomberg, jeweler and musician who wrote "March Alamogordo," are sitting in front of the original Alamogordo railroad depot. (Courtesy of TBHS.)

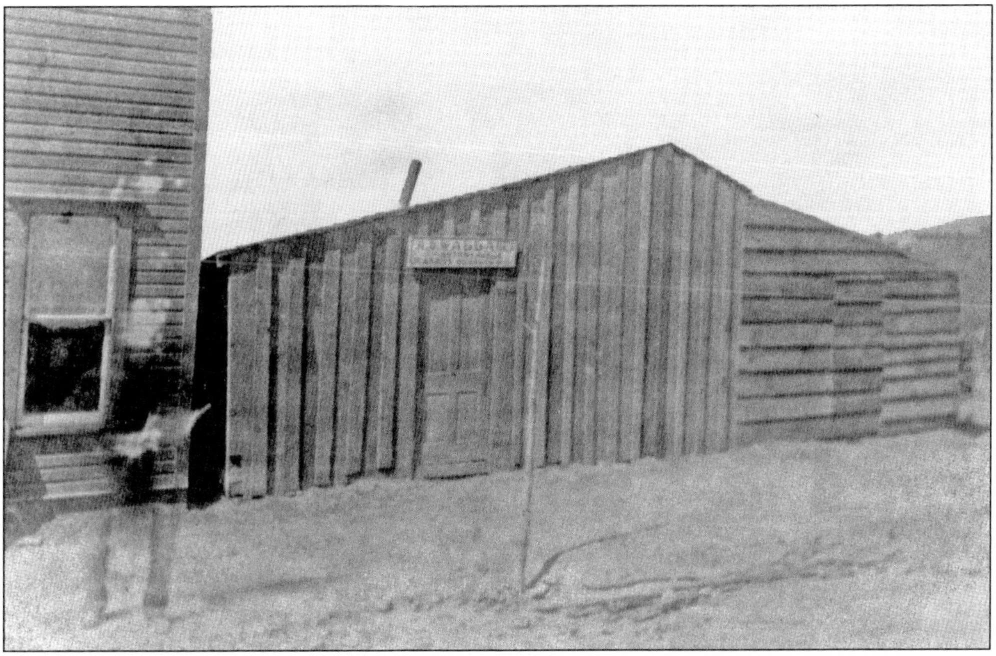

The A. D. "Pumpkin" Wallace mercantile store, the fourth building in Alamogordo, was located on Pennsylvania Avenue, south of the depot (which can be faintly seen, right background). (Courtesy of TBHS.)

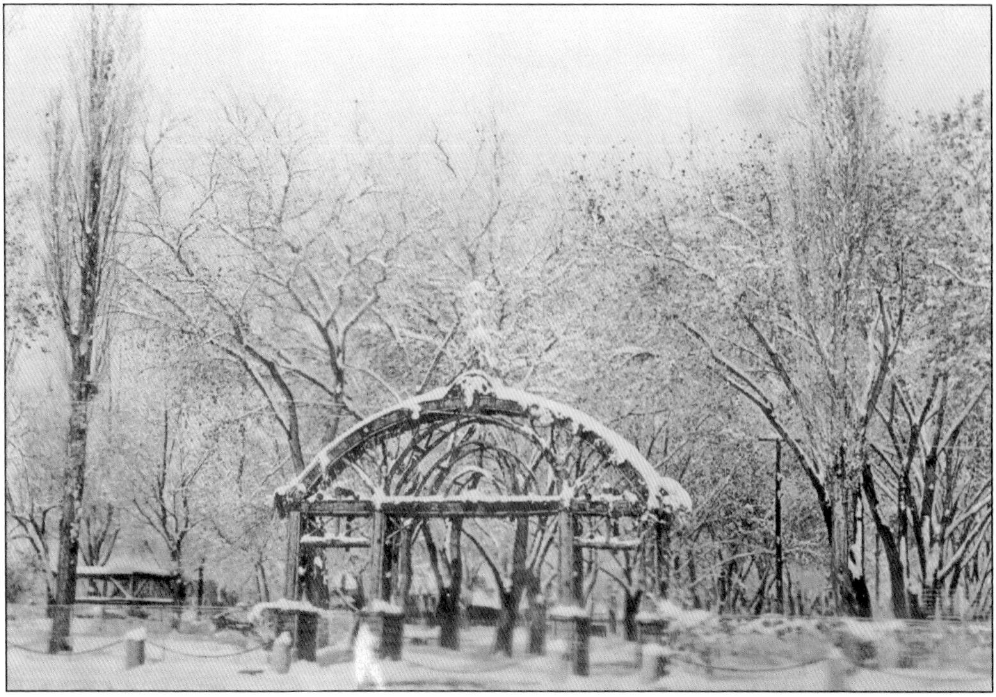

The Alameda Park Adirondack-style entry gate was built by E. M. Abbott, one of the town's first construction contractors. (Courtesy of Frances Evans.)

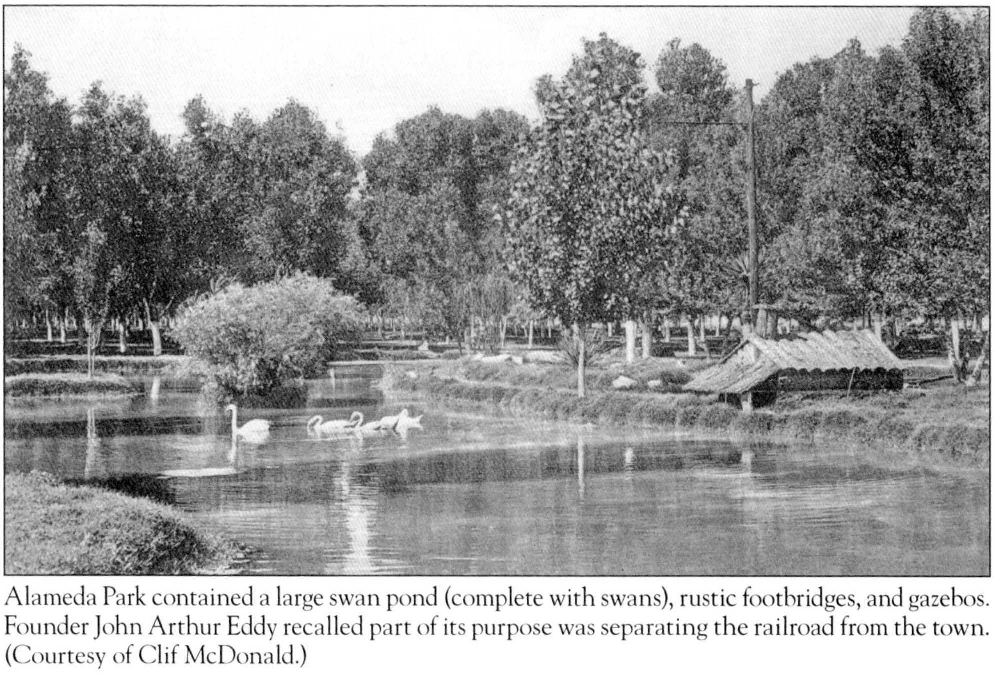

Alameda Park contained a large swan pond (complete with swans), rustic footbridges, and gazebos. Founder John Arthur Eddy recalled part of its purpose was separating the railroad from the town. (Courtesy of Clif McDonald.)

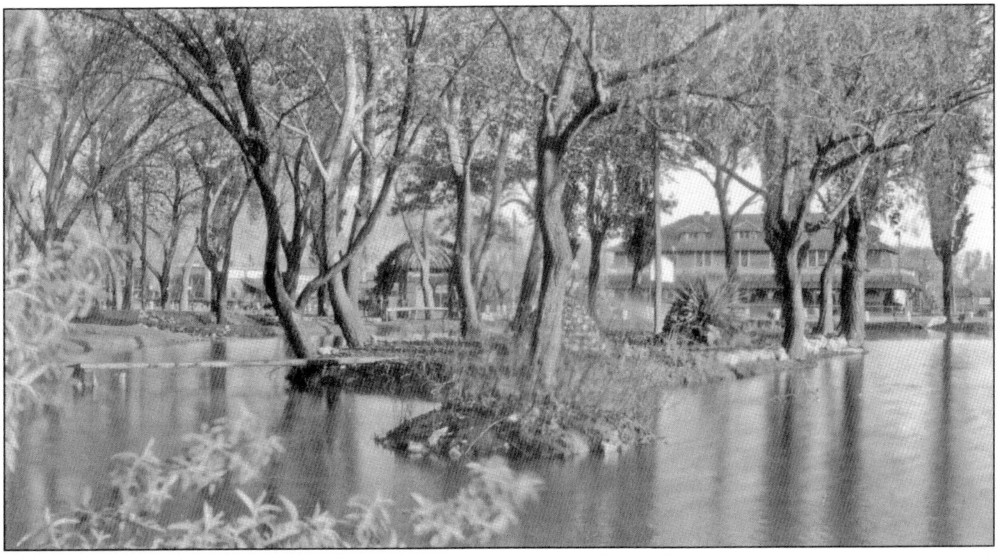

The south end of Alameda Park, with its rustic gate and pond, faced south toward the Hotel Southwestern. (Alamogordo Improvement Company Offices, courtesy of TBHS.)

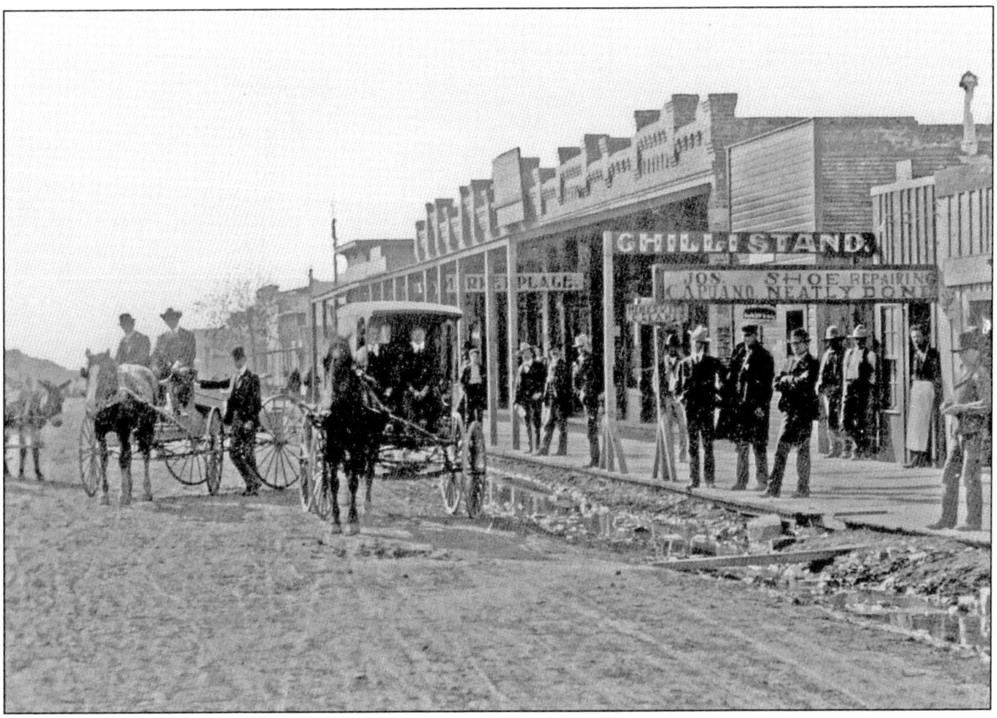

Pennsylvania Avenue (now White Sands Boulevard) is shown in this *c.* 1910 photograph near the intersection with Tenth Street. It was, and still is, the center of town. Today it is occupied by Founders Park and Alamogordo Airborne Memorial. (Courtesy of TBHS.)

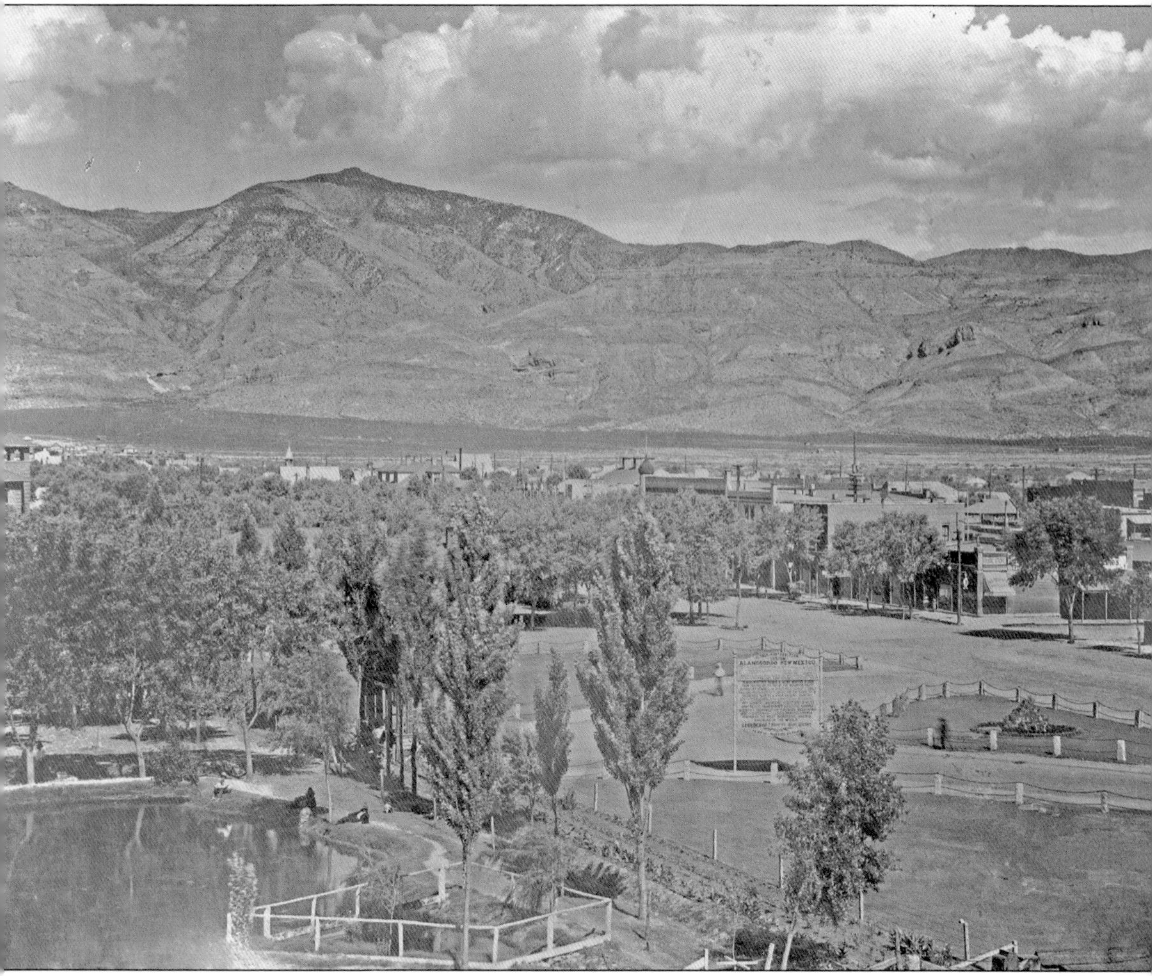

The intersection of Pennsylvania Avenue (now White Sands Boulevard) and Tenth Street anchored the central business district, which developed rapidly on Pennsylvania Avenue and New York Avenue, one block east, adjacent to its intersection with Tenth Street. The west end of Tenth Street terminated at the EP&NE depot, the entry to Alameda Park, and the railroad offices. (Courtesy of TBHS.)

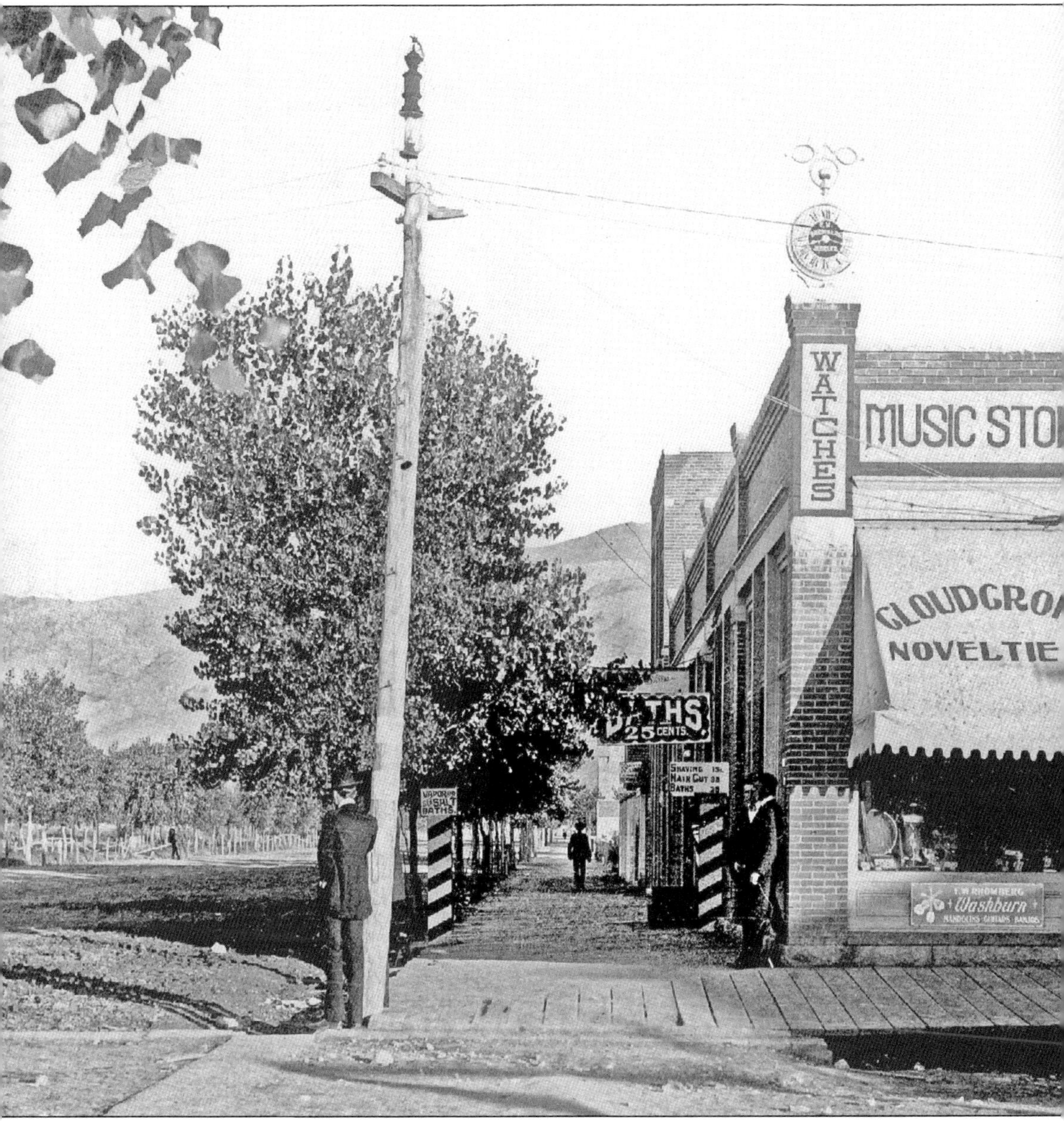

Pictured here is the southeast corner of Pennsylvania Avenue and Tenth Street looking east down Tenth Street, where the original lines of cottonwood trees can be seen. This corner is now occupied by Founders Park, which was created after the original Bennett Building—one of the oldest commercial structures in town—could not be preserved. (Courtesy of TBHS.)

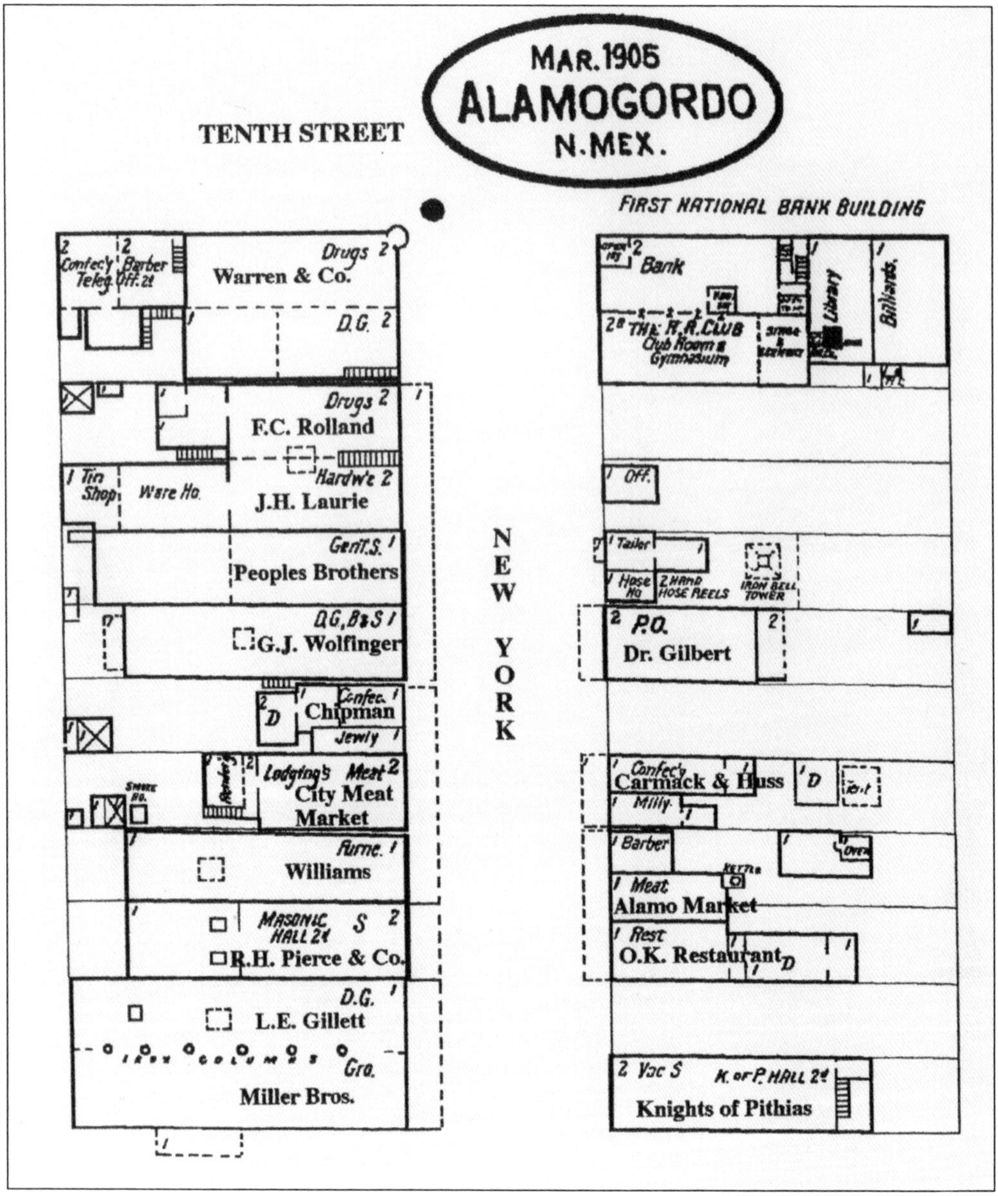

The core business district, 1905, on New York Avenue between Tenth and Ninth Streets, contained the First National Bank, the railroad club, the fire department, the post office, Dr. Gilbert's office, the Masonic and Knights of Pythias Halls, drugstores, meat markets, dry goods, confectionery shops, a barbershop, furniture, hardware, clothing and jewelry, and a restaurant. This image is based on the 1905 Sanborn Fire Insurance Company maps of Alamogordo. (Drawing by the author, 1999.)

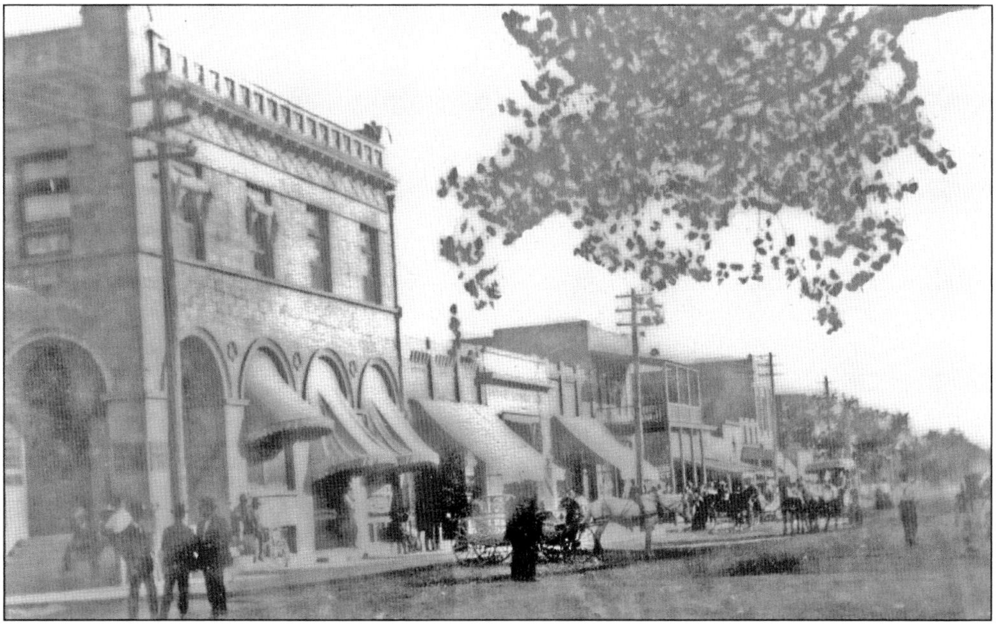

The east side of New York Avenue between Tenth and Ninth Streets is shown here. The First National Bank and the railroad club occupy the two-story building on the corner in the left foreground. (Courtesy of Millicent Shyne.)

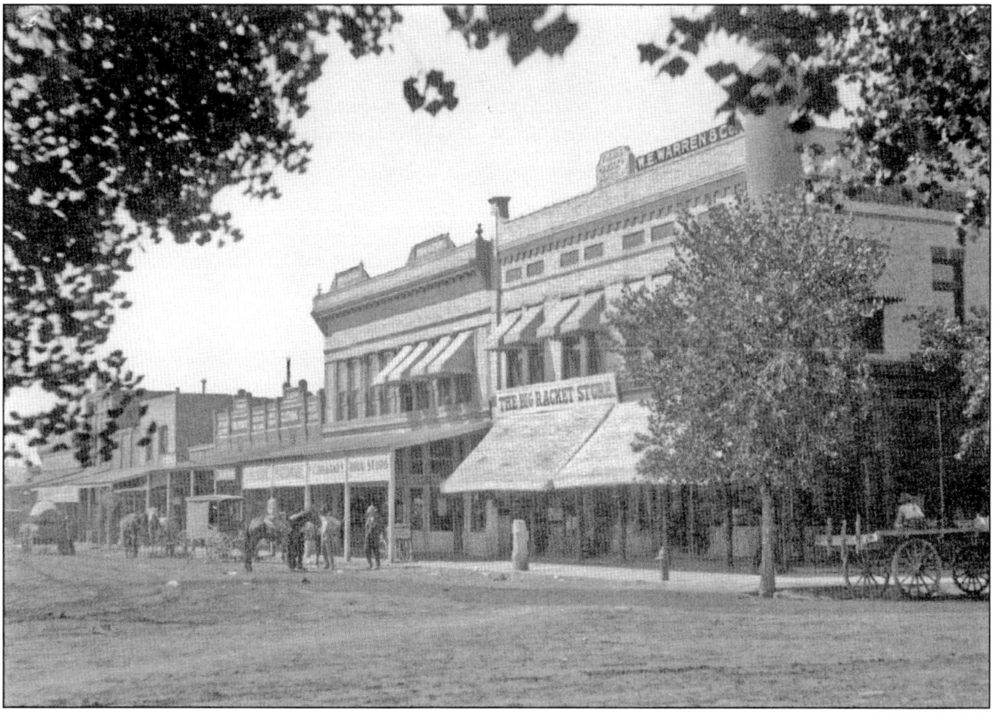

The west side of New York Avenue between Tenth and Ninth Streets is shown here. The Big Racket Store—a variety store—occupied the lower story of the Warren (Avis) Building. This structure is still prominent as a town landmark due to its cupola-topped solarium tower. (Courtesy of TBHS.)

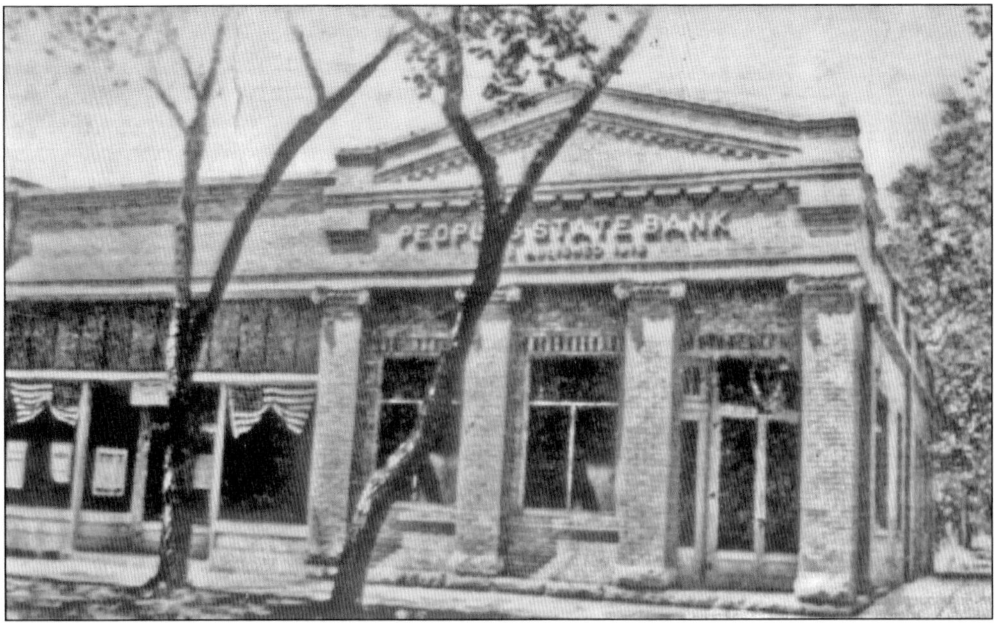

Peoples State Bank, established around 1915, was located on the northwest corner of New York Avenue and Tenth Street and is now a billiard parlor. (Courtesy of Clif McDonald.)

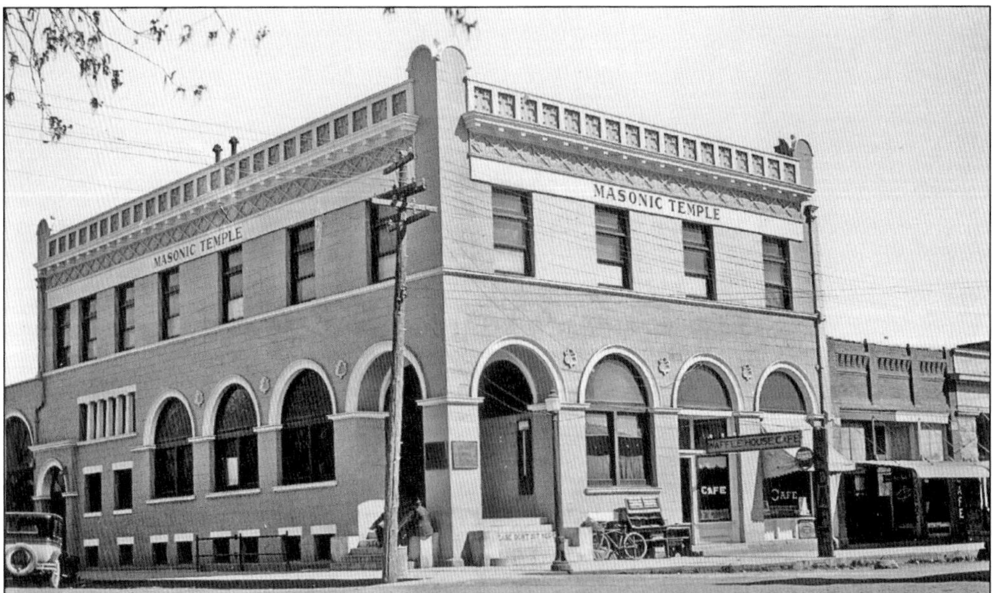

The First National Bank building, which originally housed the Railroad Club and later, the Masonic Temple on its second story, occupied the southeast corner of New York Avenue and Tenth Street. (Courtesy of TBHS.)

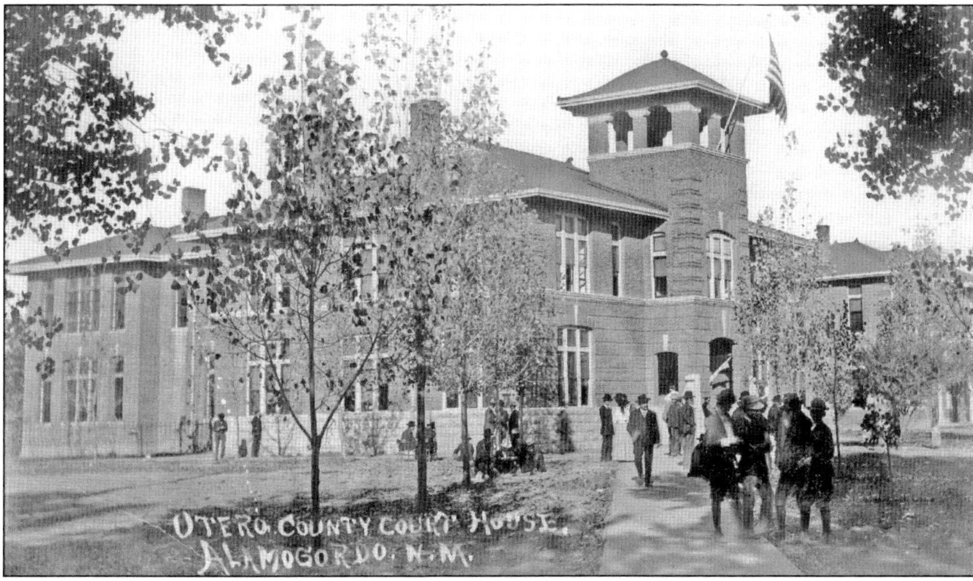

The Otero County Courthouse was located on the north side of Tenth Street, between New York and Michigan Avenues, on one of the several blocks devoted to public buildings. This photograph was taken by Jim Alexander. (Courtesy of TBHS.)

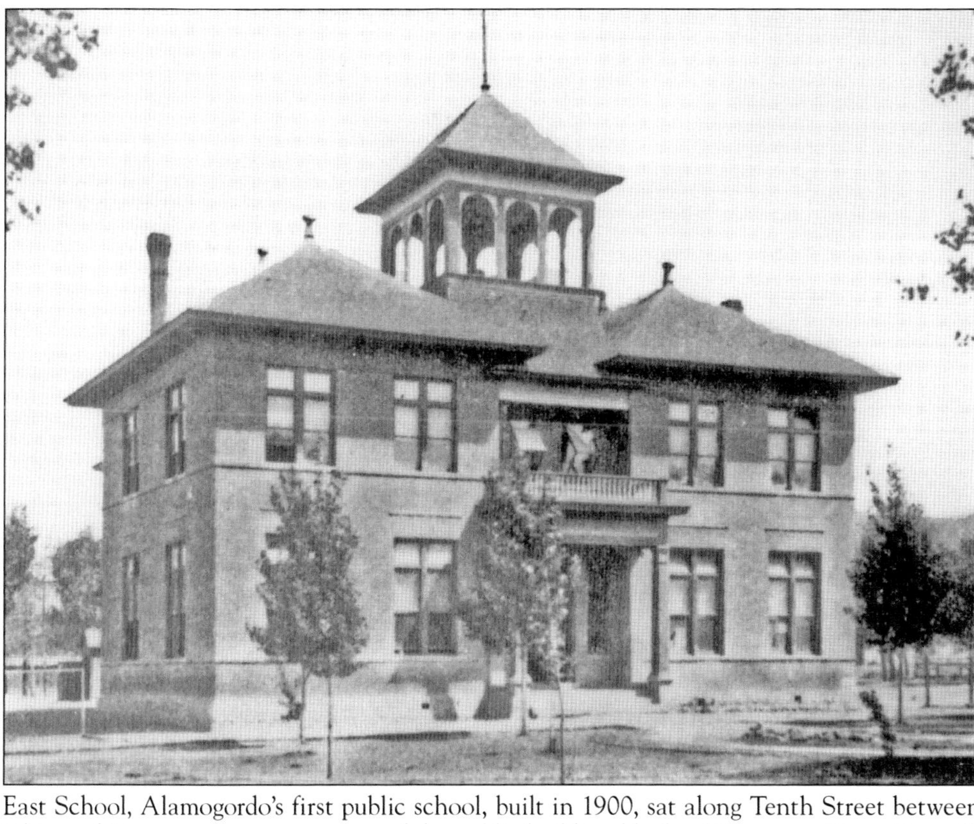
East School, Alamogordo's first public school, built in 1900, sat along Tenth Street between Ohio and Vermont Avenues on one of the public building blocks. (Courtesy of June Harwell, Alamogordo Public Library.)

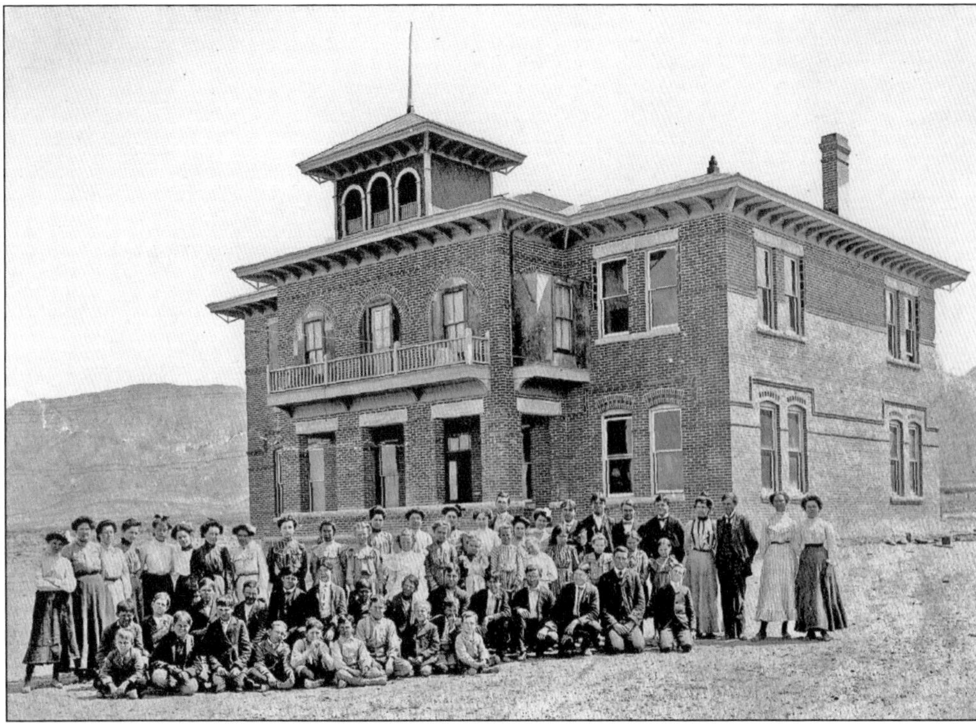

The New Mexico Baptist College at Ninth Street and College Avenue was not in existence for long. It closed in 1911. Here the 1902 faculty and students pose for their portrait. (Courtesy of TBHS.)

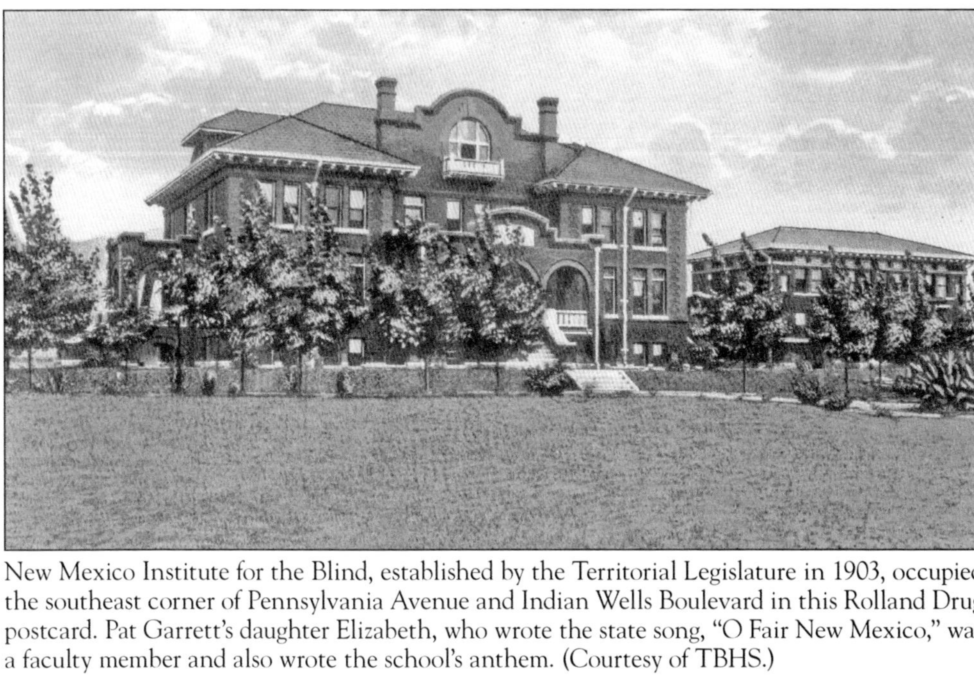

New Mexico Institute for the Blind, established by the Territorial Legislature in 1903, occupied the southeast corner of Pennsylvania Avenue and Indian Wells Boulevard in this Rolland Drug postcard. Pat Garrett's daughter Elizabeth, who wrote the state song, "O Fair New Mexico," was a faculty member and also wrote the school's anthem. (Courtesy of TBHS.)

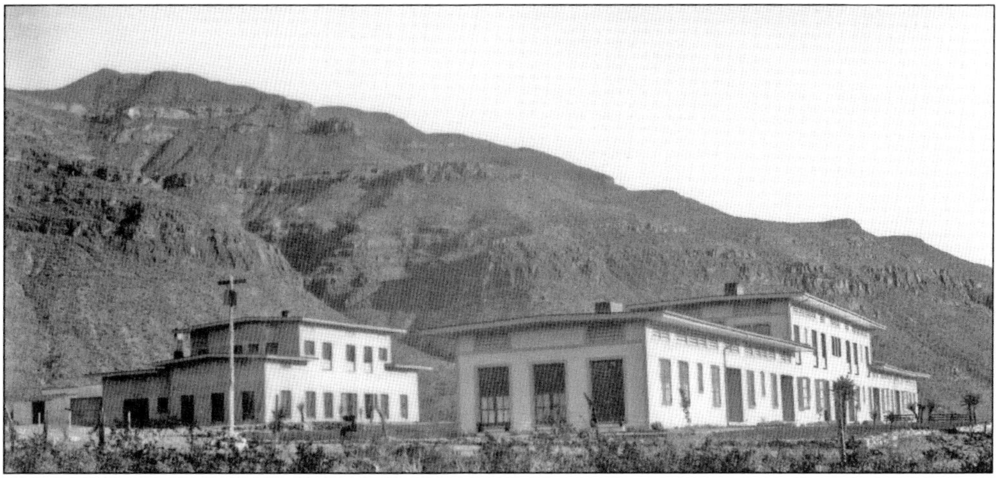

The Alamogordo Fraternal City Sanitorium, southeast of the city, opened in 1907 for tubercular patients. (Courtesy of TBHS.)

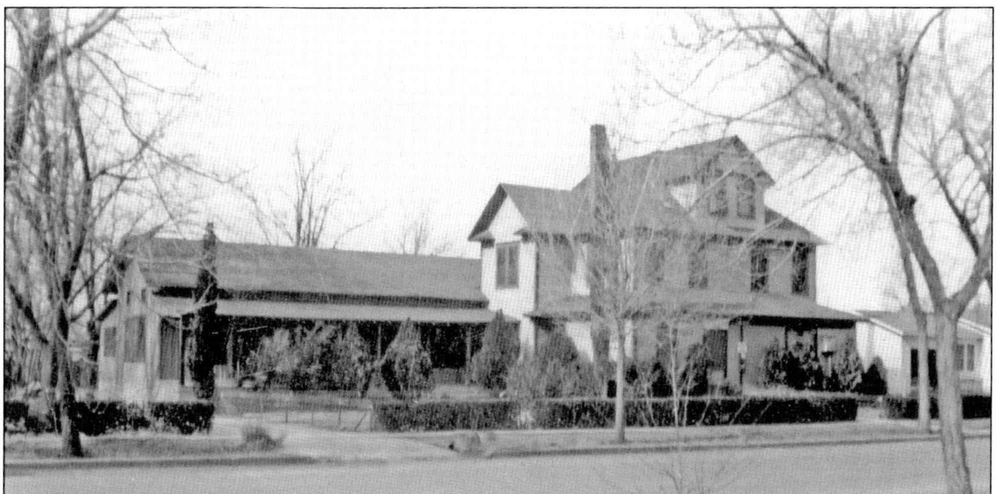

Southwest Lumber Company Hospital, originally the El Paso and Southwestern Railroad (EP&SW) hospital, was on Michigan Avenue between Thirteenth and Fourteenth Streets. It was, in fact, the town's second hospital. (Courtesy of TBHS.)

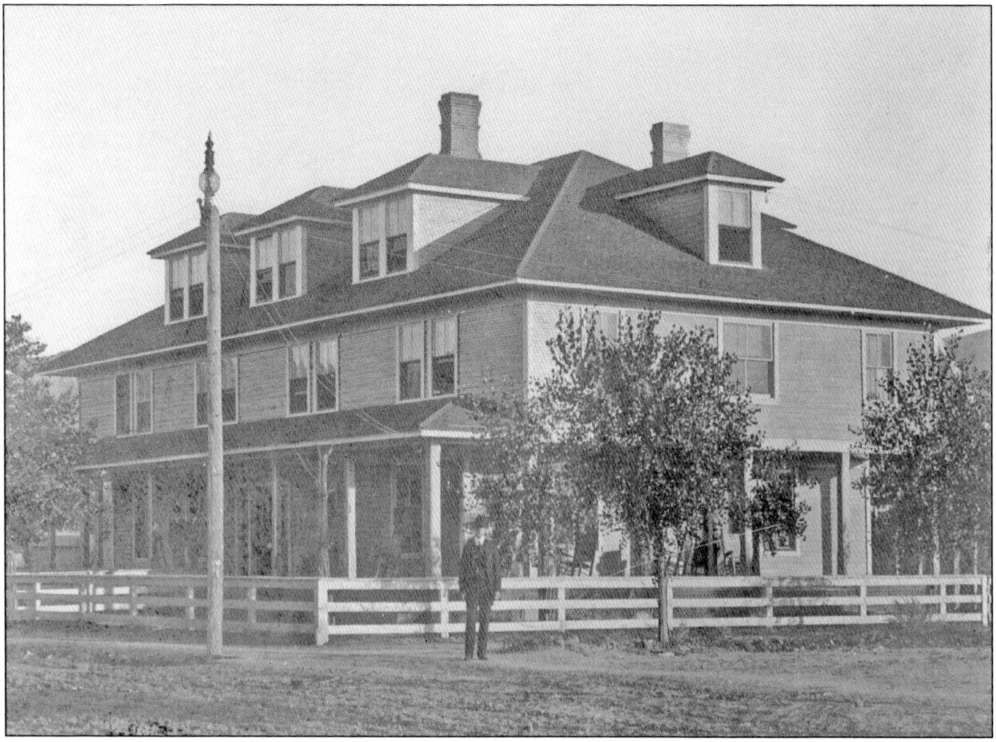

Hotel Alamogordo, at Tenth Street and Delaware Avenue, was managed by Col. J. F. Harvey and his wife, who were known for arranging galas, musicals, and moonlight concerts in the park. (Courtesy of TBHS.)

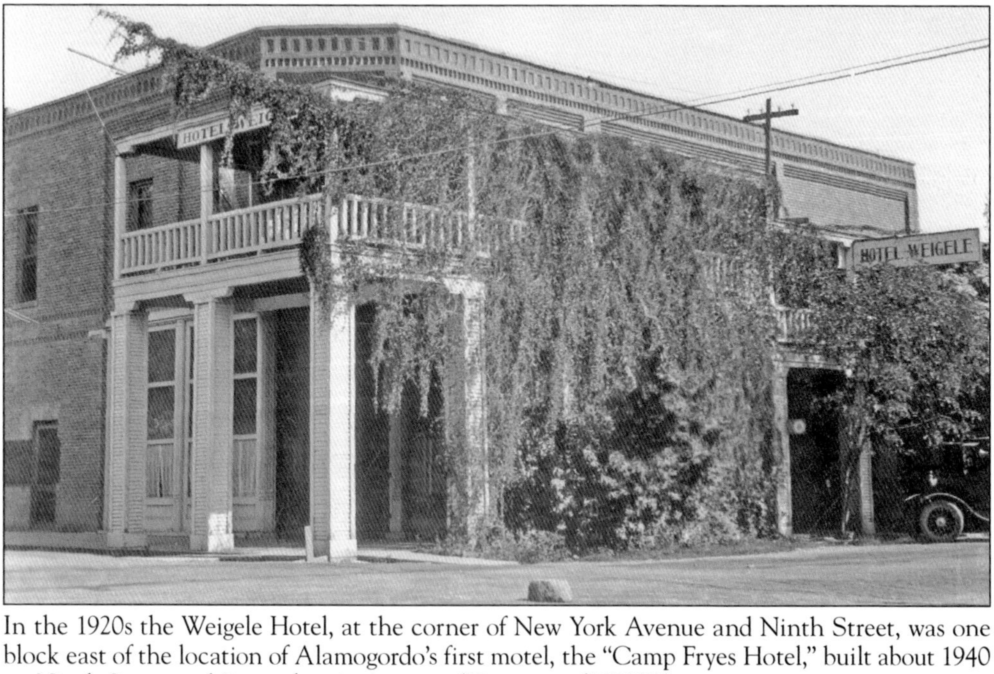

In the 1920s the Weigele Hotel, at the corner of New York Avenue and Ninth Street, was one block east of the location of Alamogordo's first motel, the "Camp Fryes Hotel," built about 1940 on Ninth Street and Pennsylvania Avenue. (Courtesy of TBHS.)

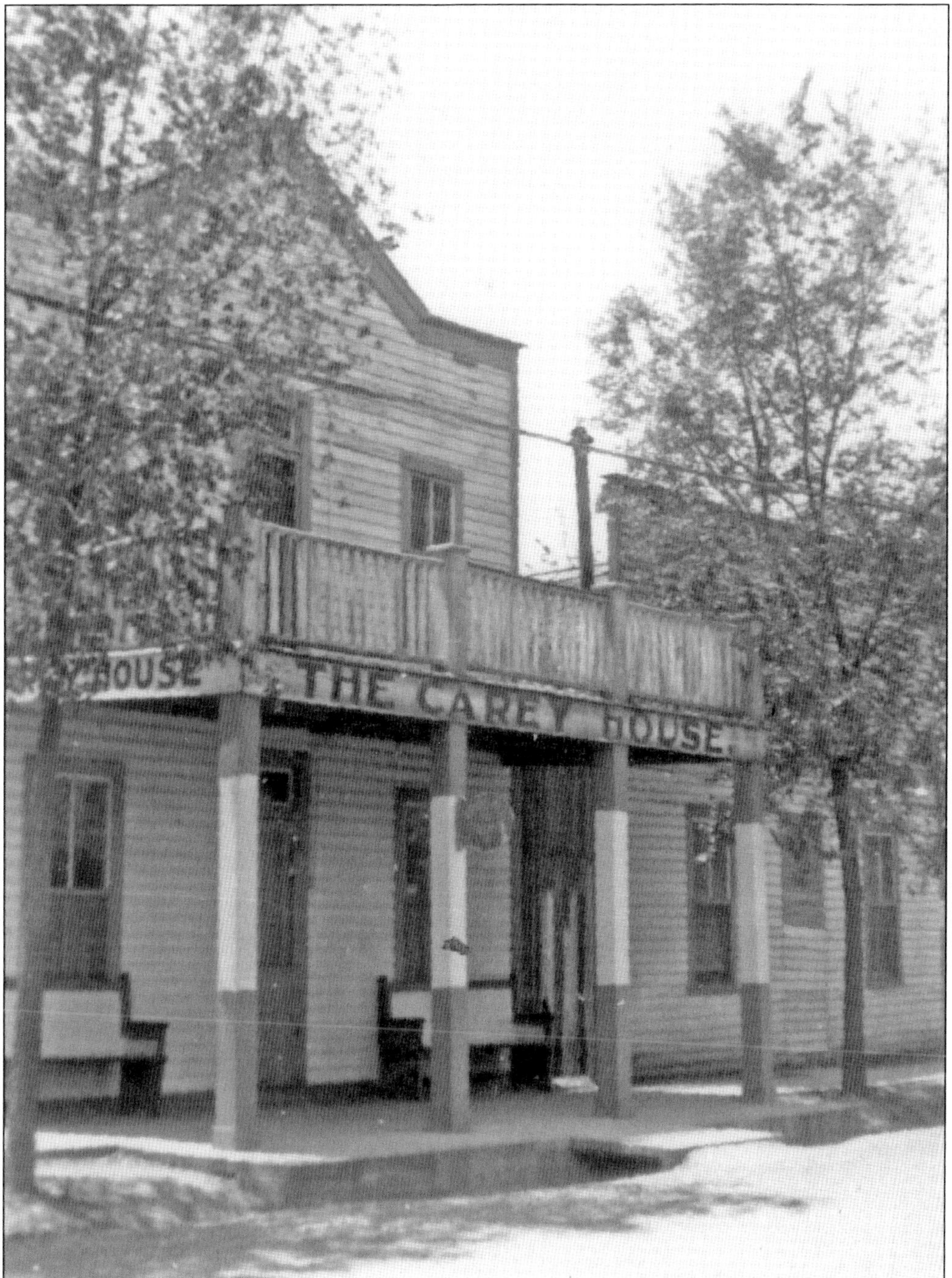

The Carey Boarding House was located on Maryland Avenue between Ninth and Tenth Streets. (Courtesy of TBHS.)

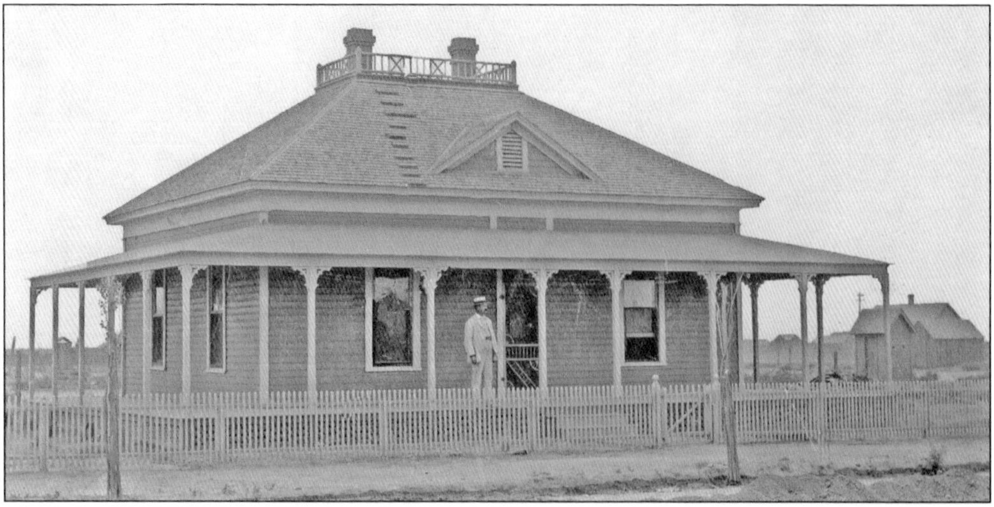

The John L. O'Shea Mansion was at the corner of Tenth Street and Virginia Avenue, pictured here in this *c.* 1898 photograph. (Courtesy of TBHS.)

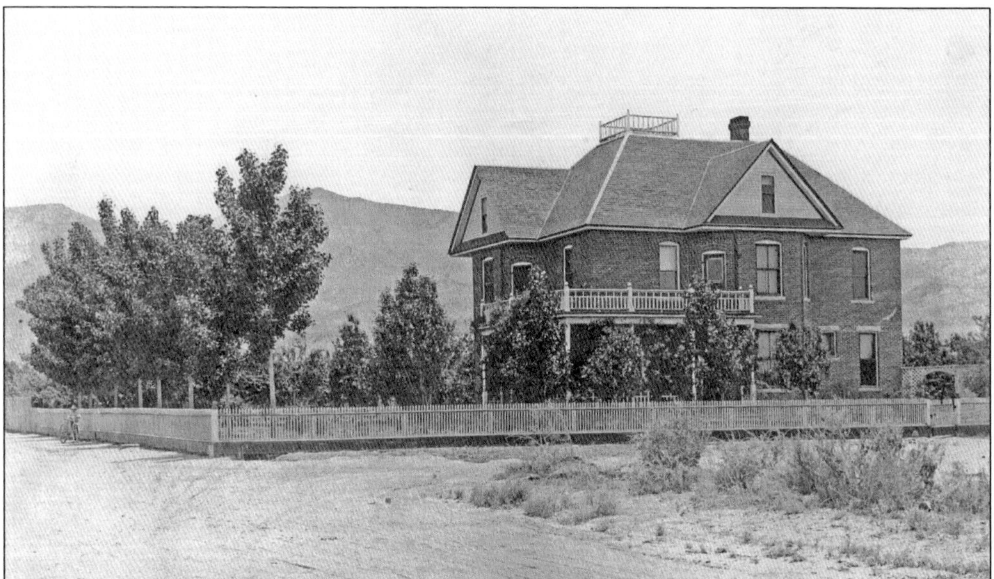

The Robert Pierce house and pear orchard were located at Tenth Street and Cuba Avenue. (Courtesy of TBHS.)

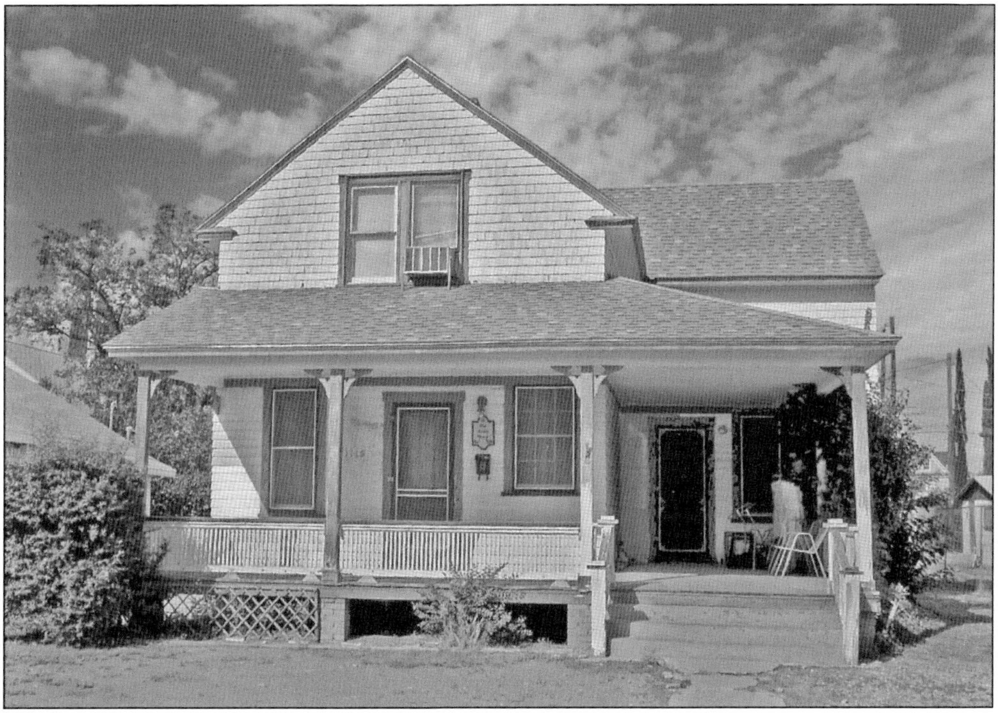

The Queen Anne/Colonial Revival Harry Ackley house (also known as the Seaman's residence) at 1115 Indiana Avenue was built by F. E. Bieldleman for Harry F. Ackley, an engineer with the EP&NE Railroad. (Author's collection.)

The A. P. Jackson house at Ninth Street and Monroe Avenue is a classic Victorian Queen Anne and Free Classic home and is one of the most detailed and best-preserved original homes in Alamogordo. It was built by A. P. Jackson himself, co-owner of the first lumberyard. (Courtesy of TBHS.)

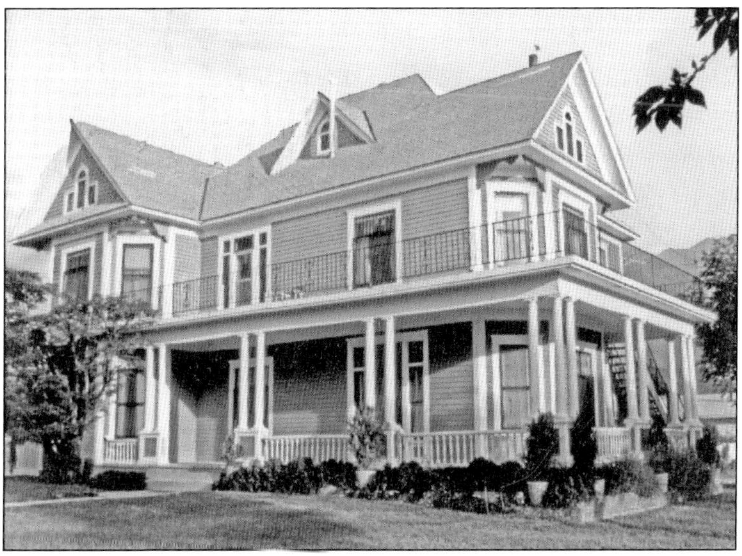

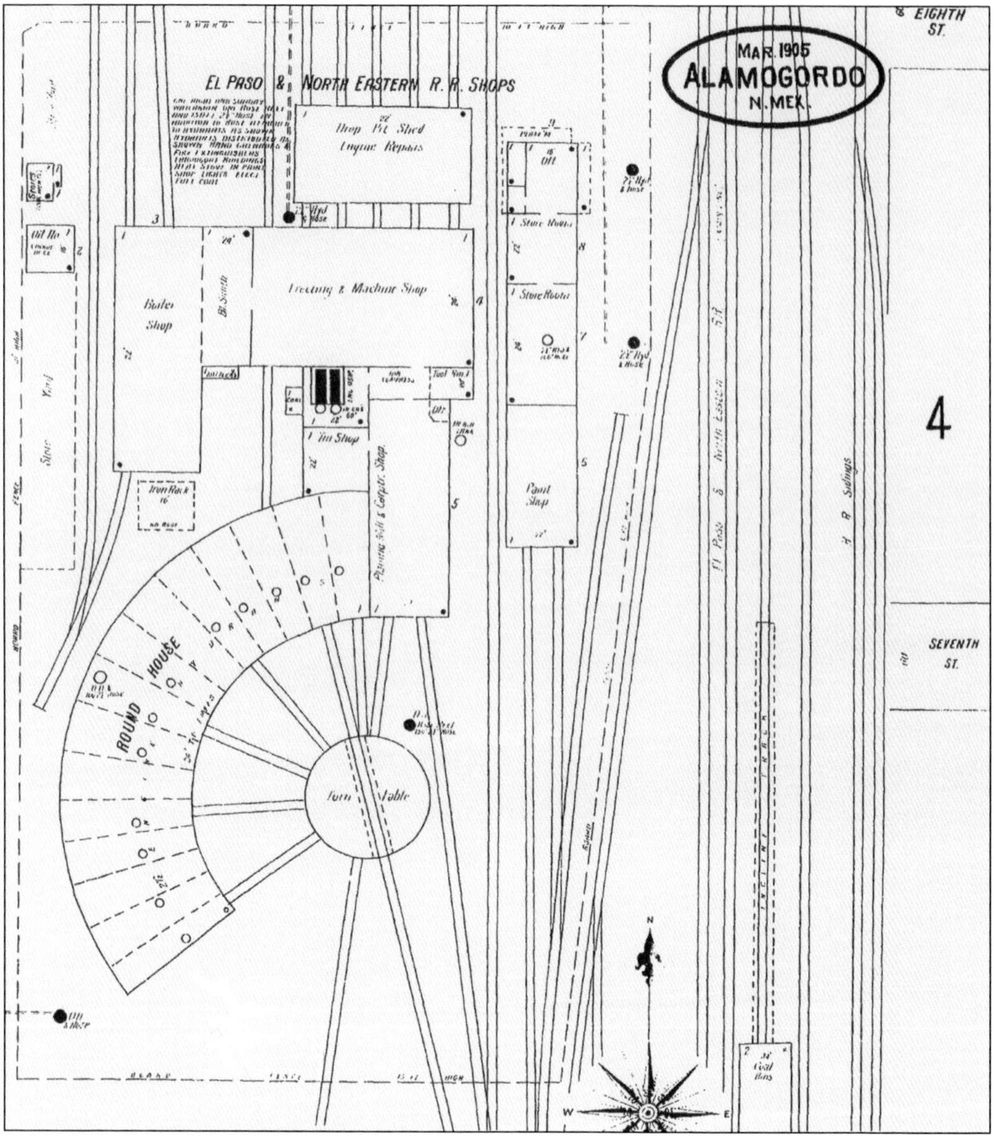

The El Paso and Northeastern Railroad (EP&NE) main yards and roundhouse were west of Pennsylvania Avenue and the railroad tracks (based on the 1905 Sanborn Fire Insurance maps). Charles B. and John Arthur Eddy realized from their initial acquisition of railroad assets (originally belonging to Jay Gould) that successful extension of the railroad to connect with the national network would require immense quantities of lumber for cross ties, trestle timbers, and supporting infrastructure. (Courtesy of Library of Congress.)

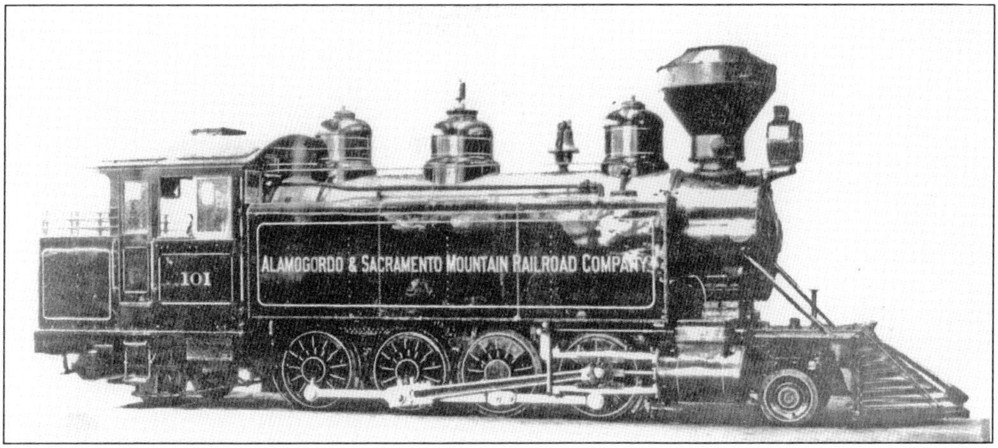

After acquiring the railroad franchise and beginning new construction, Charles Eddy organized the Alamogordo and Sacramento Mountain (A&SM) Railroad. The Baldwin Locomotive Works built the engines needed for the steep, twisted corkscrew route of the "Cloud-Climbing Railroad," completed by the end of 1898. A&SM engine No. 101, 2-8-2T Baldwin No. 16103, had two pilot wheels, eight drive wheels, two trailing wheels, a water tank, and fuel onboard. (Courtesy of Zeke Castro.)

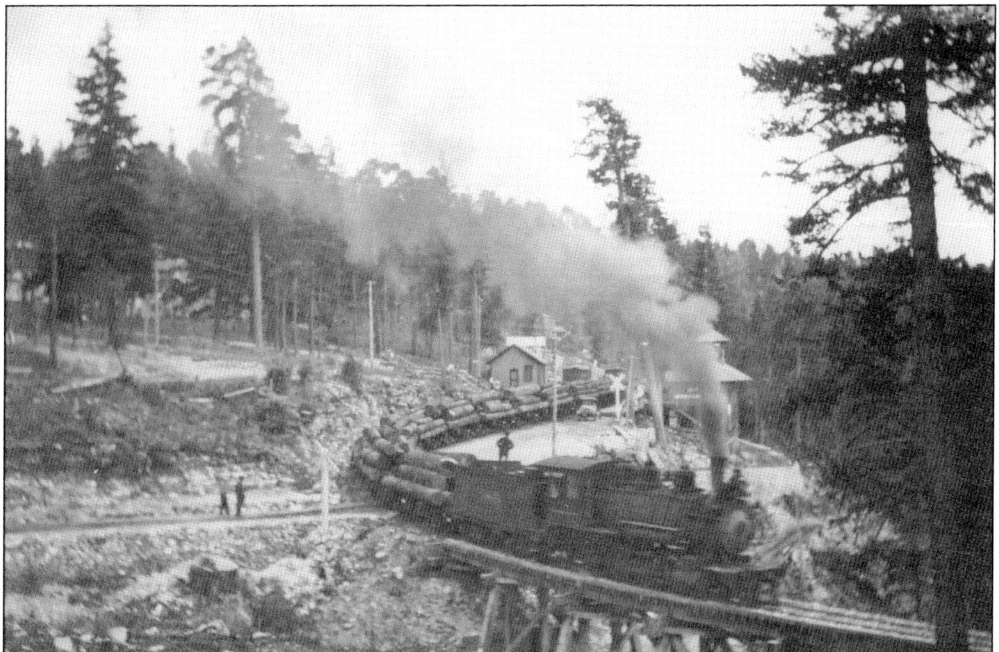

This A&SM logging train leaves the Cloudcroft depot to descend from 8,600 feet to 4,800 feet, an average grade of more than 3.5 percent in only 20 miles. Fifty-eight timber trestles, averaging 120 feet in length, were built along the route. The longest was 338 feet, with two 30-degree curves. (Courtesy of SMHS.)

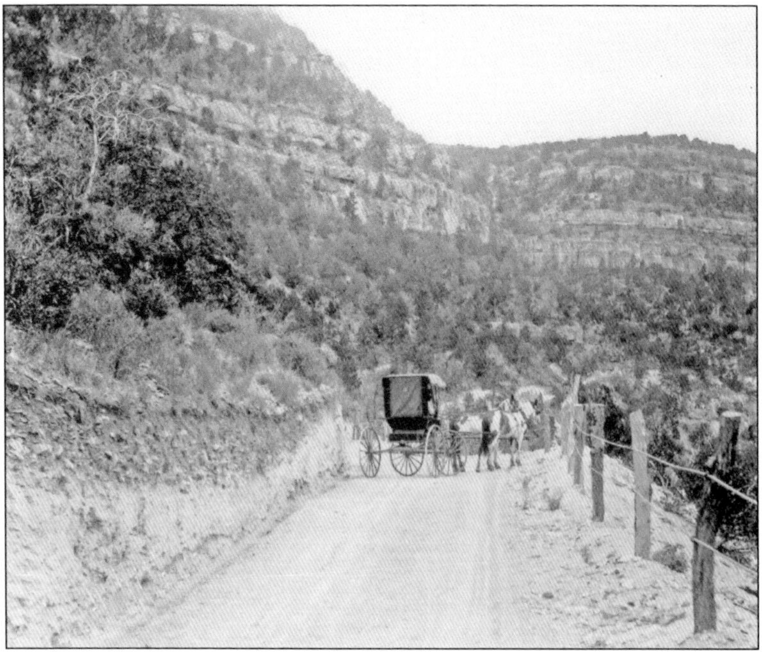

Fresnal Canyon Road—today's U.S. 82—was the only Western access route to the high Sacramento Mountains until the construction of the Alamogordo and Sacramento Mountain Railroad in 1898. (Courtesy of TBHS.)

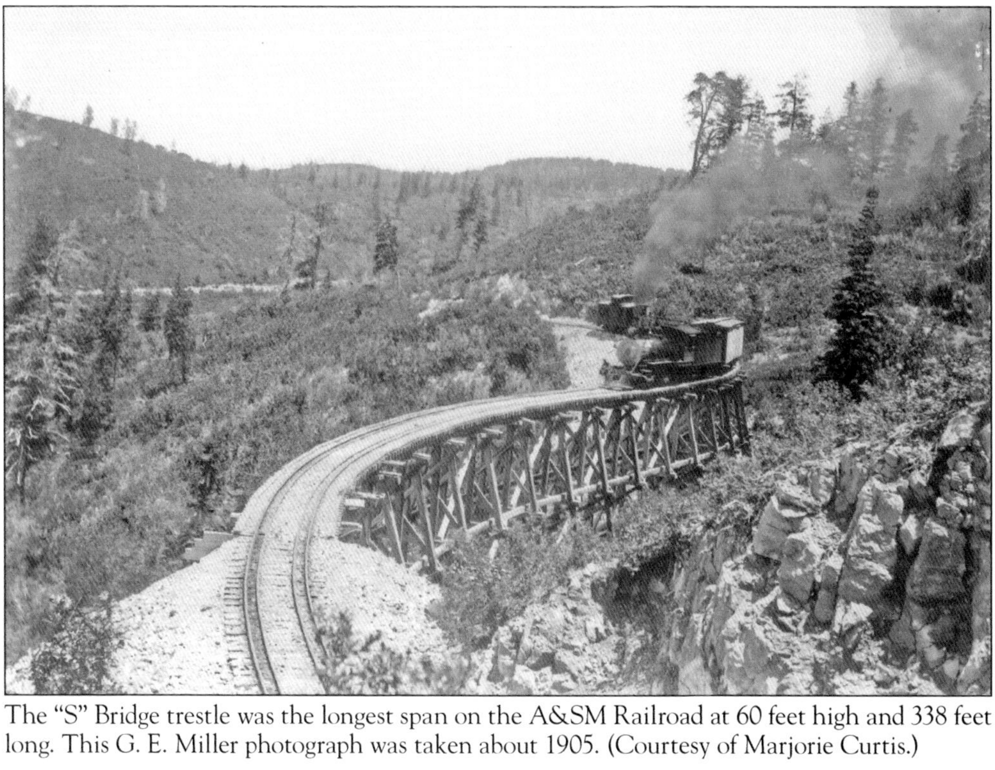

The "S" Bridge trestle was the longest span on the A&SM Railroad at 60 feet high and 338 feet long. This G. E. Miller photograph was taken about 1905. (Courtesy of Marjorie Curtis.)

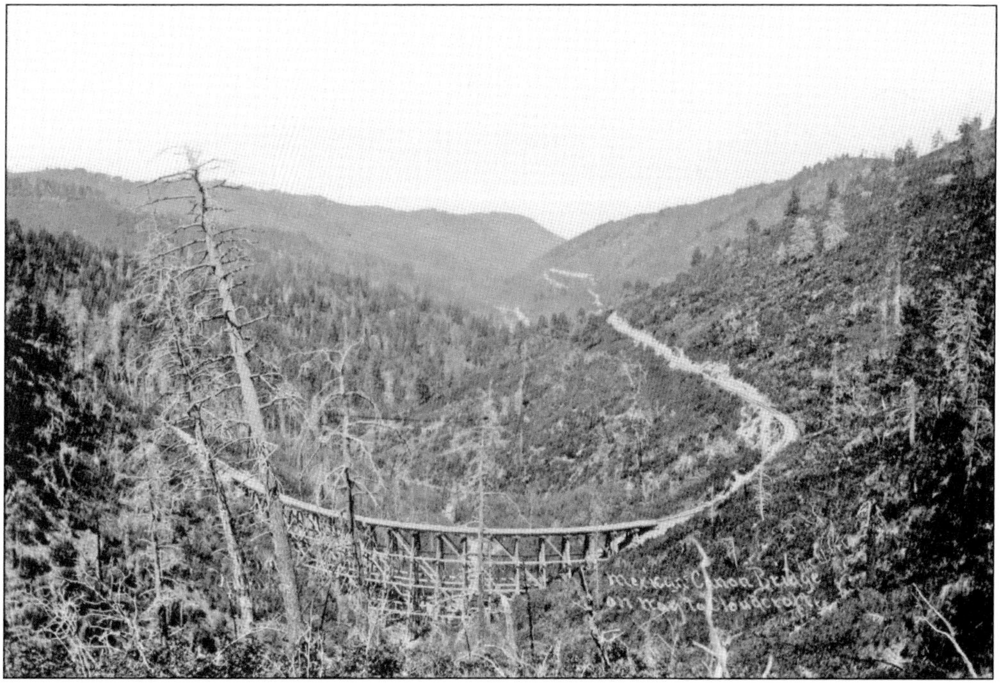

The Mexican Canyon Trestle just below Cloudcroft, seen in this photograph by Jim Alexander, is listed on the National Register of Historic Places. When the train blew its whistle on the trestle, town residents knew it would be about 15 minutes before the locomotive arrived. (Courtesy of SMHS.)

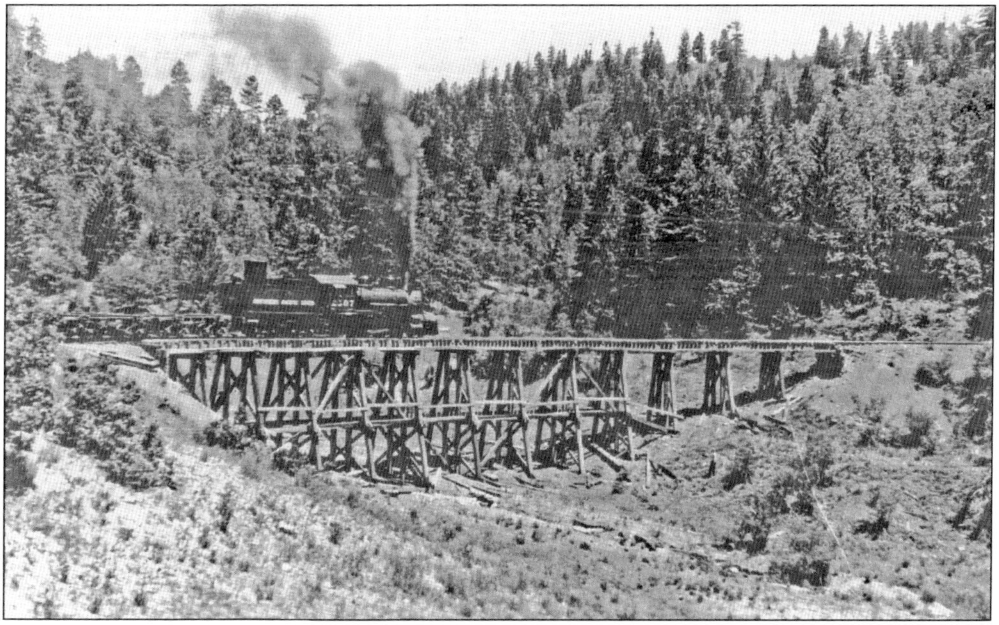

Southern Pacific Railroad Engine No. 2507 crosses one of the two trestles on the horseshoe curve at Bailey's Canyon in this 1936 photograph. (Courtesy of Zeke Castro.)

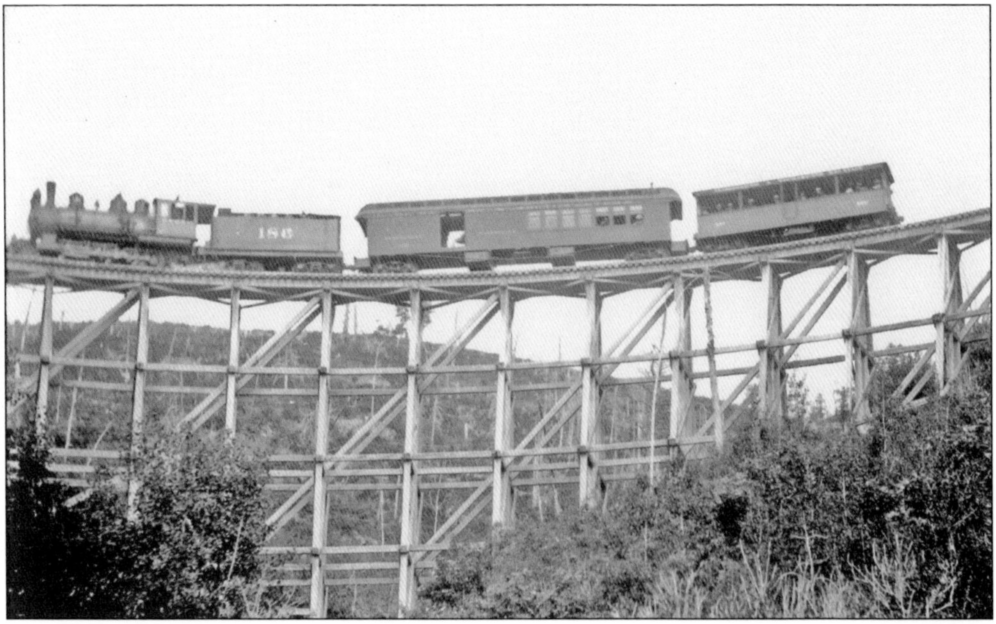

A single open-passenger Balley-Claire excursion car and mail train crosses the Mexican Canyon Trestle on its way from Cloudcroft in this photograph taken by Jim Alexander. (Courtesy of SMHS.)

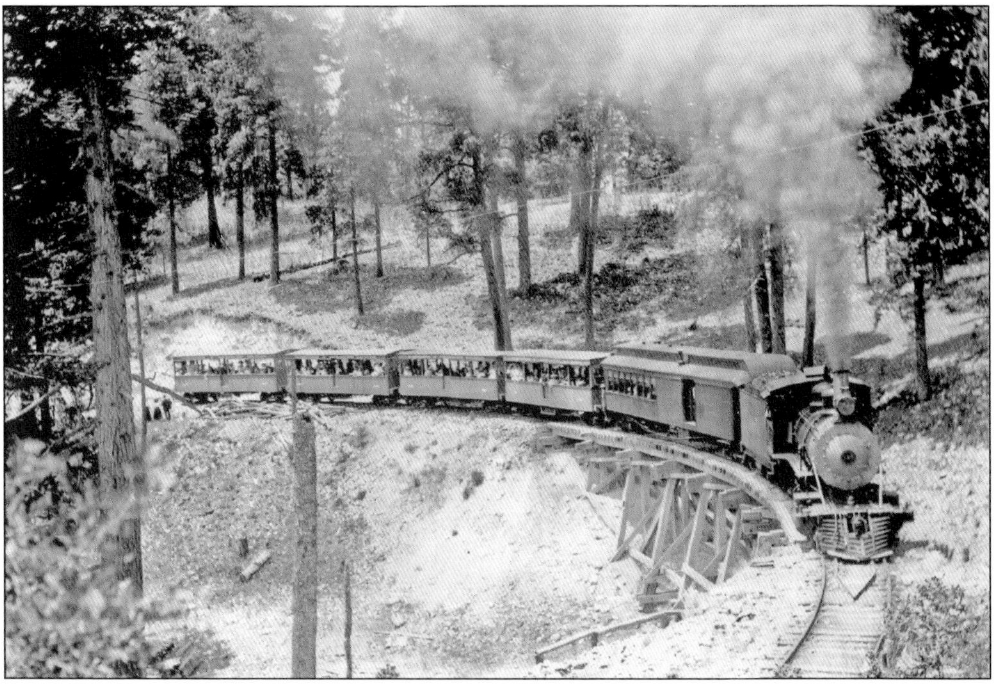

A mail car and all four passenger excursion cars approach Cloudcroft. (Photograph by Jim Alexander; courtesy of SMHS.)

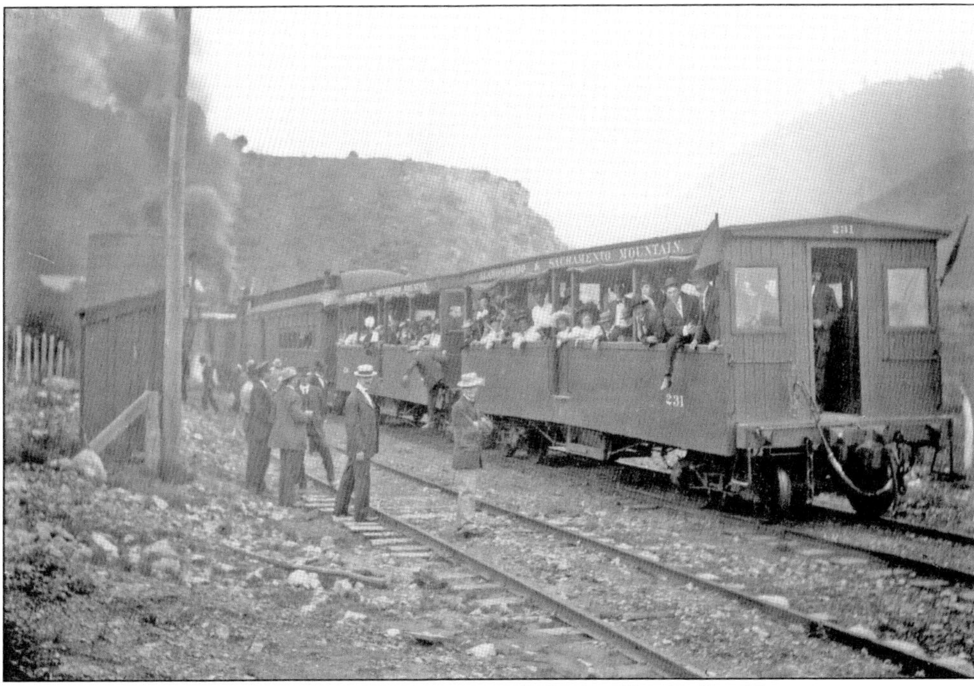

A&SM Railroad car No. 231, one of the four specially built yellow Balley-Claire excursion cars at Wooten Station, could hold 45 passengers. (Photograph by Jim Alexander; courtesy of SMHS.)

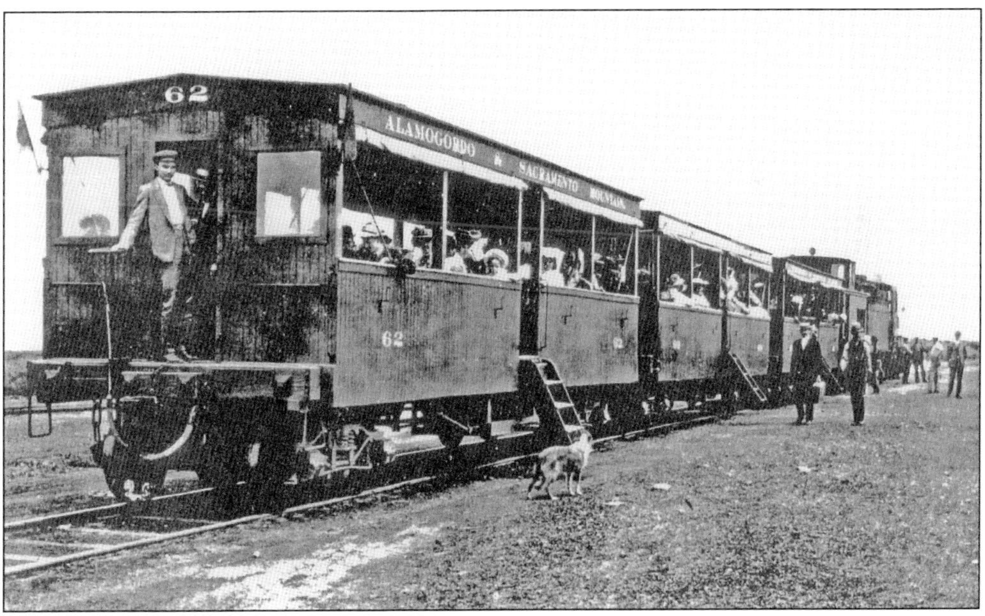

The A&SM Railroad excursion cars had side curtains in case of storms. They left Alamogordo at 9:00 a.m. with stops at local stations like High Rolls-Mountain Park, where local children would sell cut flowers to the passengers during the summer. (Courtesy of Zeke Castro.)

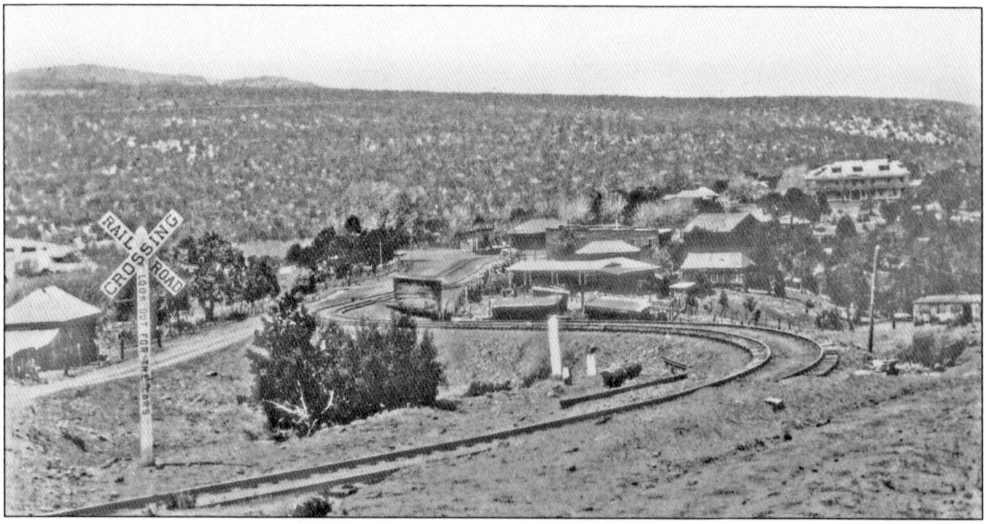

The rural community of High Rolls became a summer resort after the railroad arrived, supplementing its fruit and vegetable farming economy. The High Rolls Hotel (upper right) occupied the east end of Cottage Row, a road lined with small summer cottages. (Courtesy of Clif McDonald.)

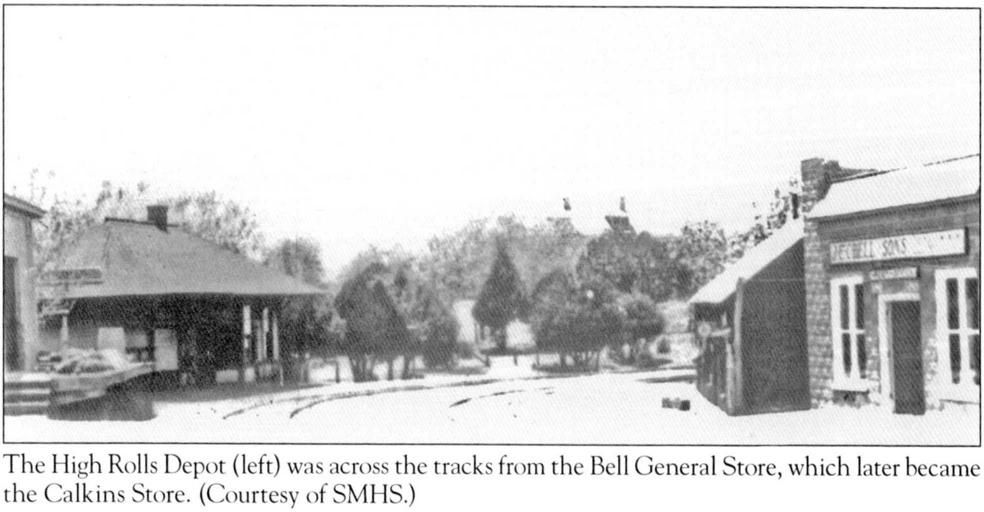

The High Rolls Depot (left) was across the tracks from the Bell General Store, which later became the Calkins Store. (Courtesy of SMHS.)

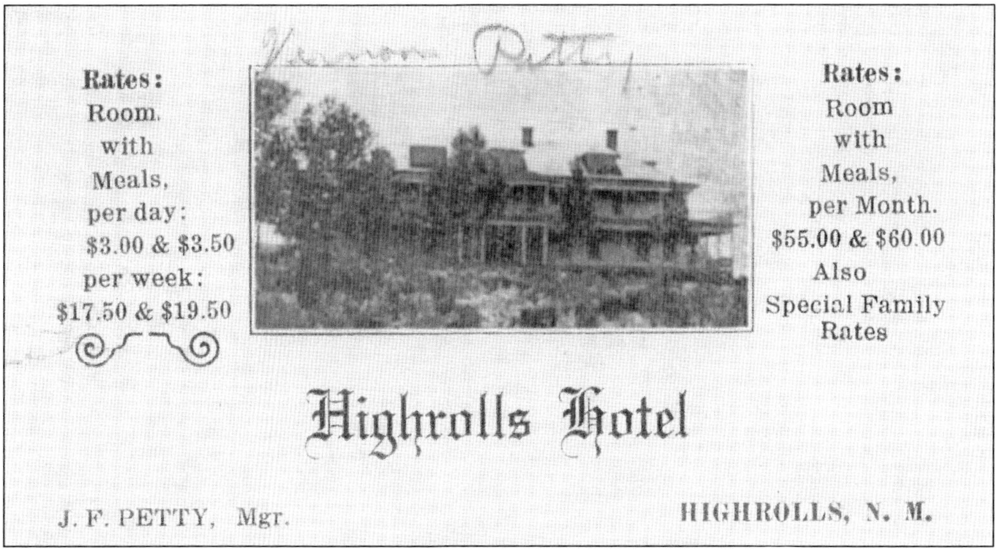

The Petty family still has one of the original High Rolls Hotel rate cards showing a photograph of the hotel with room and meal rates. (Courtesy of Vernon Petty.)

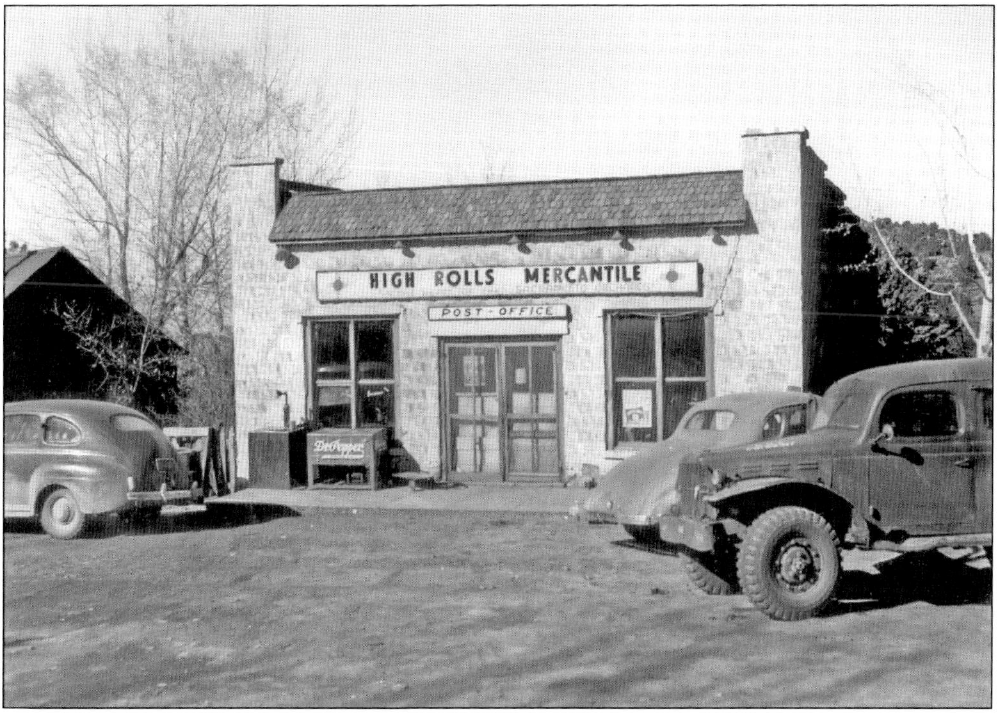

The Calkins High Rolls Mercantile was the successor to the original Bell Store next door, which was converted to a residence. (Courtesy of Cecil Calkins.)

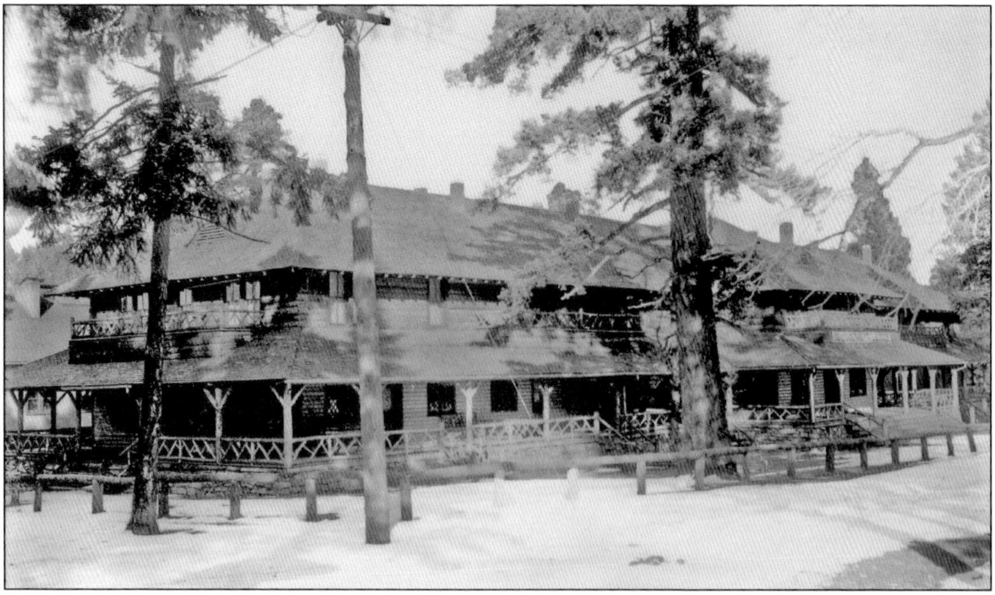

The railroad built the original two-story Cloudcroft Lodge in 1901. The lodge building was 212 feet by 80 feet with log slab sides, a surrounding rustic porch, and a wooden shingle roof. (Photograph by Jim Alexander; courtesy of SMHS.)

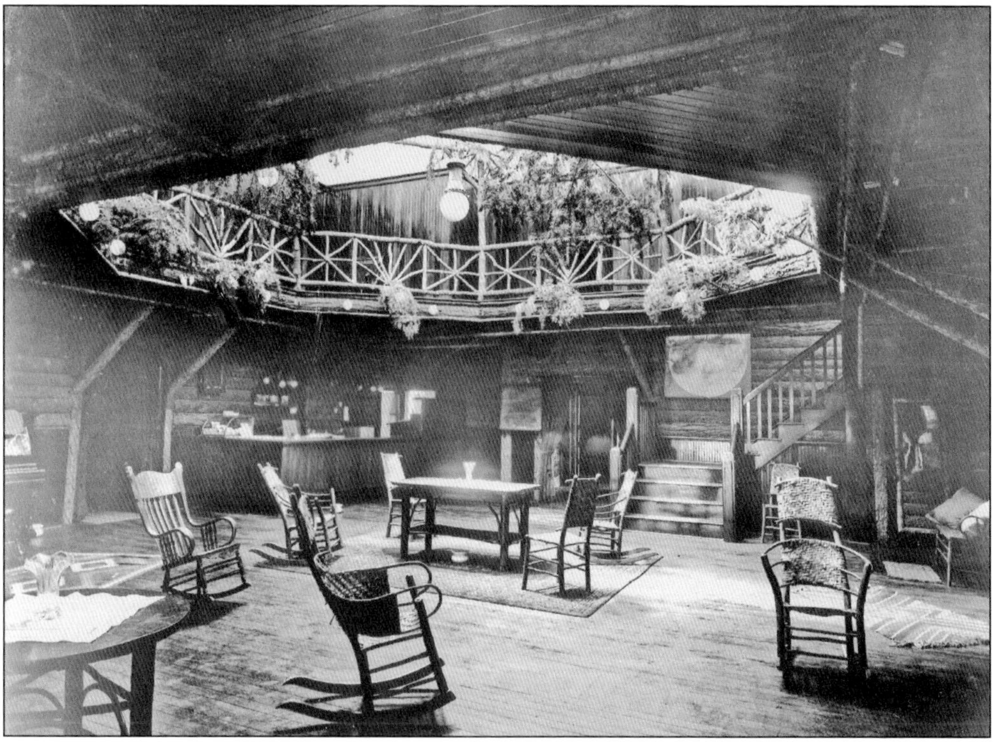

The central lobby of the Cloudcroft Lodge was furnished and appointed in a rustic Adirondack style with stick railings, caned chairs, and hanging plants. (Courtesy of SMHS.)

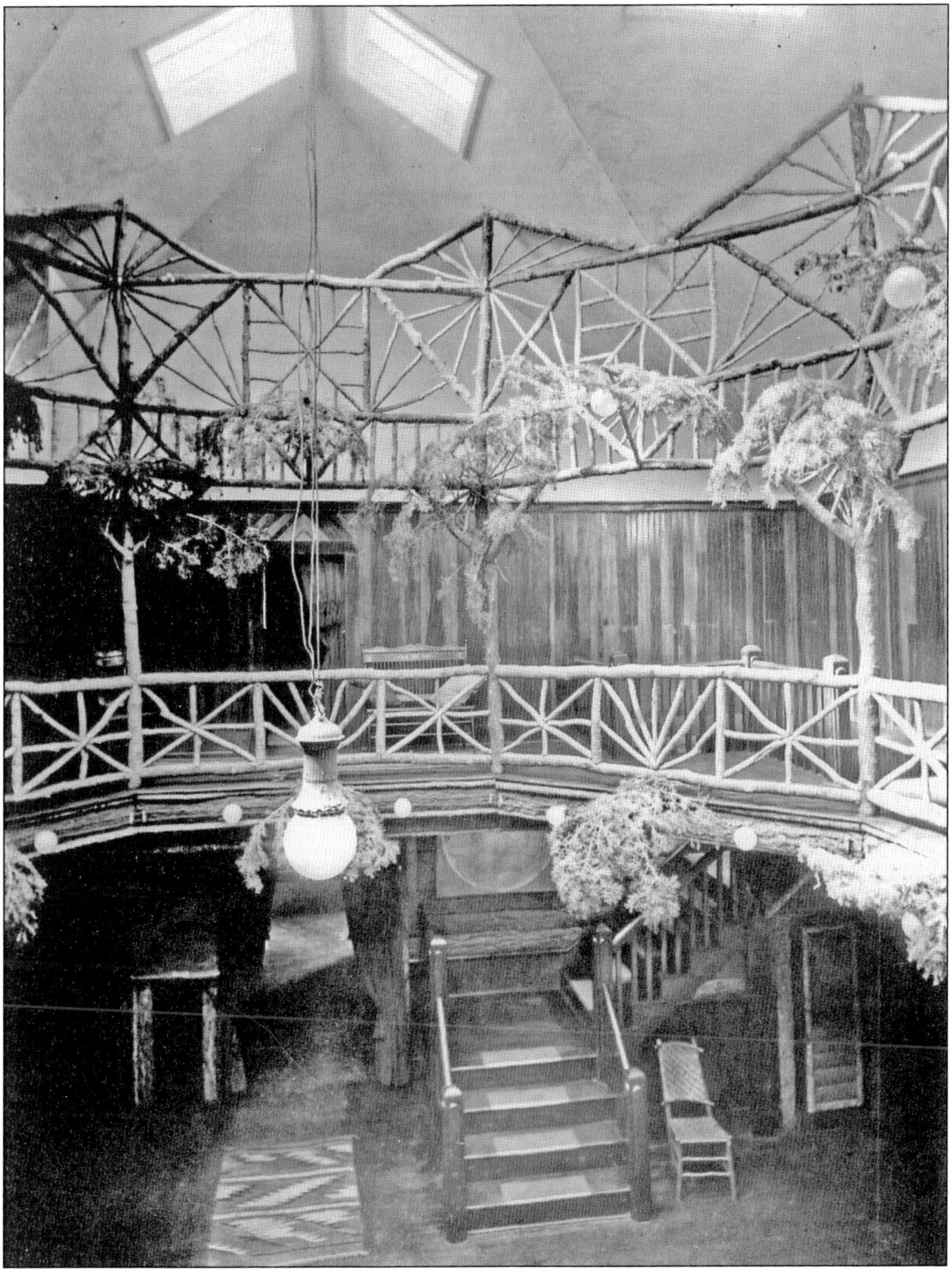

The rustic mezzanine above the lobby in the lodge was lit by skylights and often decorated with fresh pine boughs, a clear fire hazard. (Courtesy of SMHS.)

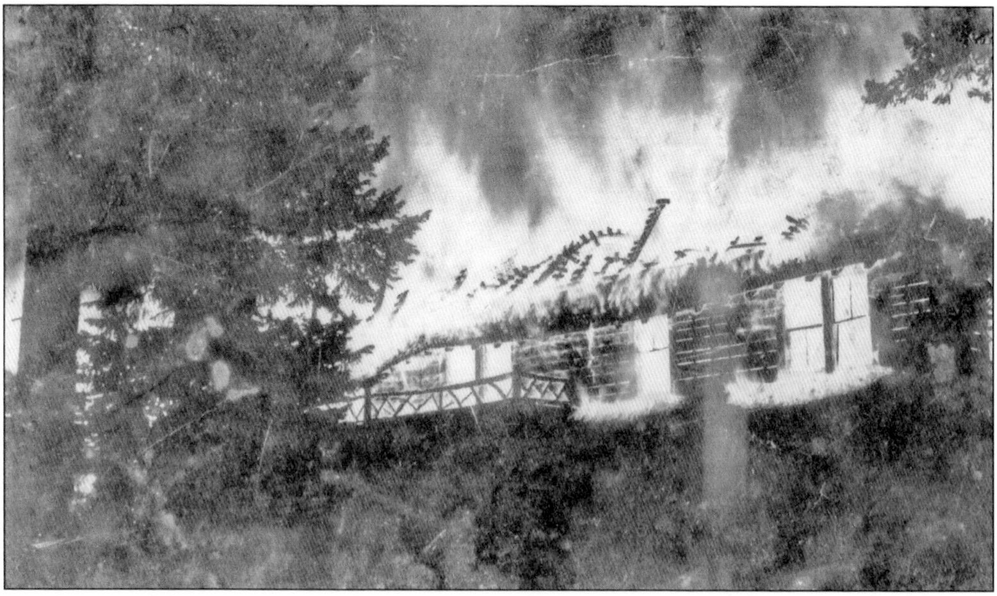

Fire devastated the original Cloudcroft Lodge at 2:00 a.m. on July 13, 1909, completely consuming the wooden building. (Photograph by Jim Alexander; courtesy of SMHS.)

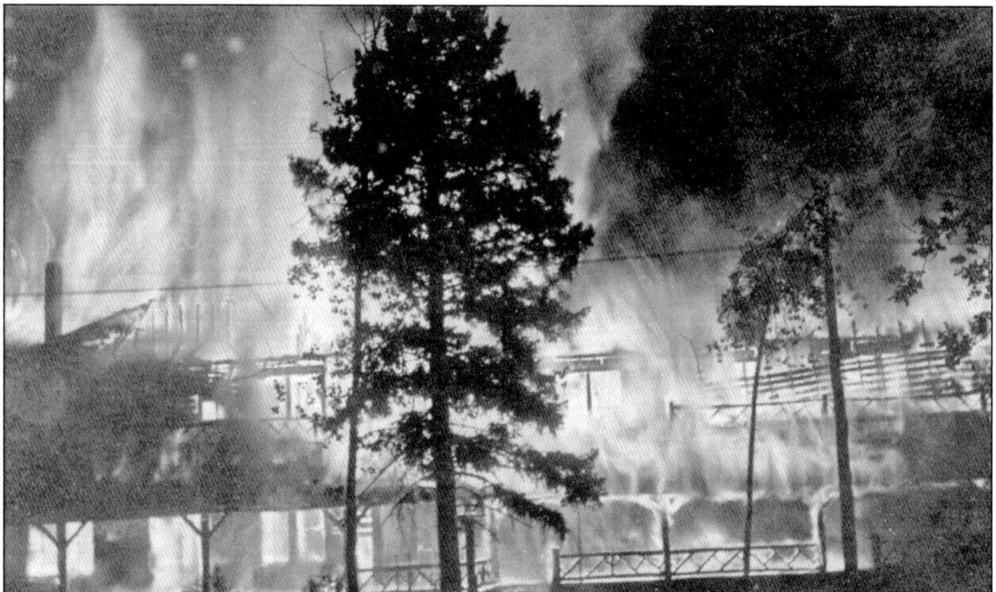

The lodge was rebuilt six blocks south of its original location, where it burned to the ground, and reopened in 1911. (Photograph by Jim Alexander; courtesy of SMHS.)

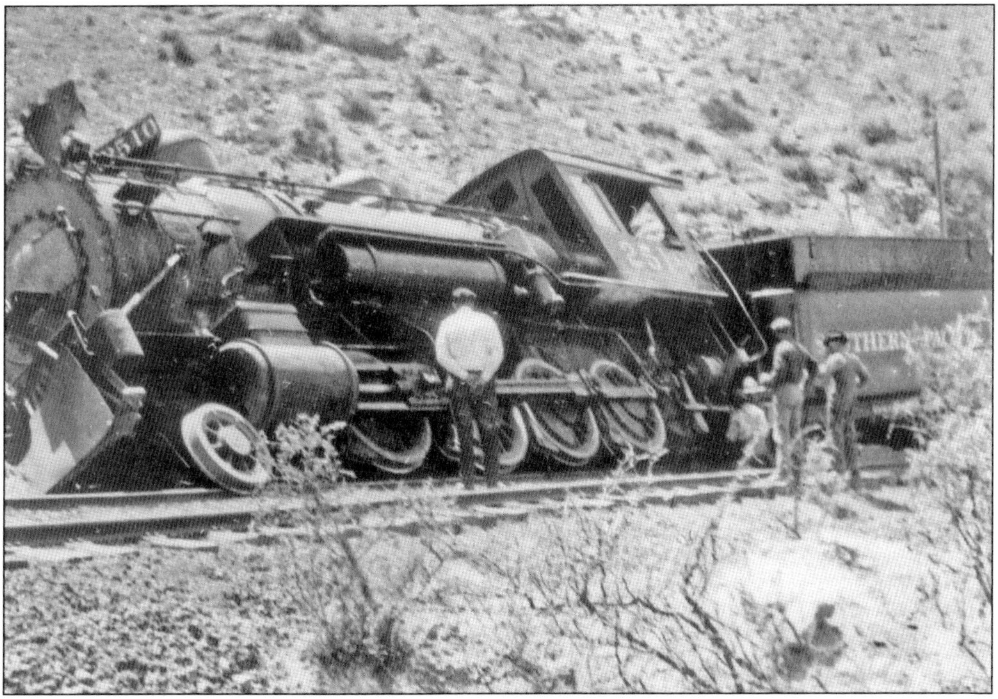

Uneven track, slumping of fill, and equipment failure occasionally caused derailment of A&SM engines and trains, like engine No. 2510, whose pony wheel axle broke. (Courtesy of SMHS.)

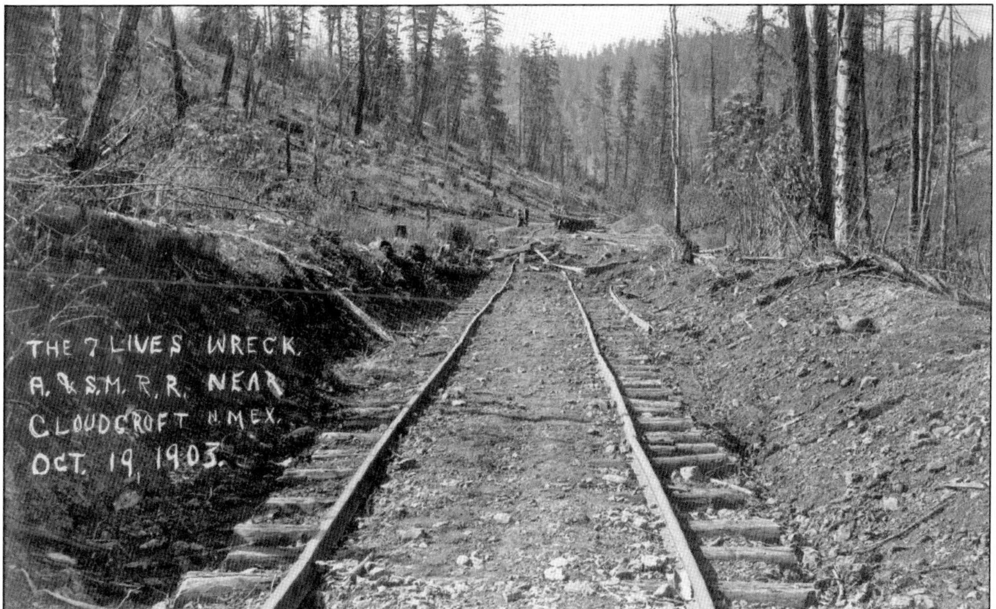

The "Seven Lives Wreck" took place near Cloudcroft on October 19, 1903. The evening train down the mountain was fully loaded with passengers and a load of logs. When the engineer tried to unsuccessfully slow for the steep grades, he realized he did not have sufficient air pressure. He reversed the engine and jumped, as did most of the passengers, but three were killed immediately, four more died from injuries, and thirteen others were seriously injured. (Courtesy of TBHS.)

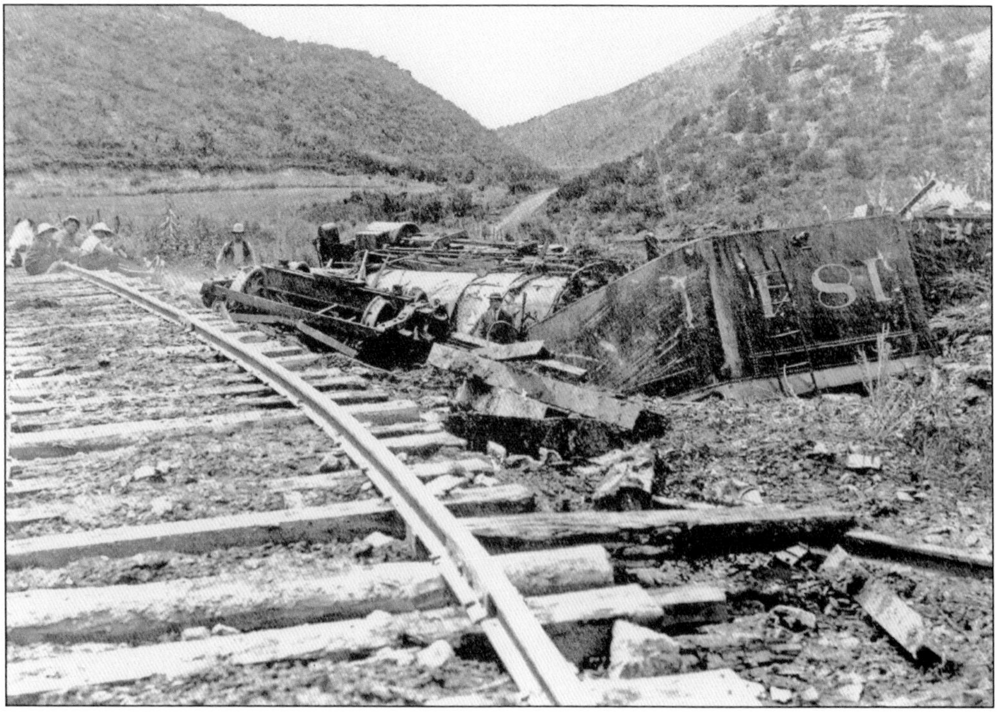

SP No. 2508 (EP&NE No. 55; EP&SW No. 184) wrecked near Wooten in about 1907. Engineer F. M. Weldy was killed in the wreck when the train slid on the steep grade because of wet rails. (Courtesy of SMHS.)

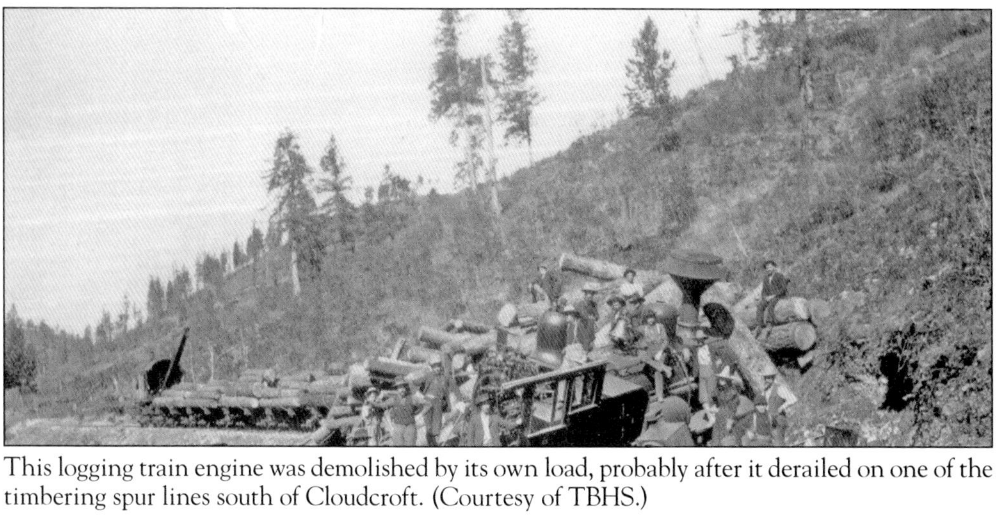

This logging train engine was demolished by its own load, probably after it derailed on one of the timbering spur lines south of Cloudcroft. (Courtesy of TBHS.)

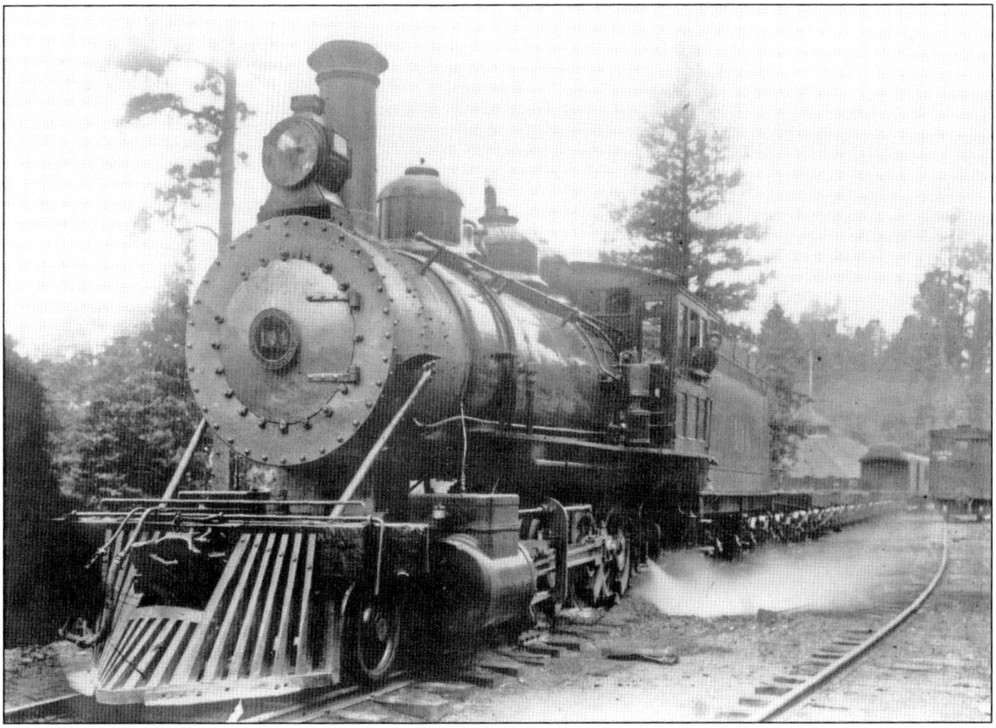

A&SM Railroad Engine No. 104, with two pilot wheels and eight 46-inch drive wheels, was built by Baldwin in 1899. It produced 160 pounds per square inch of steam pressure, weighed about 70 tons, and could pull about 15 tons. (Courtesy of Clif McDonald.)

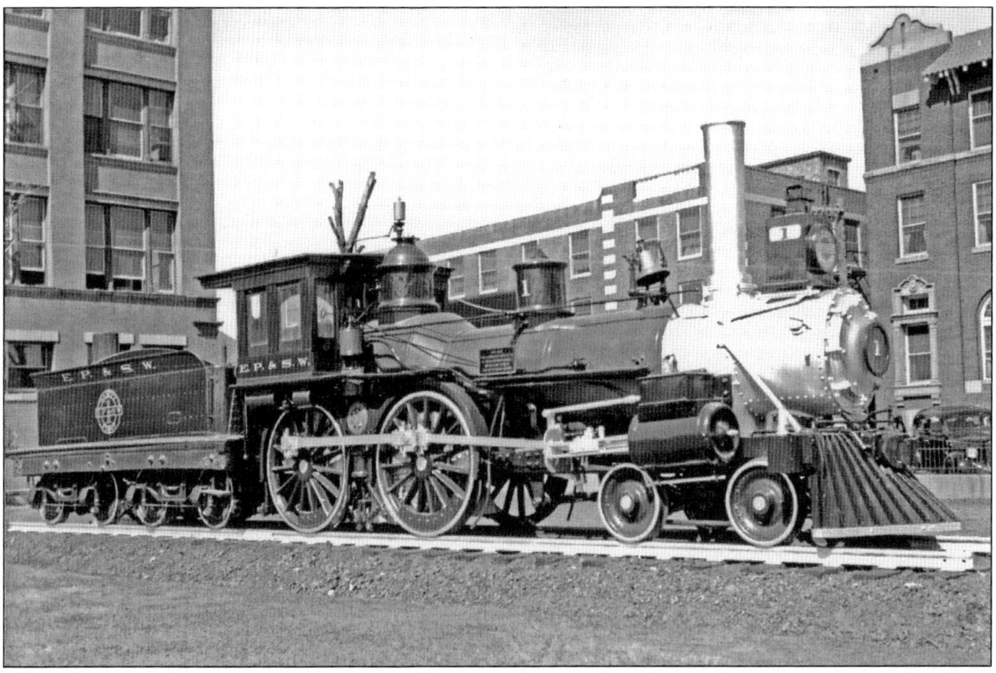

This El Paso and Southwestern Engine, shown in this c. 1946 photograph, was preserved and put on display in El Paso, Texas. (Courtesy of TBHS.)

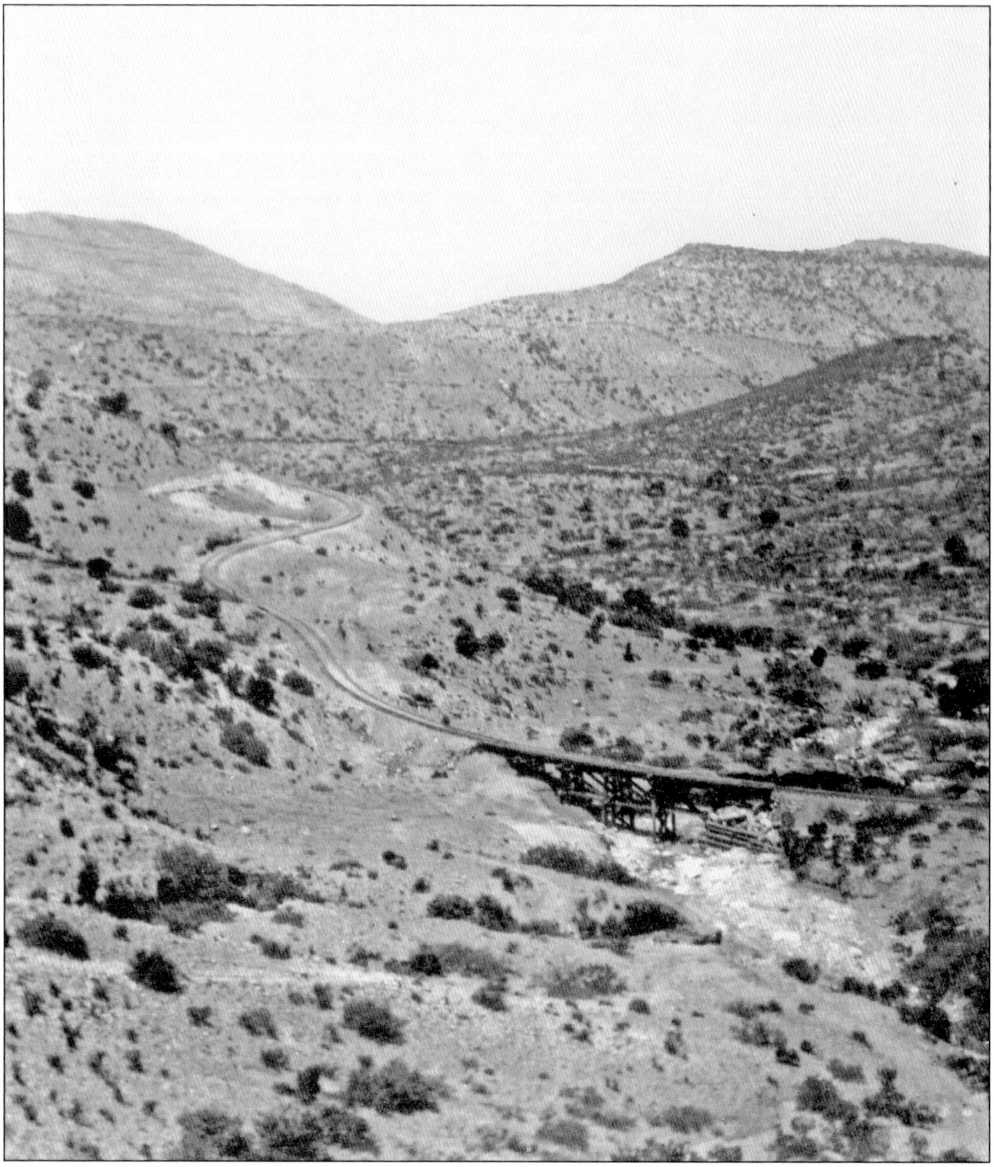

Most of the "corkscrew" Alamogordo and Southwestern route was transformed into highways after this, the last scheduled train, descended from Cloudcroft on September 12, 1947. (Courtesy of TBHS.)

Two

THE RANCHING ERA

Alamogordo grew rapidly. In 1905, its population had reached 3,500. The railroad brought tourists to the mountains and opened markets for farm products, timber, and minerals, especially lead and copper. The Alamogordo and Sacramento Mountains Railroad encouraged the growth of the several mountain communities and brought apples, cherries, and vegetables down to the new city for distribution or shipment elsewhere. The Edgar Cadwallader orchards alone had more than 30,000 fruit trees. The railroad also allowed expansion of southern New Mexico's growing cattle industry and an Angora goat industry in the nearby San Andres Mountains.

The city was laid out in quadrants with a formal grid of streets similar to New York or Philadelphia. It lacked the central plaza characteristic of Hispanic New Mexico's older towns and had a preplanned ethnic neighborhood, known as Chihuahuita, between First and Third Streets and Railroad to Texas Avenues. From its beginning, Alamogordo was a mixture of Hispanics, Native Americans, European Americans, Asians, and African Americans, some of whom were retired Buffalo Soldiers. In 1899, a syndicate of local Chinese bought the Denver Dining Parlor in Alamogordo, adding it to several others in neighboring towns. The town also boasted three Chinese laundries. At that time, segregation was officially prohibited in the territory, and the de facto segregation of the first schools was more a matter of proximity and convenience than policy. In 1901, the Mexican School, later known as the Dudley School, at Sixth Street and Maryland Avenue, listed an average of 150 pupils in first, first "high," and second grades. Dudley probably served African Americans and other ethnic minorities as well. After the first few grades, those students were mainstreamed into the core school system. Real segregation in the schools did not come until 1928. A segregated black school was constructed at Fourth Street and Pennsylvania Avenue and later moved to Fourth Street and Delaware Avenue, where it became known as the Delaware School. African American segregation lasted until 1949, when the first four black students were admitted to the high school.

At its height, the crown jewel of the southern New Mexico cattle industry was Oliver M. Lee's Circle Cross Ranch centered in the Sacramento Mountains. Just before its collapse into bankruptcy in 1929, the Circle Cross Cattle Company controlled more than 1 million acres of rangeland. It and many of its competitors were broken up into smaller, controlled range ranches during the Great Depression.

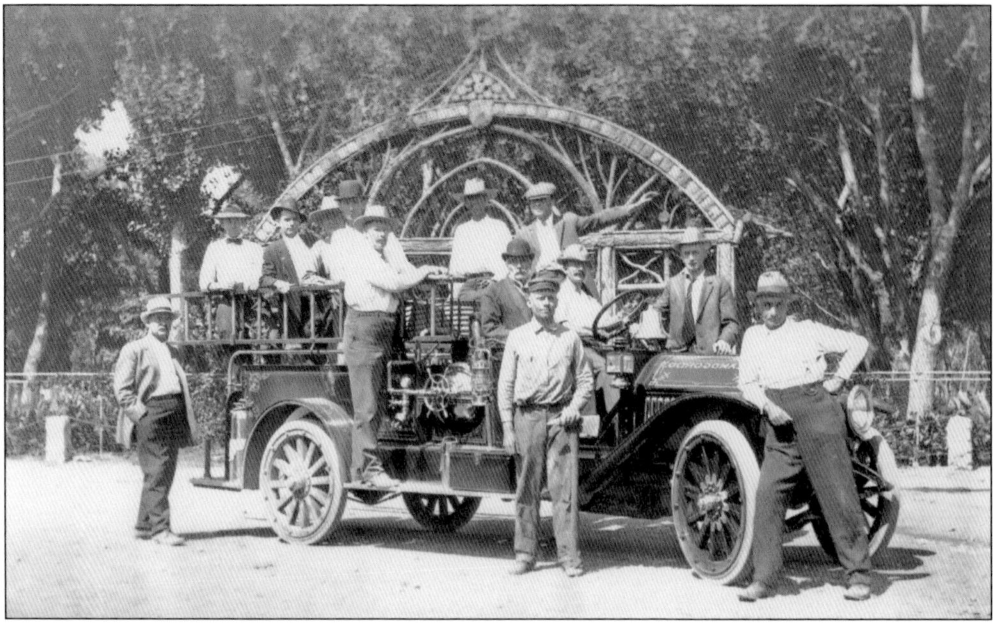

Alamogordo bought its first fire truck for $3,000 in 1914 from the Anderson Coupling and Fire Supply Company in Kansas City, Missouri. In 1912, F. C. Rolland was chief, with volunteer firemen Emmett Hancock, J. J. Hill, Stanley Holden, Charles Hickman, Frank Bufkin, T. A. Pace, Marshall Parker, John Tweed, and Mel Walters. (Courtesy of TBHS.)

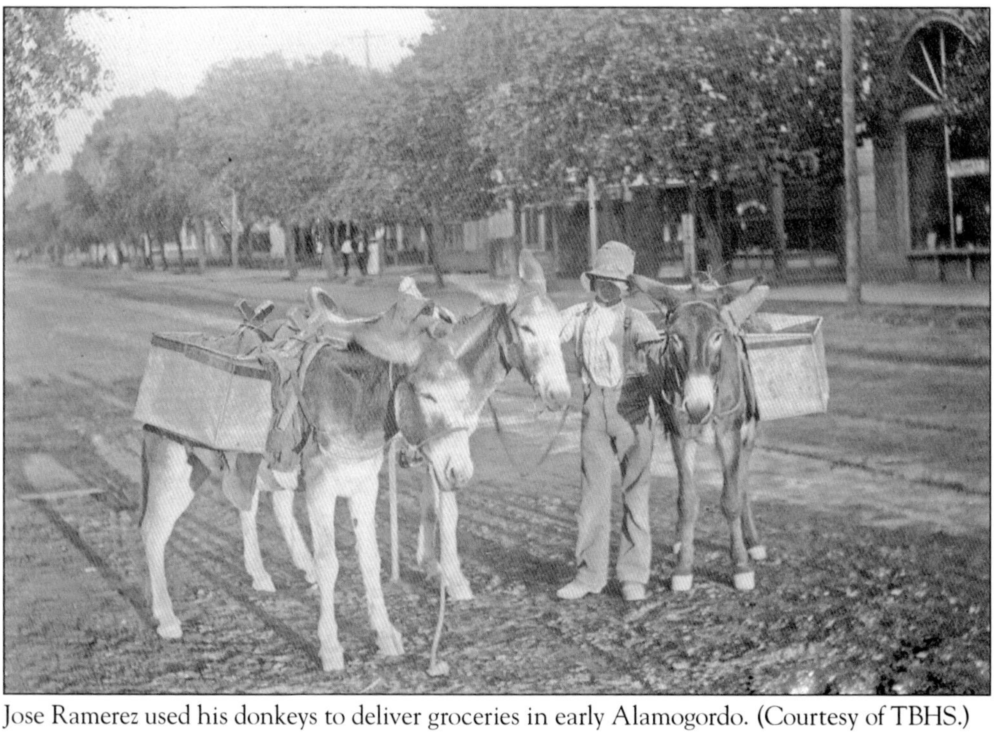

Jose Ramerez used his donkeys to deliver groceries in early Alamogordo. (Courtesy of TBHS.)

Jose Guieterrez delivers hay for carriage horses on New York Avenue in about 1902. (Courtesy of Davis Baca.)

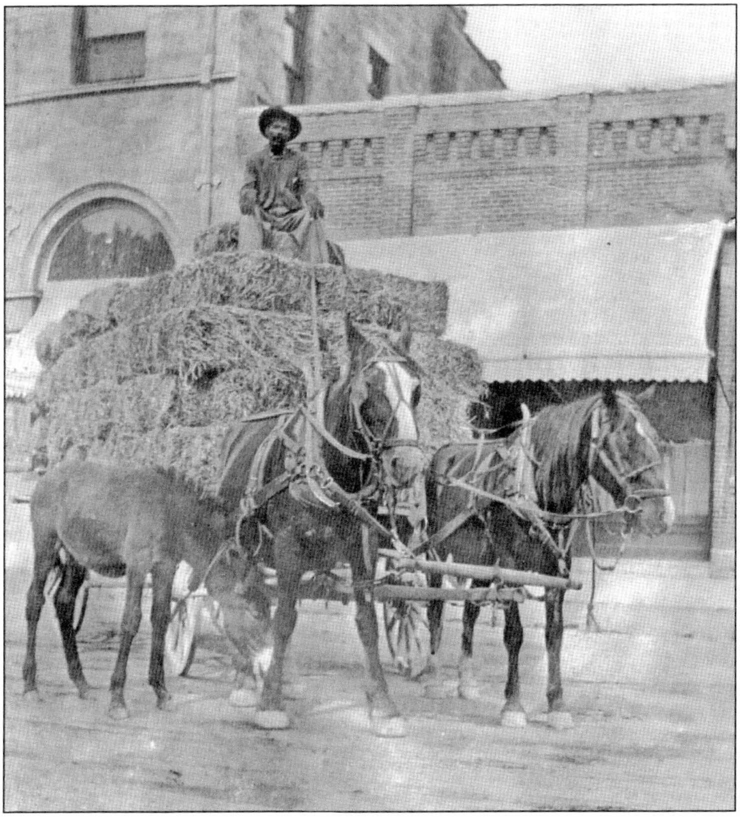

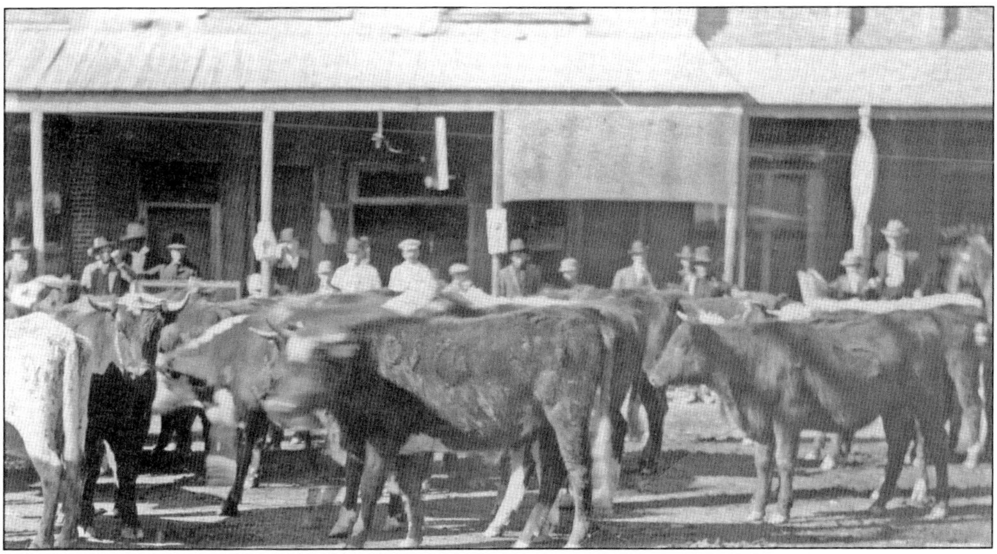

This postcard, postmarked 1909, identifies "30 head of cattle for the cash market" on New York Avenue. (Courtesy of Clif McDonald.)

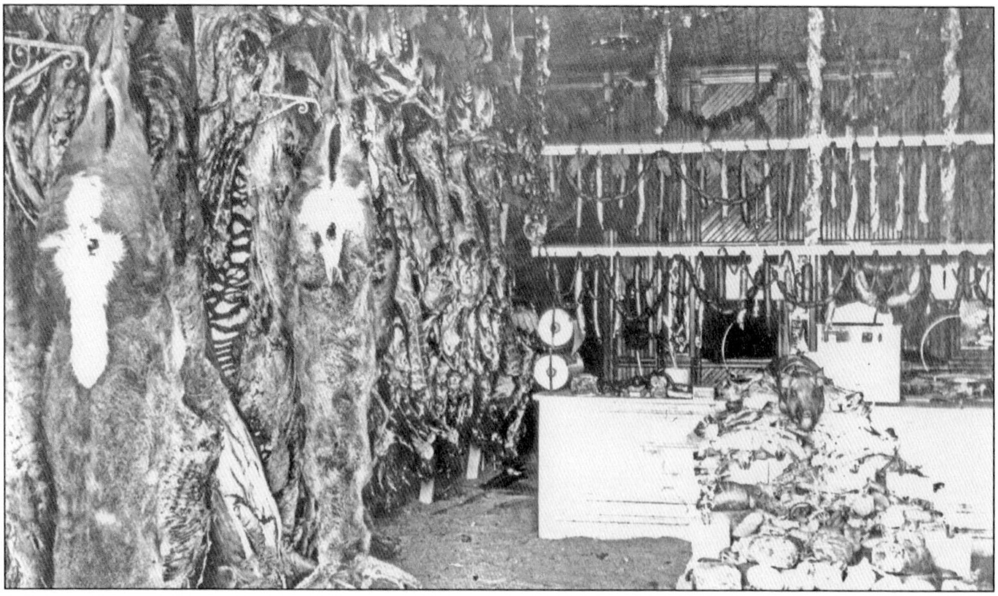

George Richardson and Oliver M. Lee, whose Dog Canyon Ranch supplied meat for the building of the railroad, operated the City Meat Market on New York Avenue in early Alamogordo. They sold venison, pheasant, pork, and sausage, as well as beef. (Courtesy of Davis Baca.)

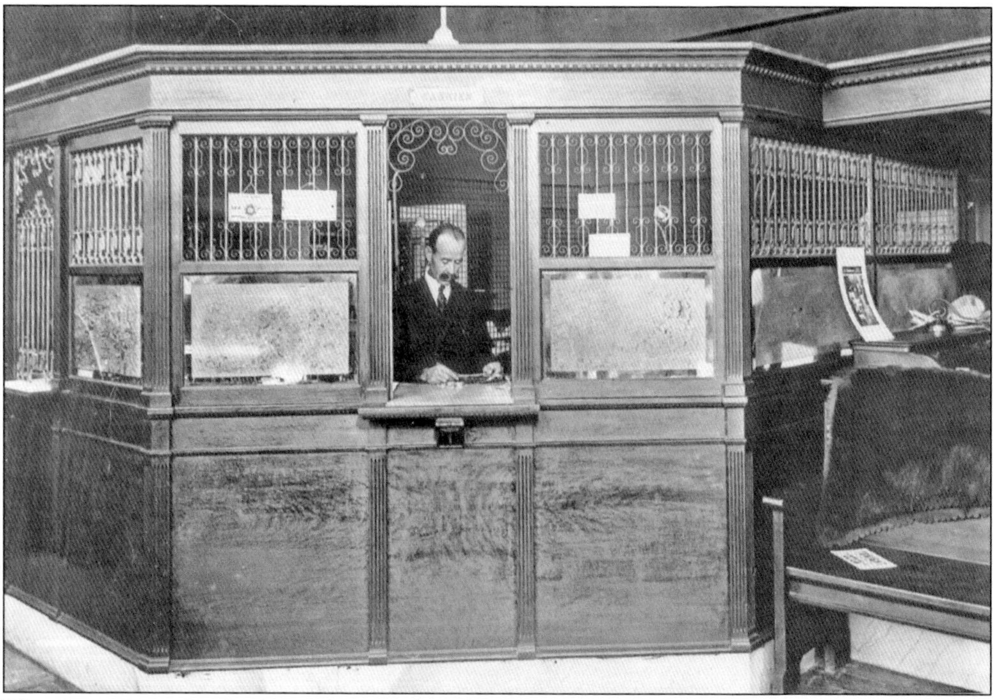

The Otero State Bank, shown here with cashier E. H. Wayland, operated at Tenth Street and New York Avenue. (Courtesy of Alamogordo Public Library.)

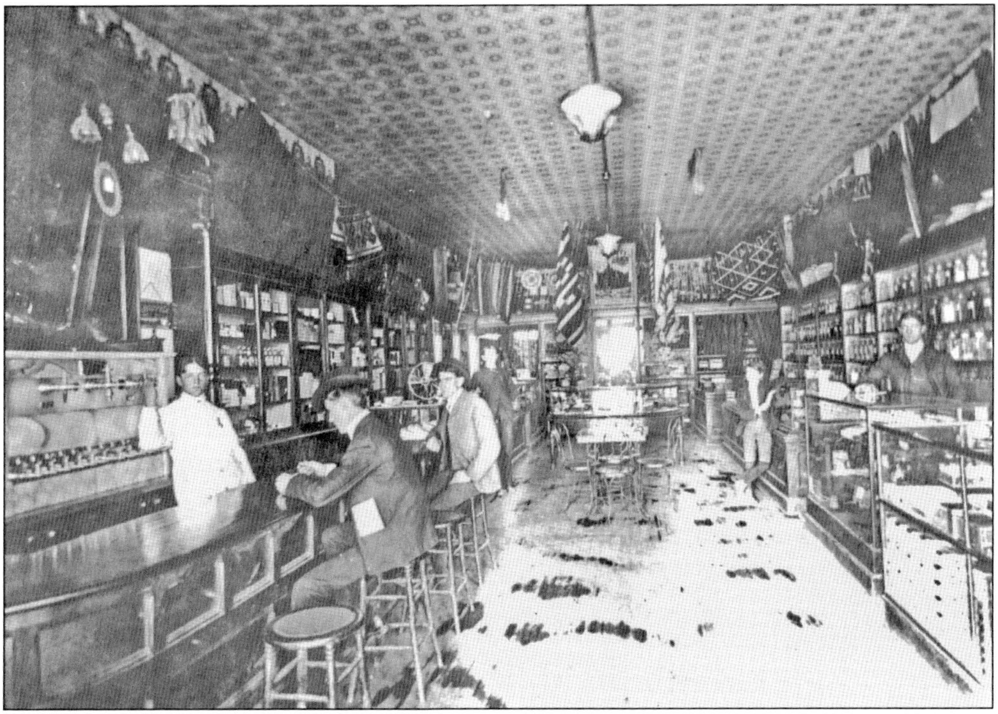

Druggist Frank Rolland purchased his employers' Aragon Brothers Drug Store in New York Avenue's Sutherland Building and opened F. C. Rolland's Drugs and Curios in 1901. The store had a soda fountain as well as a pharmacy, and Navajo rugs were hung from the wall and ceiling. (Courtesy of Clif McDonald.)

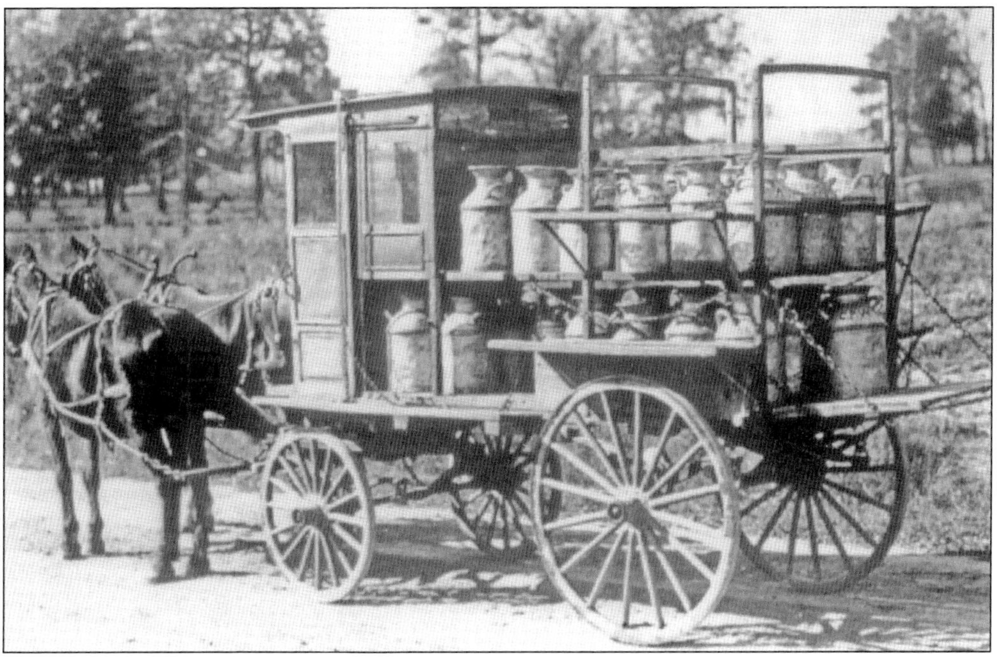

Horse-drawn milk wagons like this one delivered dairy products to Cloudcroft residents during its early days. (Courtesy of Clif McDonald.)

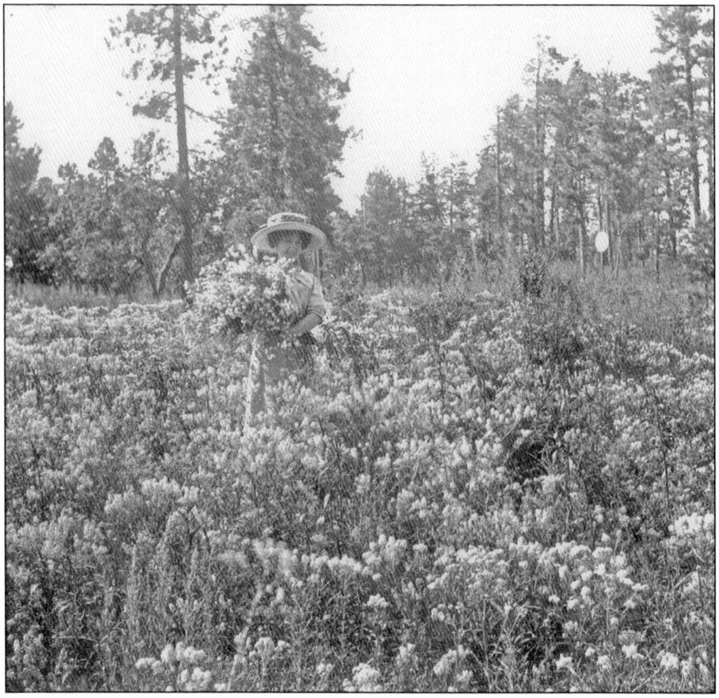

This woman is harvesting summer wildflowers. Cut flowers and vegetables were major summertime products in the mountain communities along the A&SM "Cloud-Climbing" Railroad. (Photograph by Jim Alexander; courtesy of SMHS.)

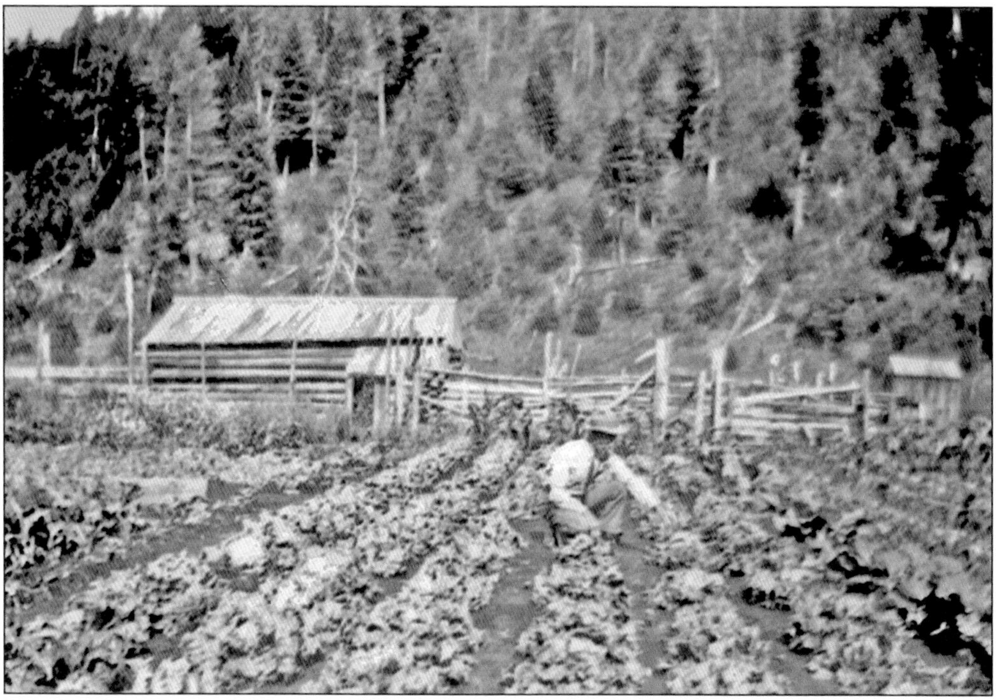

This local farmer, probably W. Buckner, tends his commercial lettuce garden around 1927. The Buckner homestead was along Agua Chiquita Creek near Weed, New Mexico, on the east side of the Sacramento Mountains. (Courtesy of Ruby Buckner.)

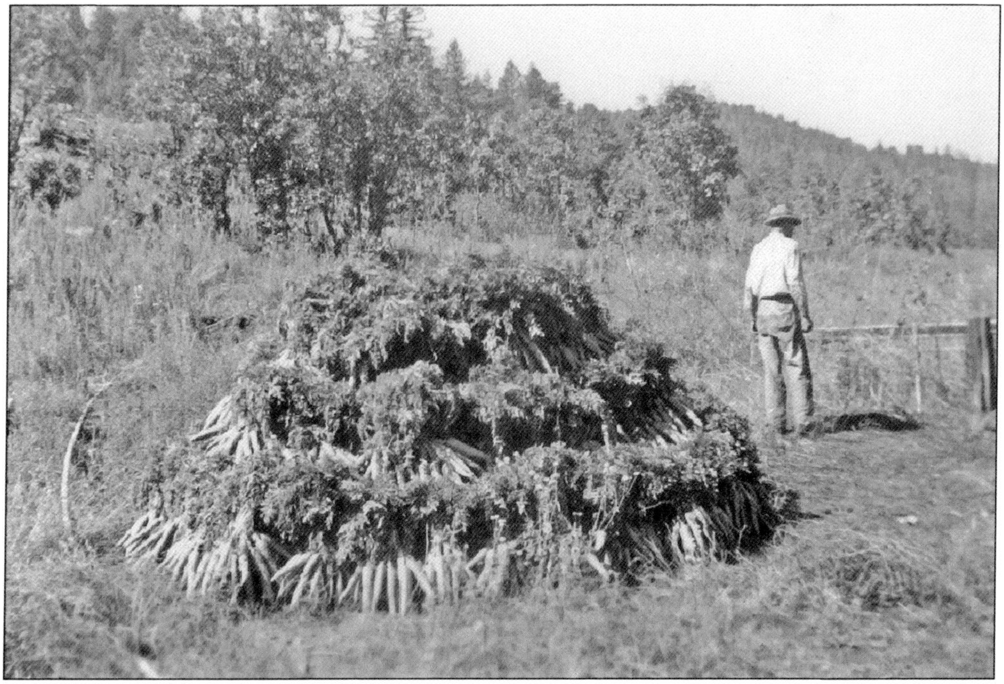

Bert Davis was known for his carrots, which he grew in Cox Canyon, near Cloudcroft. He is shown here with a large pile of his harvest that was sold locally. (Courtesy of the Carner family.)

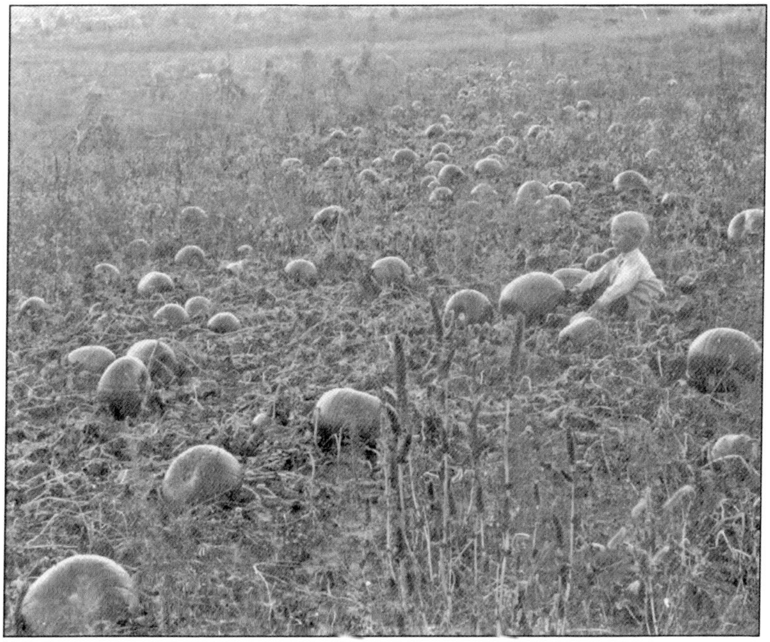

This large, successful pumpkin patch is watched over by this youngster, simply identified as "Charlie," probably at the G. E. Miller farm in the Sacramento Mountains. G. E. Miller took this photograph in 1908. (Courtesy of Rick Miller.)

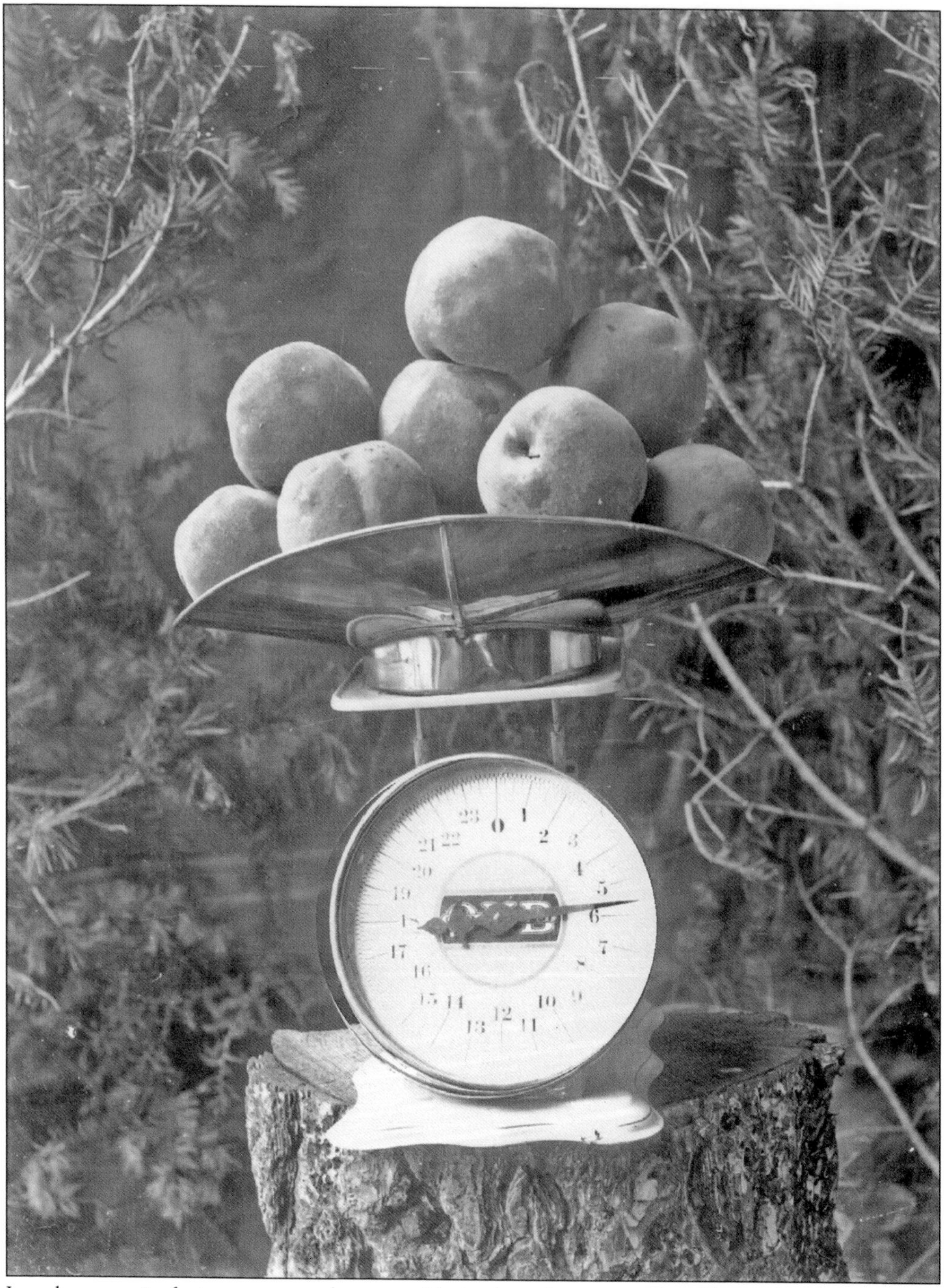

Local mountain fruit growers took great pride in their fruit crops. Jim Alexander photographed these dozen peaches that weighed nearly 6 pounds. (Courtesy of SMHS.)

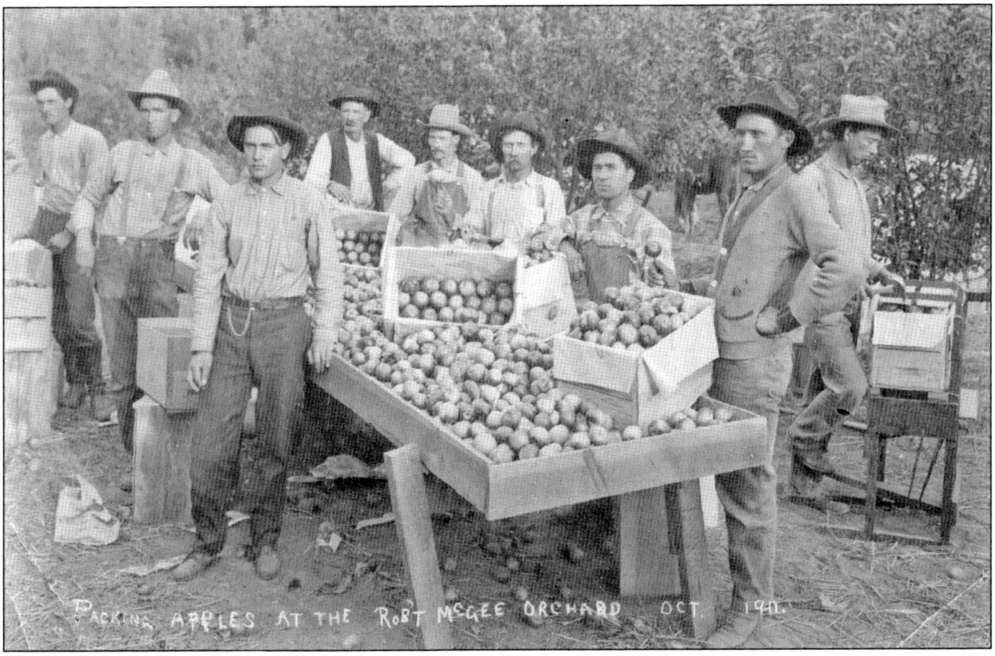

Picking, sorting, and packaging local apples was a major fall industry in the mountain communities. G. E. Miller photographed the McGee orchard crew, which included, from left to right, Allen Clayton, Monroe Brantley, Frank Latham, Fred Brantley, Jasper Scott, Tony Curtis, Monte Keith, Charlie Clayton, and Melvin Dollins. (Courtesy of Marjorie Curtis.)

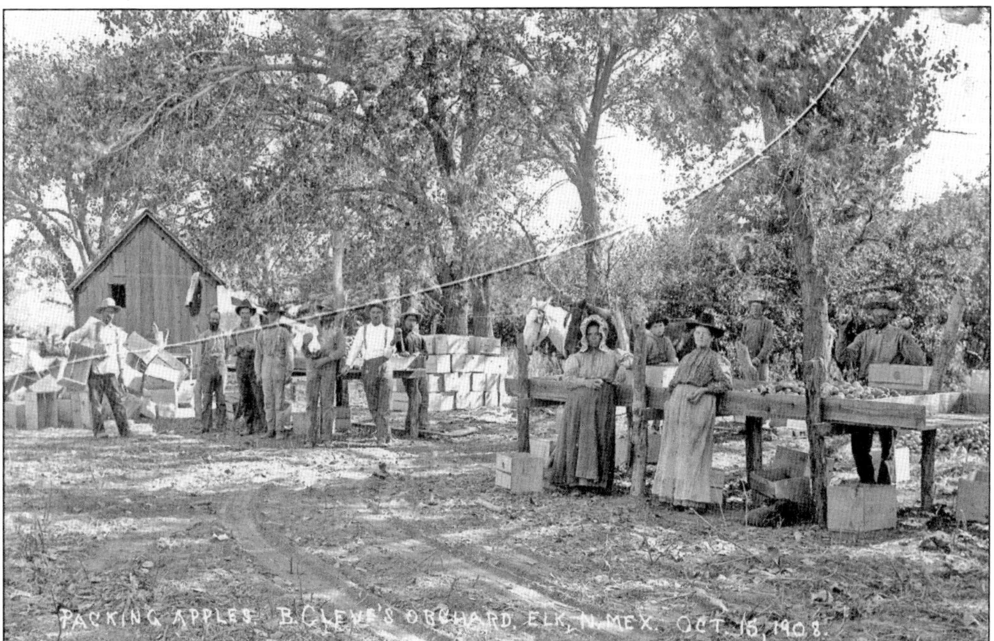

G. E. Miller also photographed apple packing at the Bernard Cleve Orchards in 1908. Bernard Cleve owned the CX Ranch store and the Cottonwood Farm on the lower Penasco River near Elk, where he operated a mercantile and was postmaster and Lincoln County commissioner. (Courtesy of TBHS.)

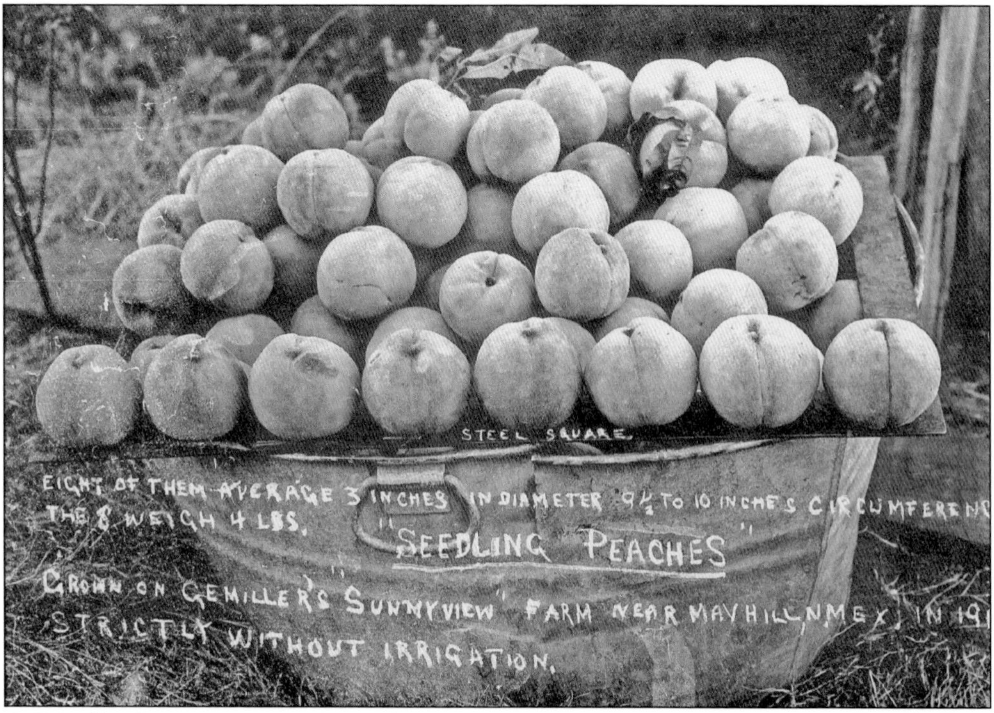

G. E. Miller also grew prize peaches on his Sunnyview Farm near Mayhill. These "seedling peaches" averaged 3 inches in diameter and weighed about half a pound each. (Courtesy of SMHS.)

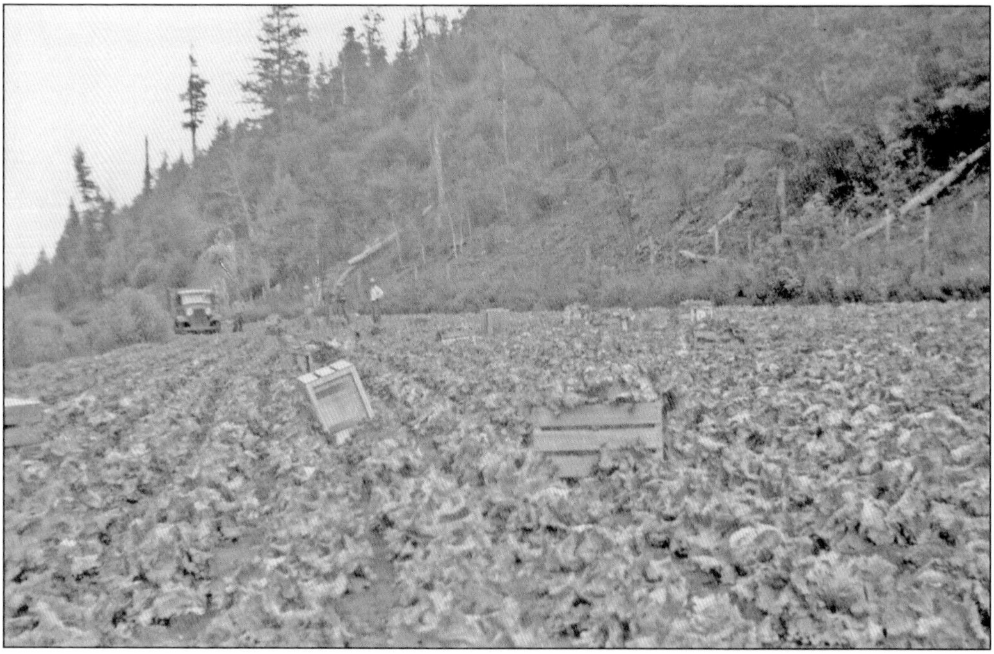

Roy Roach and his three sons—Vance and twins Valon and Vaughn—harvest lettuce on their farm on the upper Peñasco River around 1940. Much of the lettuce and apple crop was accumulated at the old Apple Barn in High Rolls for railroad shipment until the A&SM discontinued service in 1947. (Courtesy of Clif McDonald.)

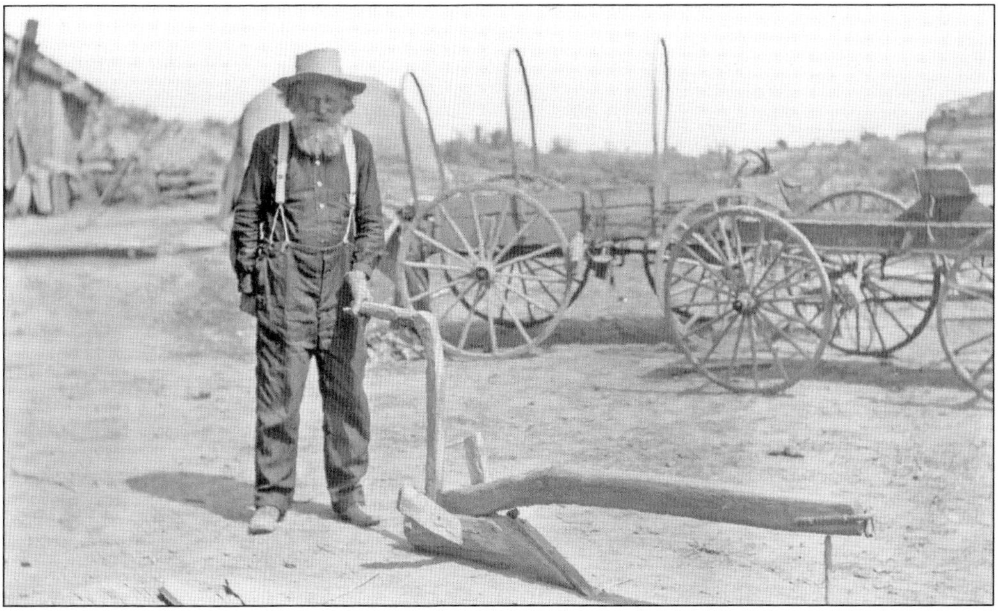

For more than 300 years, Hispanic New Mexicans used simple, traditional technology for agriculture, like this traditional wooden plow. With the growth of the cattle industry, modernized equipment was introduced to cultivate vast fields of alfalfa, hay, and oats in addition to the human staple, wheat. (Courtesy of Tularosa Village Historical Museum.)

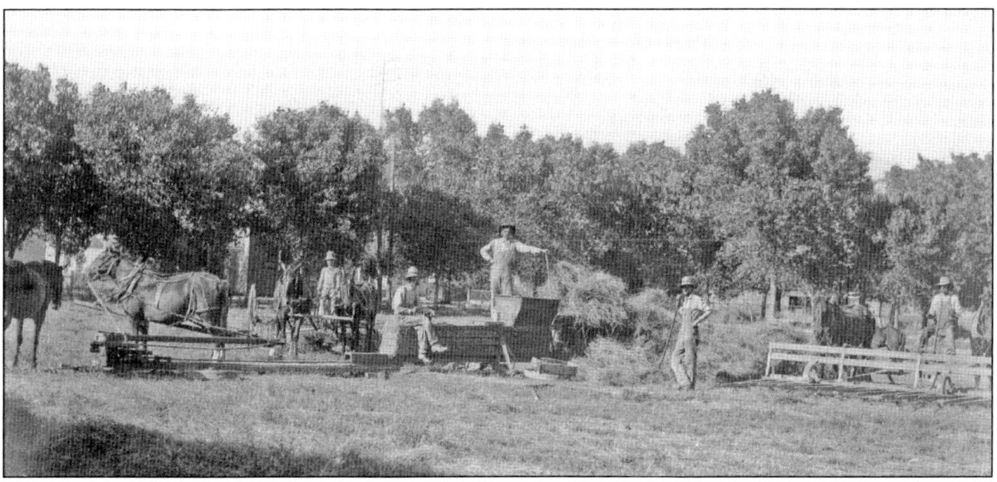

As the open range disappeared in the face of barbed wire fencing and the homesteading movement, cattle and horse ranching became more dependent on agricultural production of hay and grain. Commercial farming of grain crops expanded around Alamogordo and its satellite communities in the basin lowlands, joined by an expanding nut-orchard industry. These farms depended on irrigation water from mountain streams, which was gradually captured in pipelines and canals, or "acequias." (Courtesy of TBHS.)

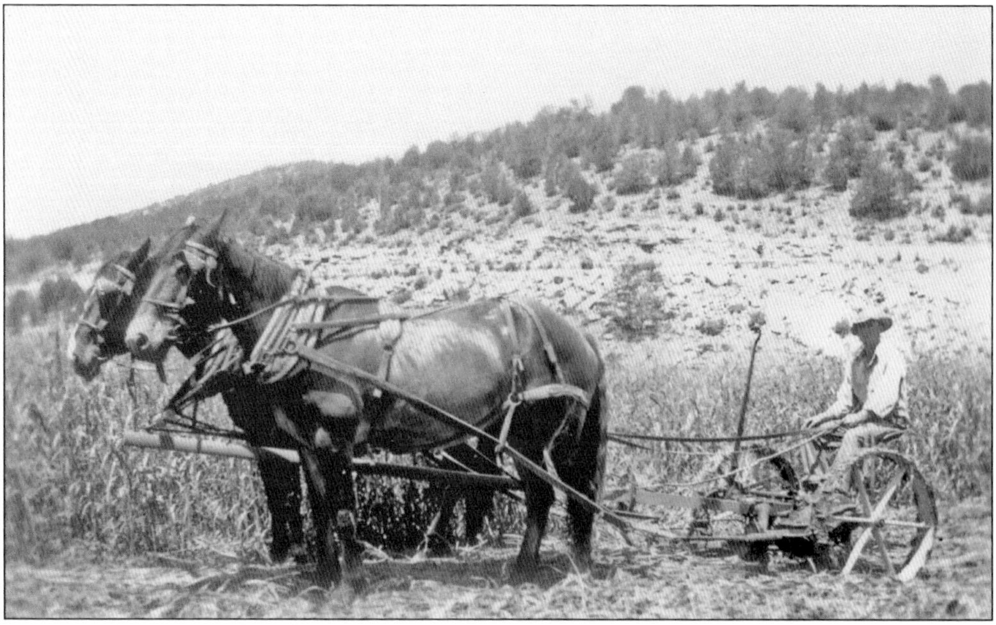

Farming also expanded in the mountains, where Kenneth Potter Jr. is shown here working his family's fields, 3 miles east of Mayhill. (Courtesy of Marjorie Curtis.)

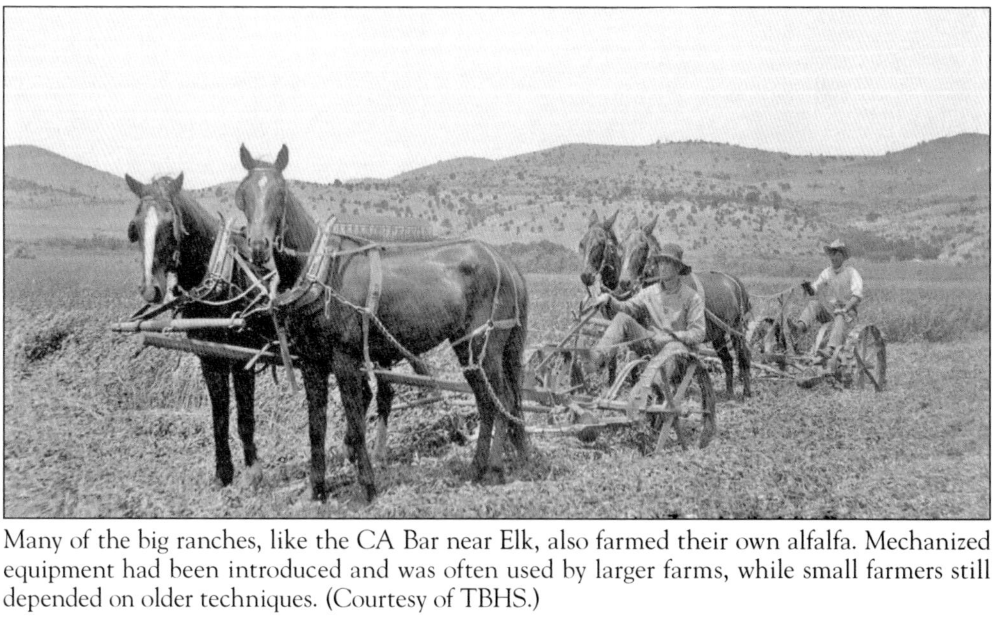

Many of the big ranches, like the CA Bar near Elk, also farmed their own alfalfa. Mechanized equipment had been introduced and was often used by larger farms, while small farmers still depended on older techniques. (Courtesy of TBHS.)

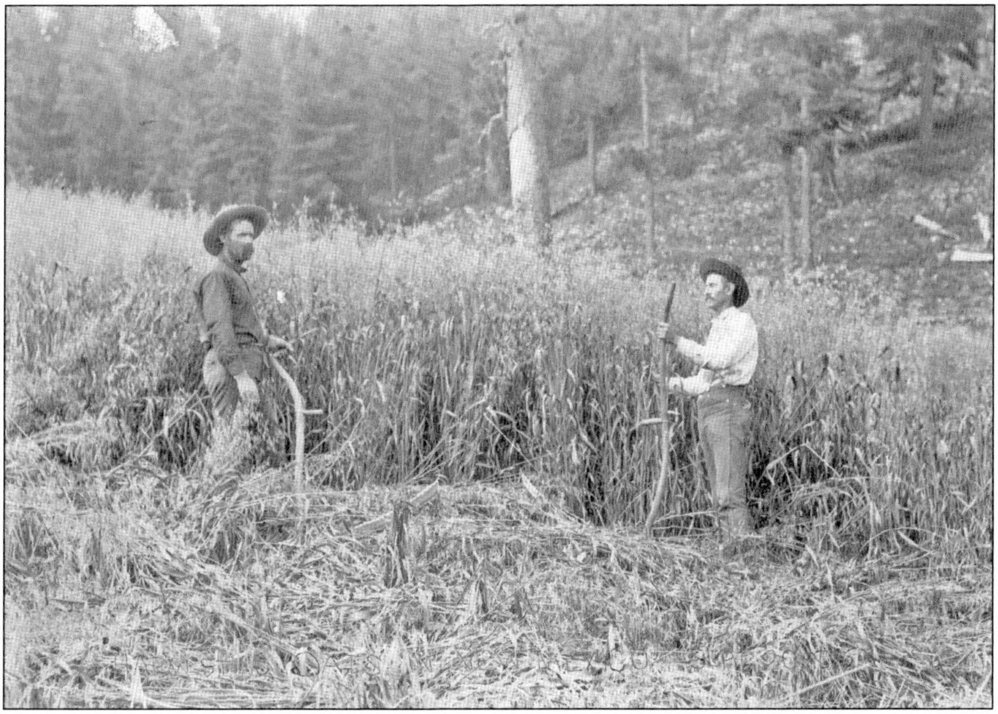

G. E. Miller photographed himself and Riley Baker cutting hay in Hay Canyon on the west side of the Sacramento Mountains near Weed. Both Miller and Baker are using traditional scythes in 1893. This was before the railroad brought modern equipment to the region. (Courtesy of TBHS.)

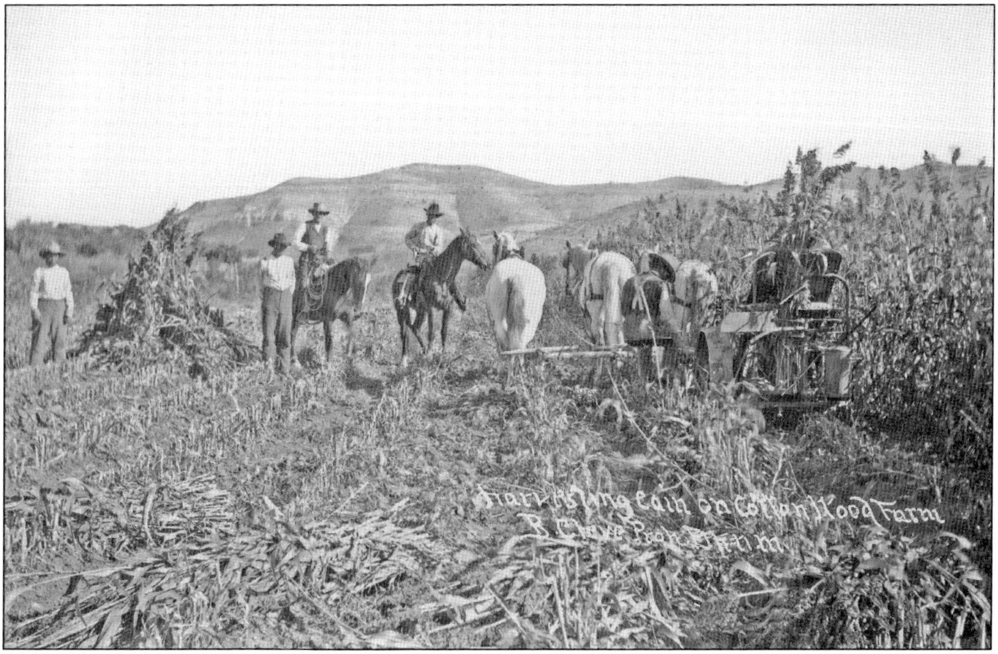

Cowhands and farmhands cut the cane crop on Cleve's Cottonwood Farm near Elk, New Mexico. (Courtesy of SMHS.)

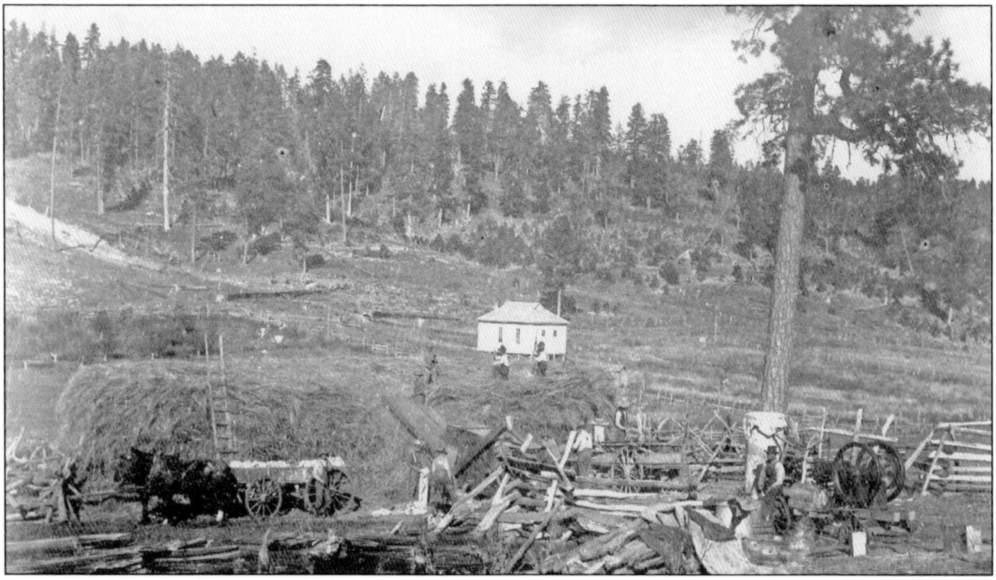

Upland farms also produced grain crops, which were threshed in a variety of techniques. Here G. E. Miller photographed the wheat crop being threshed at Tate Baird's farm in the Sacramento Mountains on October 10, 1910. (Courtesy of Marjorie Curtis.)

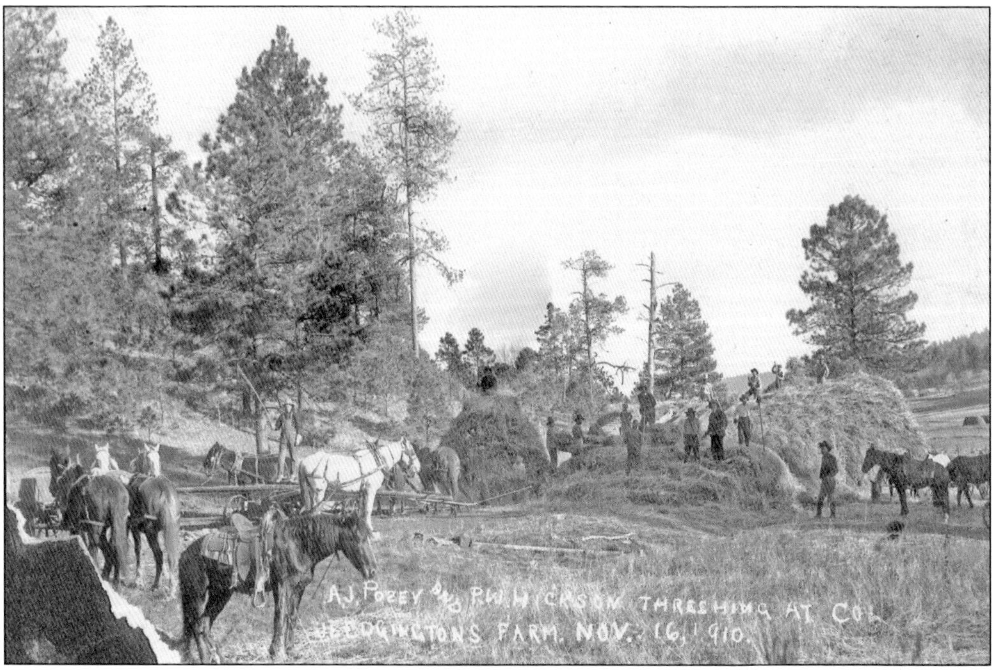

G. E. Miller also photographed A. J. Posey and P. W. Hickson threshing at Col. J. E. Edgington's farm on November 16, 1910. (Courtesy of Marjorie Curtis.)

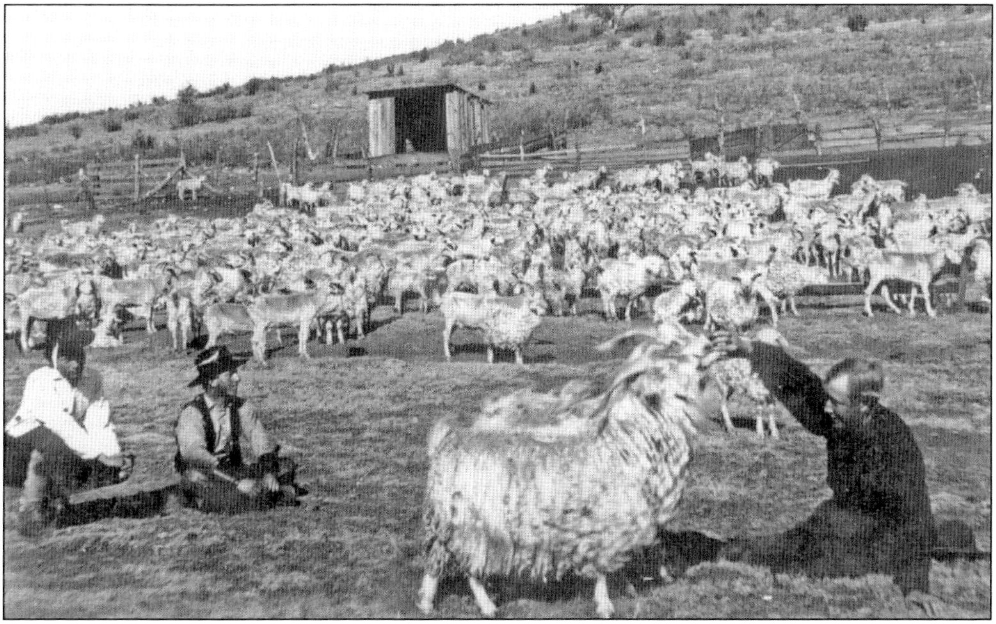

Many of the small upland family ranches began raising Angora goats for their wool and meat early in the century. The Angora goat economy became a major industry across the Tularosa Basin in the San Andres Mountains. (Photograph by G. E. Miller; courtesy of Rick Miller.)

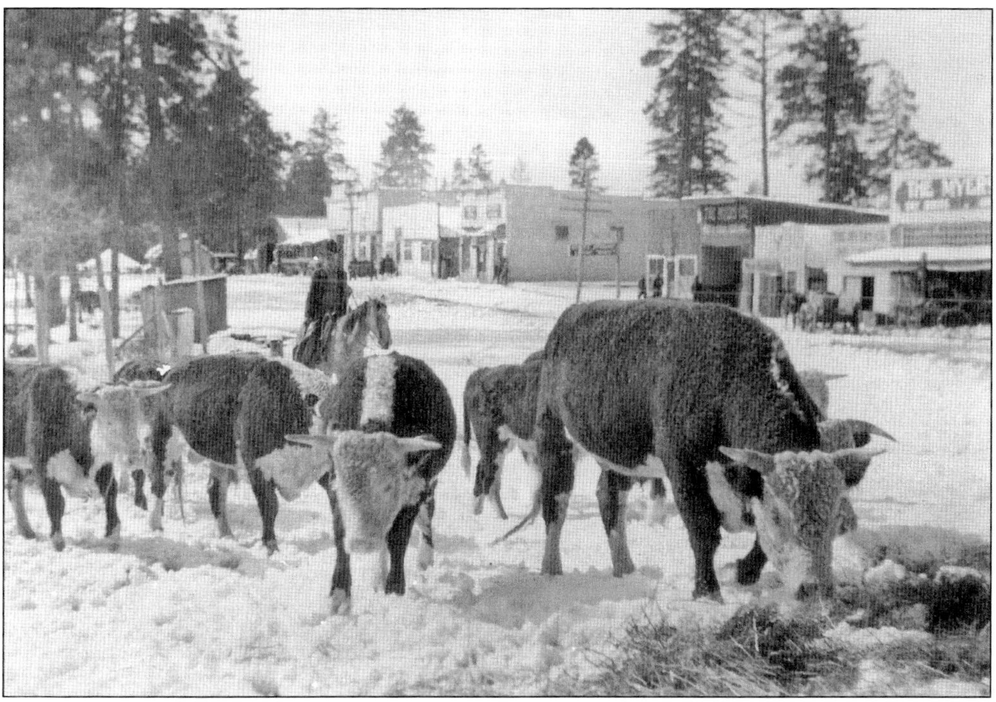

Small families still ranched cows in the mountain uplands. These cows are grazing in the main street of Cloudcroft about 1924. (Courtesy of SMHS.)

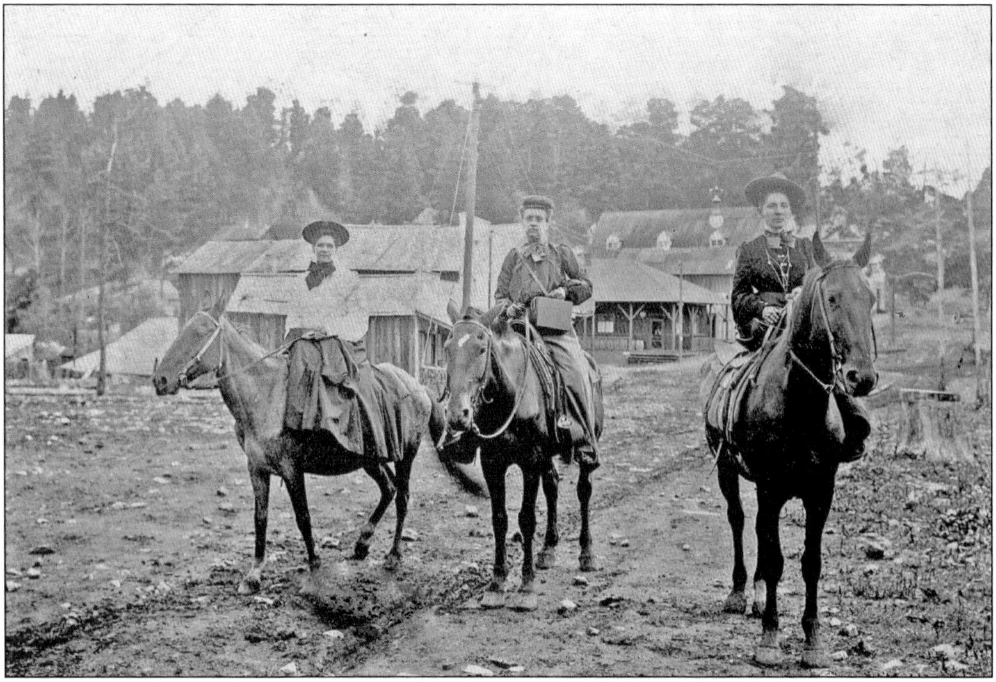

Horseback riding was also a popular pastime for local residents and tourists in the streets of Cloudcroft. Here, from left to right, an unknown woman, Kate Smith, and Anna Breckheimer tour Cloudcroft, riding sidesaddle. (Courtesy of SMHS.)

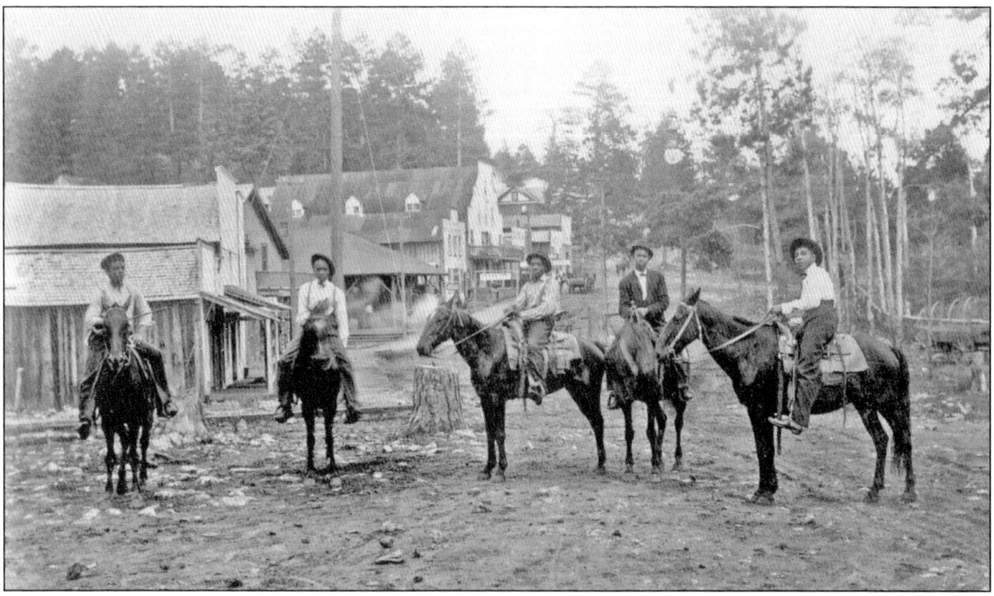

These three riders may have been working as lumberjacks for the New Mexico Tie and Timber Company when G. E. Miller photographed them in Cloudcroft about 1905. (Courtesy of SMHS.)

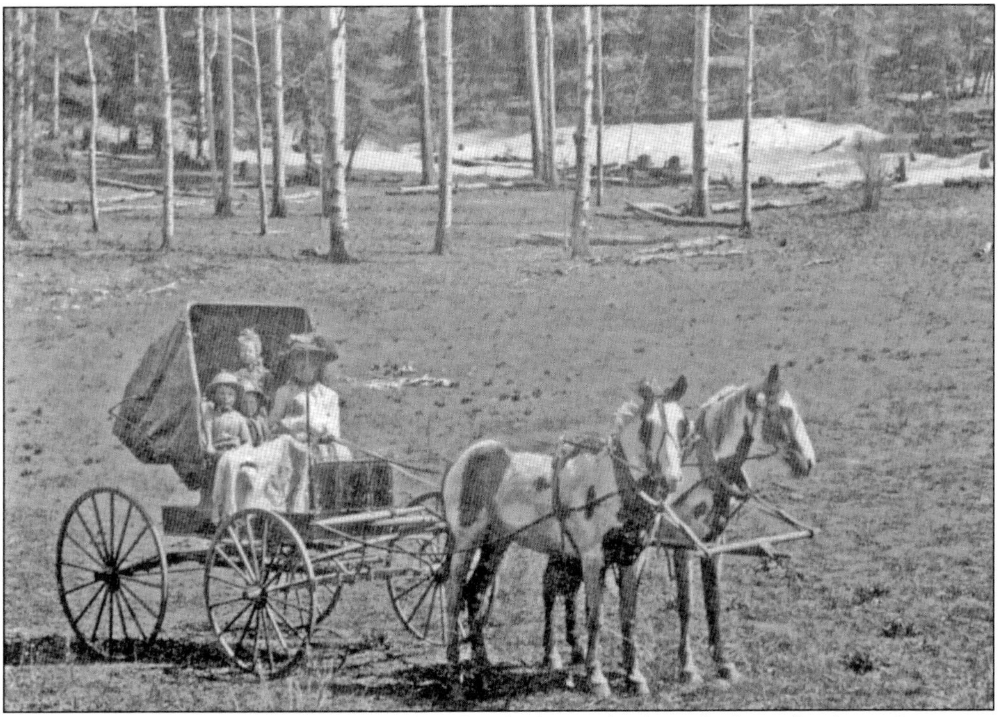

Local resident Lila Mae Buckner takes her family for a ride through the upland meadows near Cloudcroft on April 27, 1913, in the family carriage drawn by their "Wee Ponies" Paint and Pinto. With her are her four children, Aleck, Olive, Dorothy, and baby Raymond. (Courtesy of Ray and Ruby Buckner.)

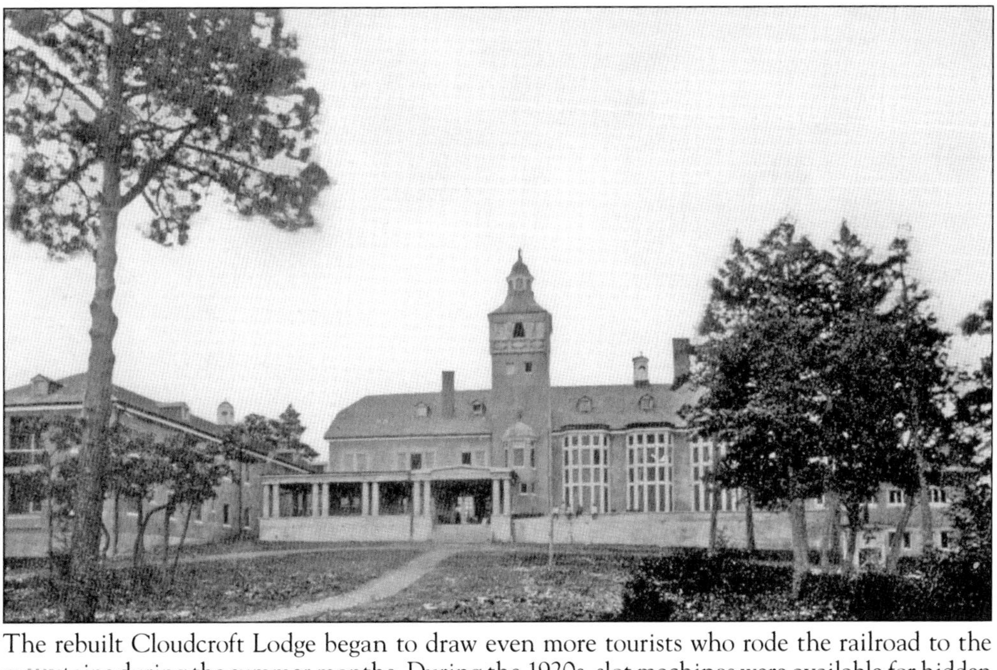

The rebuilt Cloudcroft Lodge began to draw even more tourists who rode the railroad to the mountains during the summer months. During the 1920s, slot machines were available for hidden gambling. (Courtesy of Ray and Ruby Buckner.)

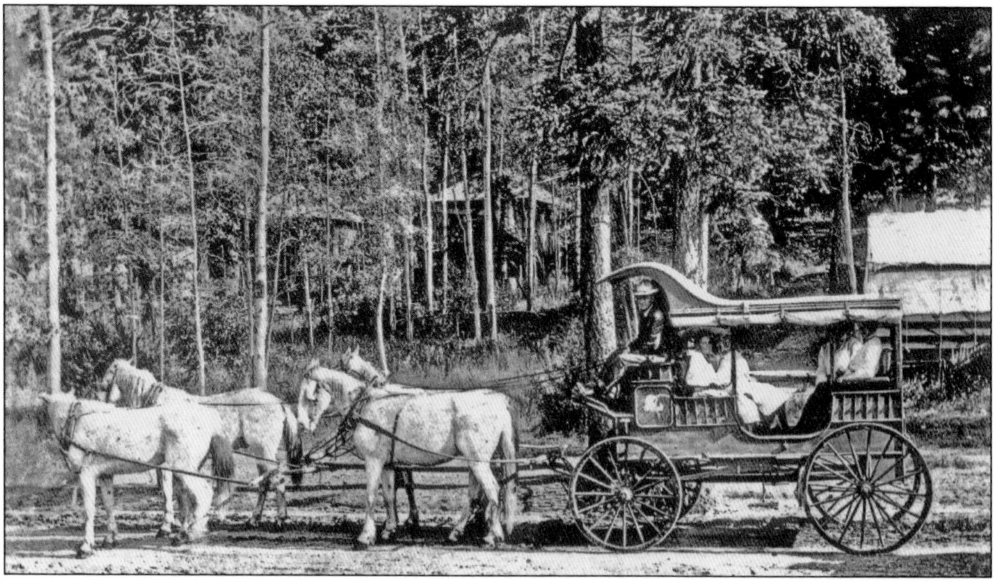

Carriage tours to the Mescalero Apache Tribal Reservation were a regular service provided for tourists staying in Cloudcroft during the summers. The Mescalero, the only native people still residing in southern New Mexico, were a major attraction. Tourists could attend the mid-summer dances, purchase crafts and curios, and sample traditional foods during their visit. (Courtesy of Clif McDonald.)

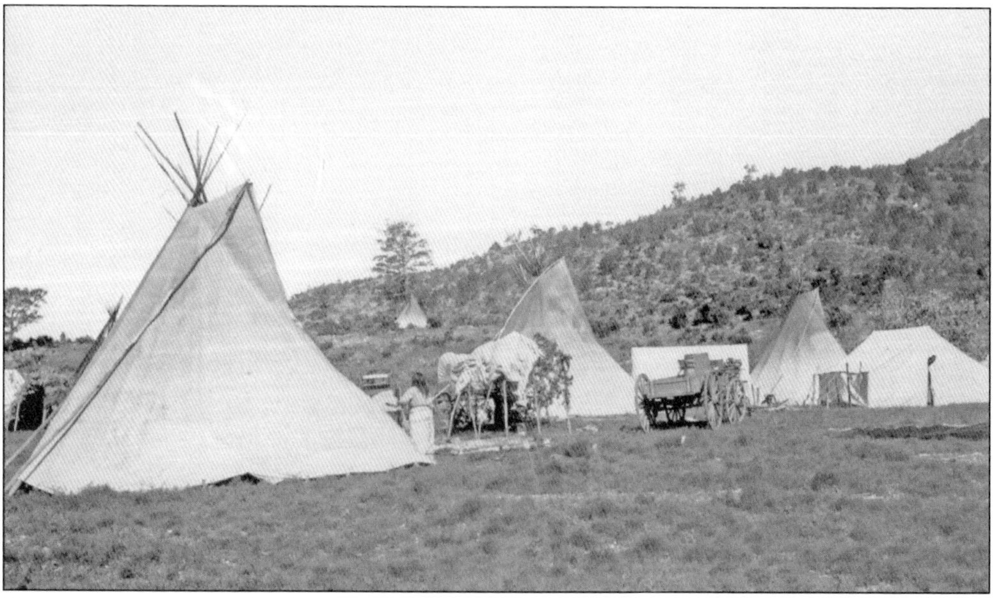

During the summer months, the Mescalero Apache used Plains-style tepees for mobile residences that could be located where they were collecting wild crops. (Courtesy of Ray and Ruby Buckner.)

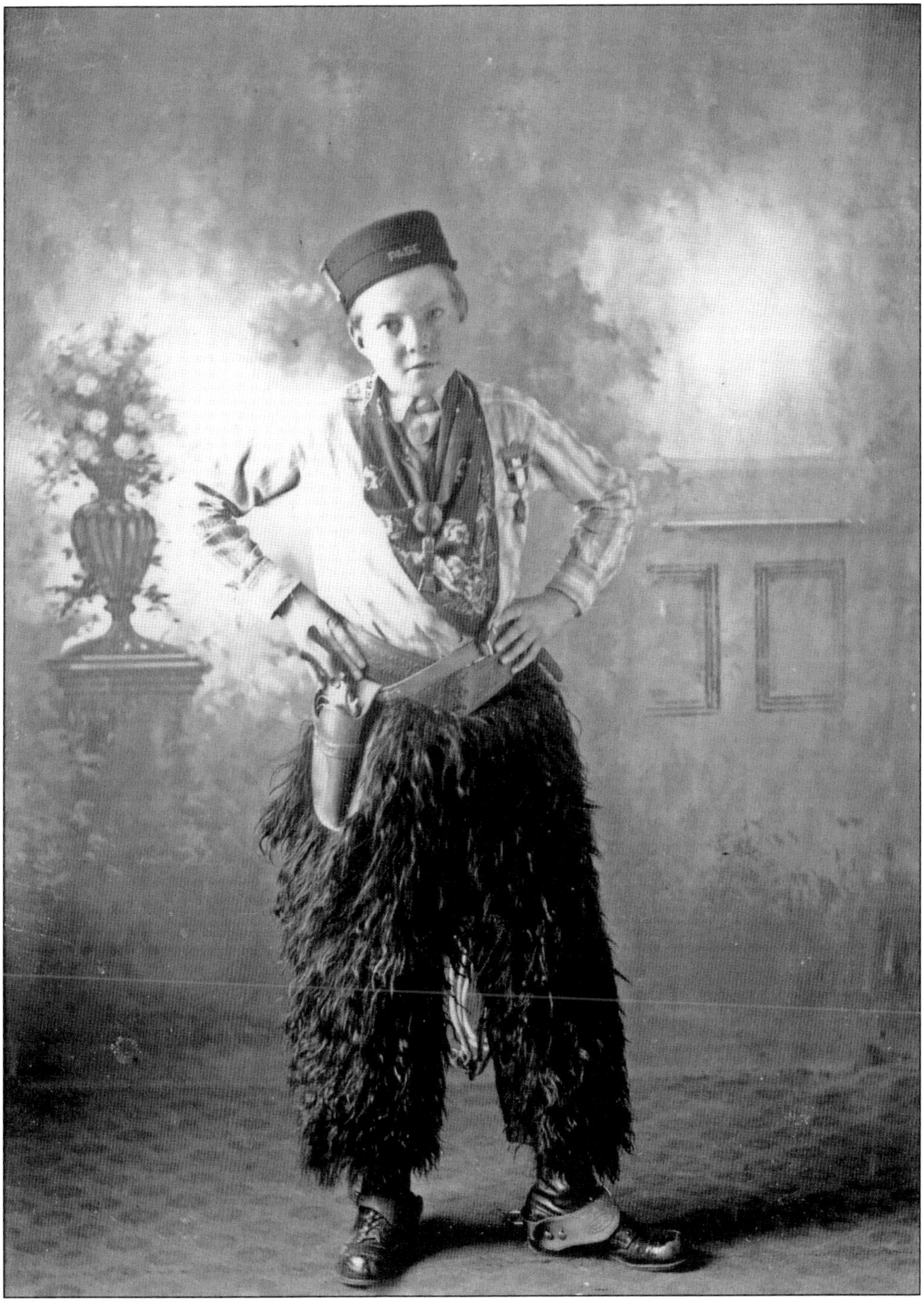

Just as they do today, early tourists and summer hotel staff visiting Cloudcroft enjoyed dressing up as cowboys or Native Americans to have their portrait taken. Here bellhop Emmett L. Ammons has donned a pair of "woolies"—chaps made from angora hide with the wool outside—spurs, a bandana, a pistol belt, and a decorative medal of some sort. (Glass negative by Jim Alexander; courtesy of SMHS.)

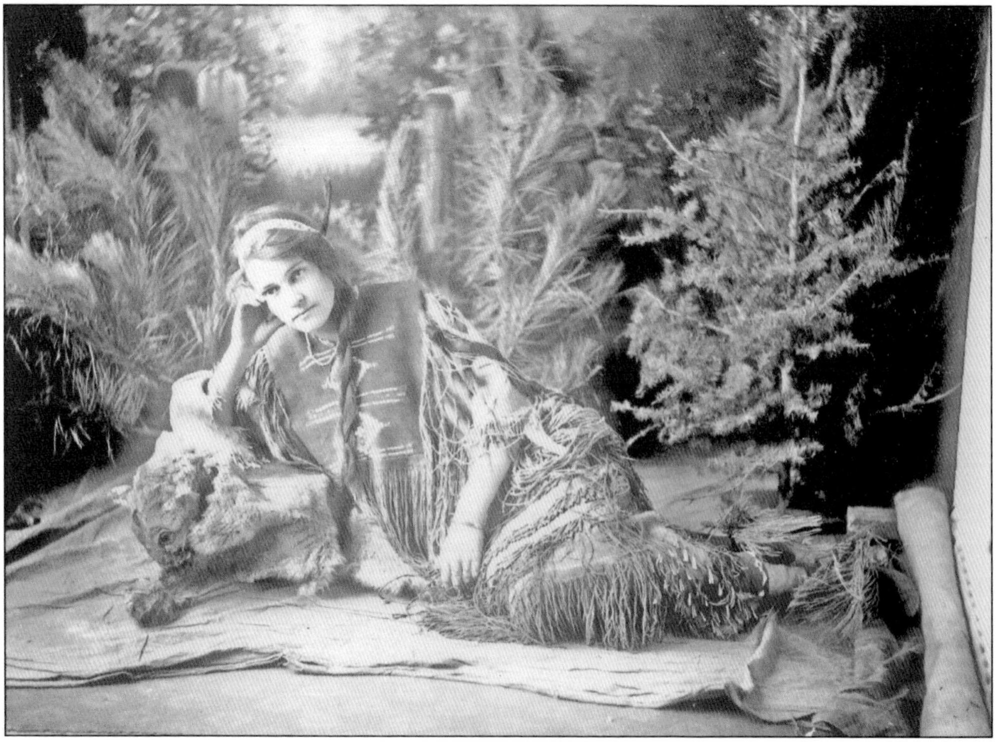

Jim Alexander provided his tourist customers with a variety of costume possibilities in his Cloudcroft summer studio. Native American maiden and cowgirl costumes were quite popular among the younger women. A reclining position was also common. (Glass negative by Jim Alexander; courtesy of SMHS.)

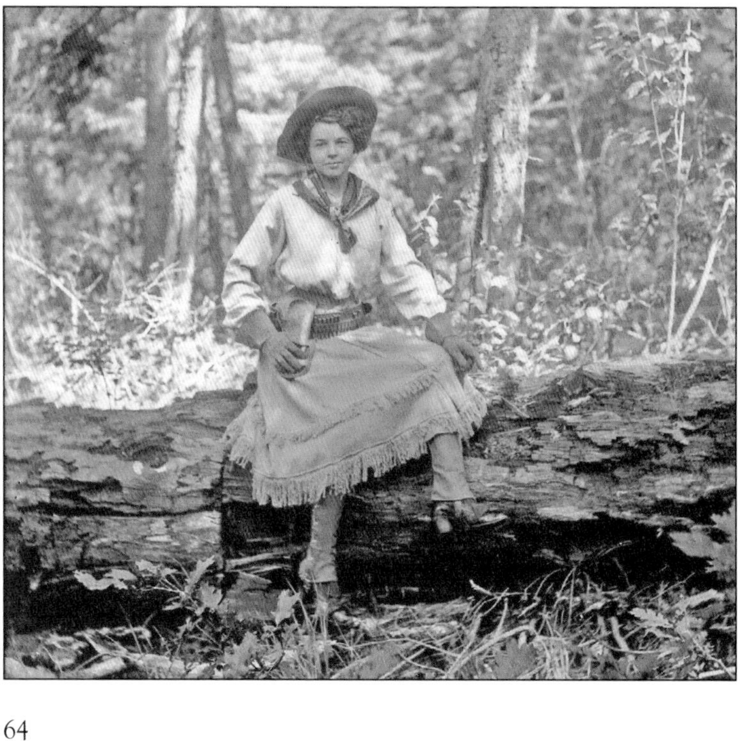

Jim Alexander often photographed his younger clients outside among the towering pines that dominated the community of Cloudcroft. (Glass negative by Jim Alexander; courtesy of SMHS.)

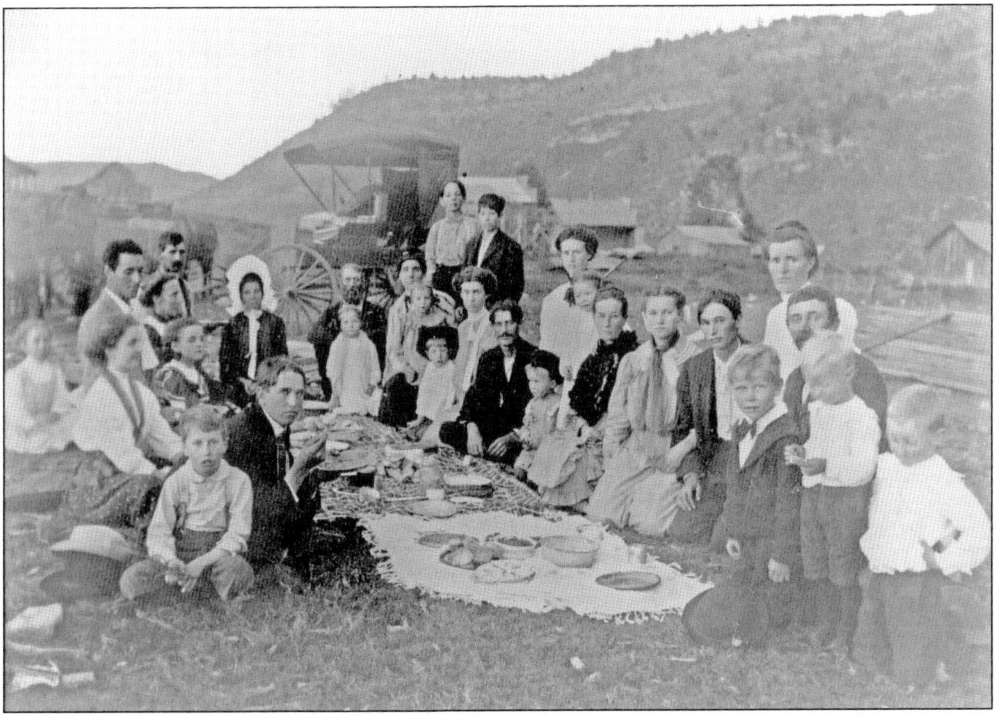

Large family picnics were a popular summertime diversion. Here G. E. Miller captured members of his own family, and the Dockray, Browning, Posey, and Curtis families. (Courtesy of Marjorie Curtis.)

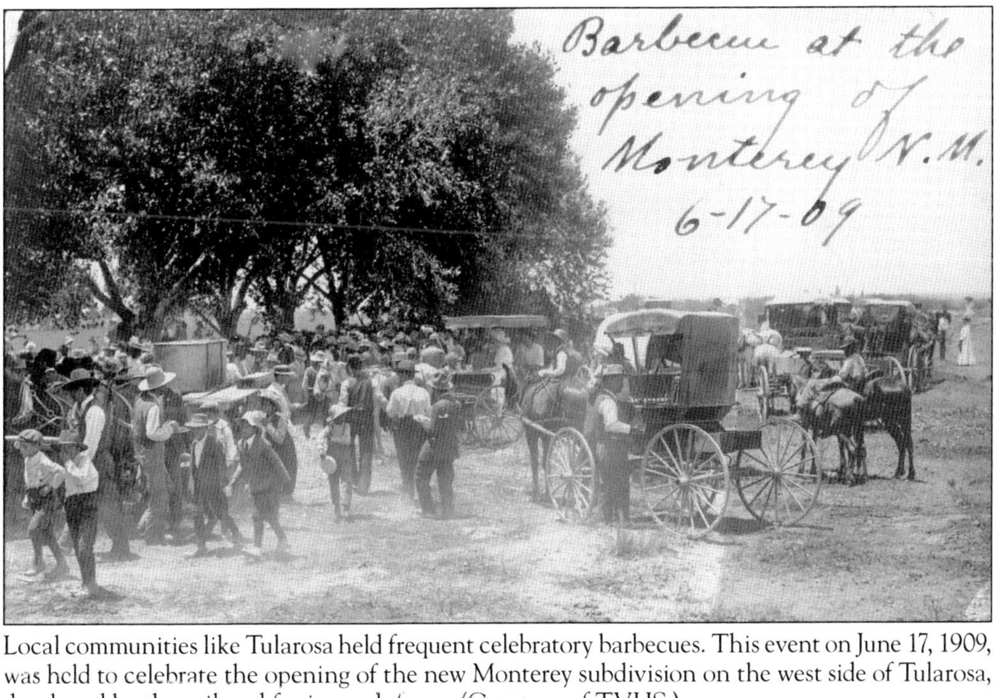

Local communities like Tularosa held frequent celebratory barbecues. This event on June 17, 1909, was held to celebrate the opening of the new Monterey subdivision on the west side of Tularosa, developed by the railroad for its work force. (Courtesy of TVHS.)

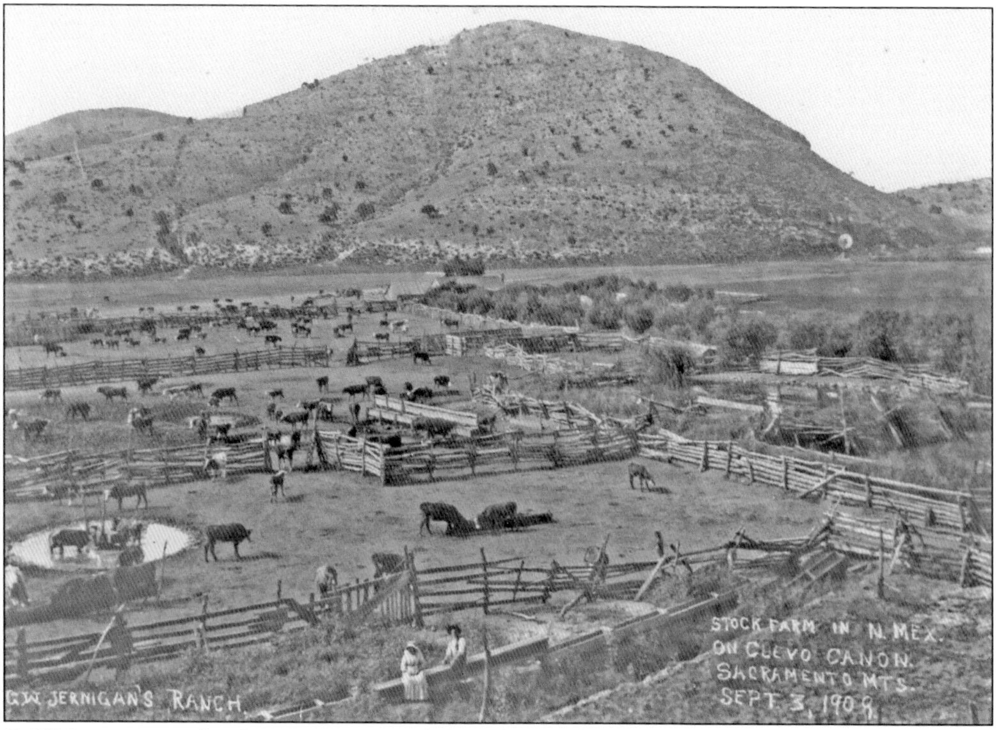

G. W. Jernigan ran his Cuevo Cañón stock farm (or ranch) in the Sacramento Mountains, shown here in 1908, where his family raised premium rodeo stock later in the century. At the end of the 19th century, large corporate ranches and small family ranches expanded into southern New Mexico. (Courtesy of the Carner family.)

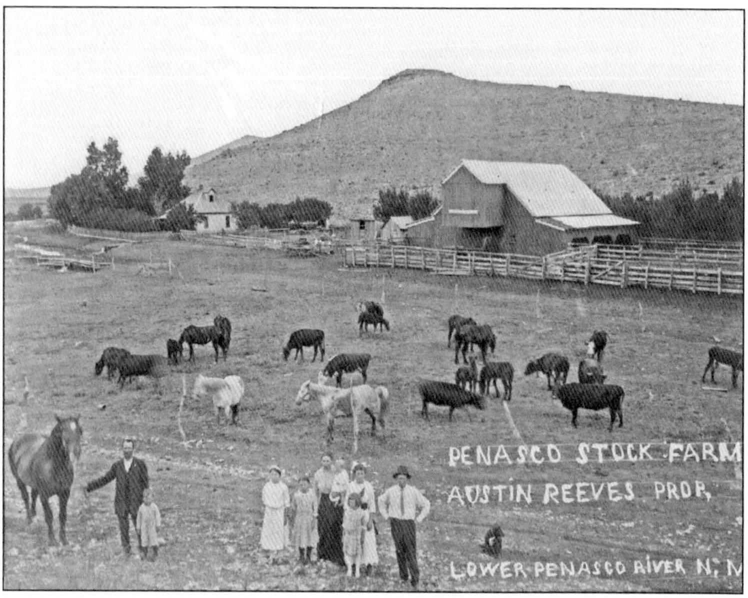

Austin and Eula Reeves and their children raised horses and cattle on their Penasco stock farm, where they posed for their portrait around 1915. Many of these upland family ranches had failed economically by the 1920s. (Courtesy of the Carner family.)

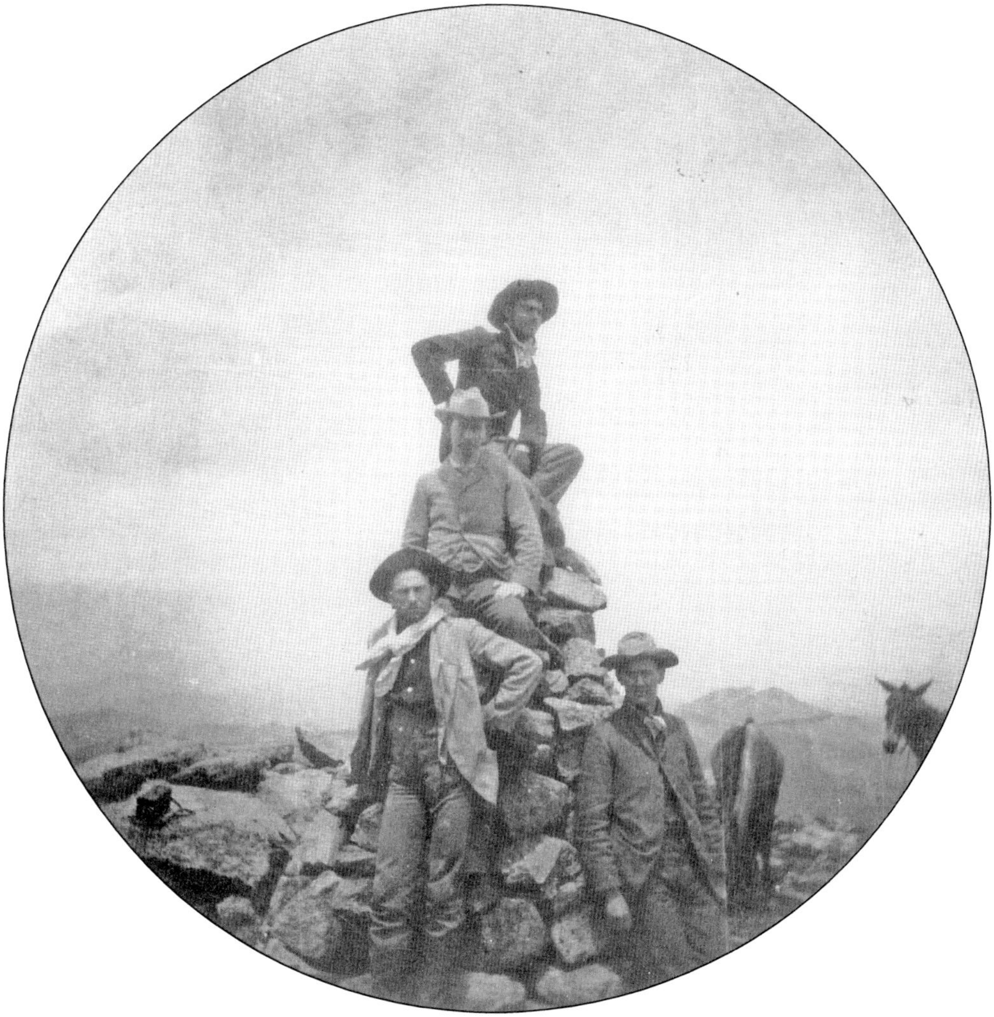

Identified as "Old Cowboys," (top down) Dr. Joyner, J. F. and John Hinkle, and Adair, pose atop a rock cairn at 12,000 feet on White Mountain (Sierra Blanca) in 1896. The West Texas cattle industry was brought into Southeast New Mexico with the Goodnight-Loving Trail up the Pecos River. The first large southeast New Mexico ranch was John Chisum's South Spring Ranch, which established the town that became Roswell, New Mexico. (Courtesy of HCSNM.)

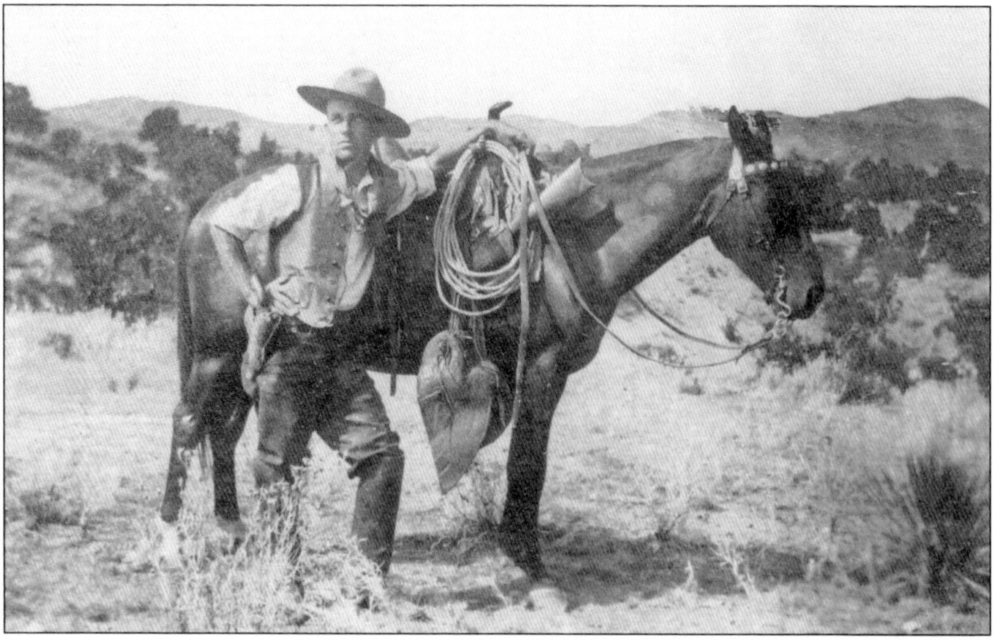

Arthur Truex and his family had a small ranch in the Three Rivers area during the 1920s. One of Eugene Rhodes's characters described the cowboy as follows: "take the typical cowboy. There positively ain't no sich person. Maybe so half of 'em's from Texas and the other half from anywhere and everywhere else." (Courtesy of TBHS.)

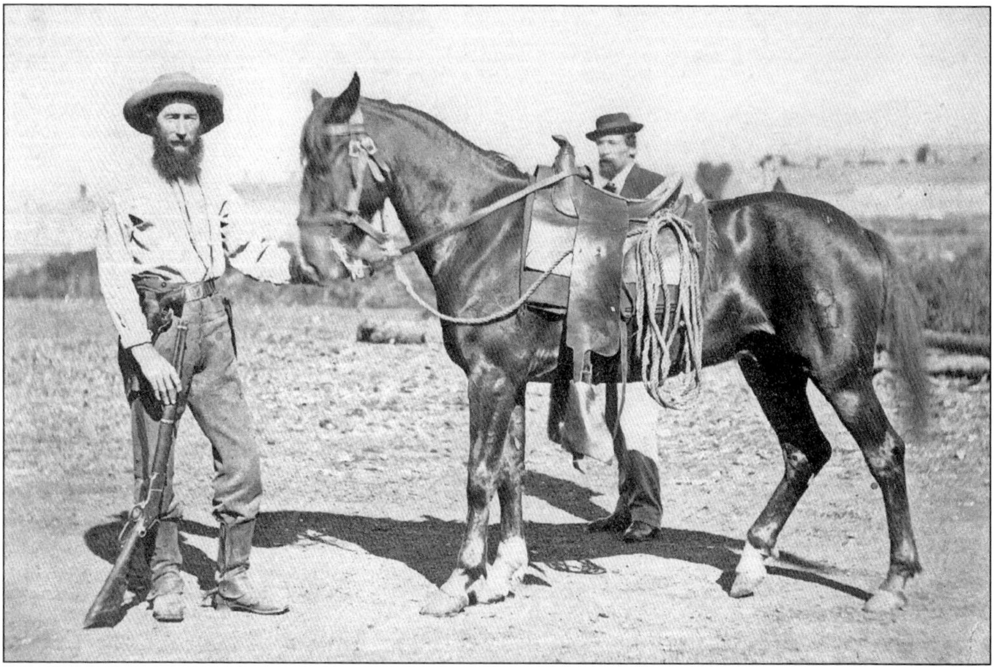

The character description by Eugene Rhodes continues: "But they're all alike in just one thing—and that is that every last one of them is entirely different from all the others. Each one talks as he pleases, acts as he pleases and—when not at work—dresses as he pleases. On the range though, they all dress pretty much alike" like this typical unknown *waddie*. (Courtesy of TVHS.)

Bronc-busters like Dick Ballard, here getting on a wild pony in 1935, were prized for their skill at breaking horses for ranching use. Horses were the essential tools for ranching, especially in the days of open range, when huge areas were subject to roundup. Today their use is declining, as small motorcycles and four-wheelers are replacing them. (Courtesy of HCSNM.)

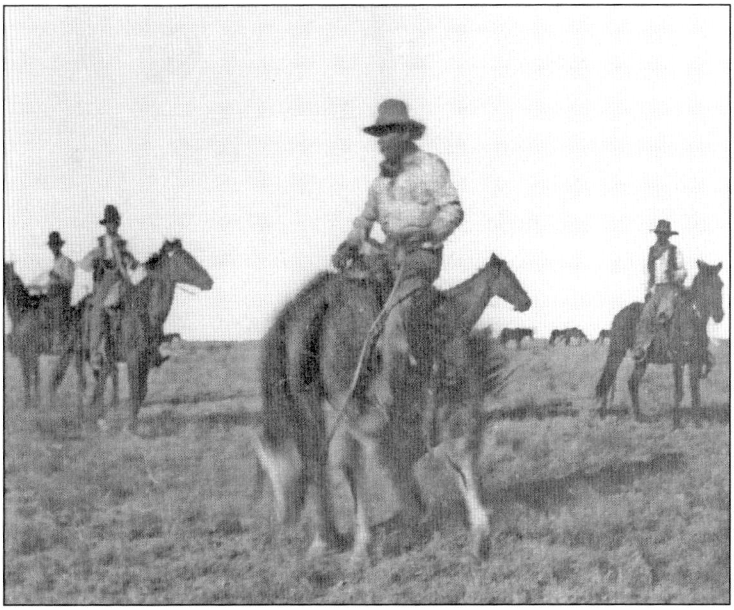

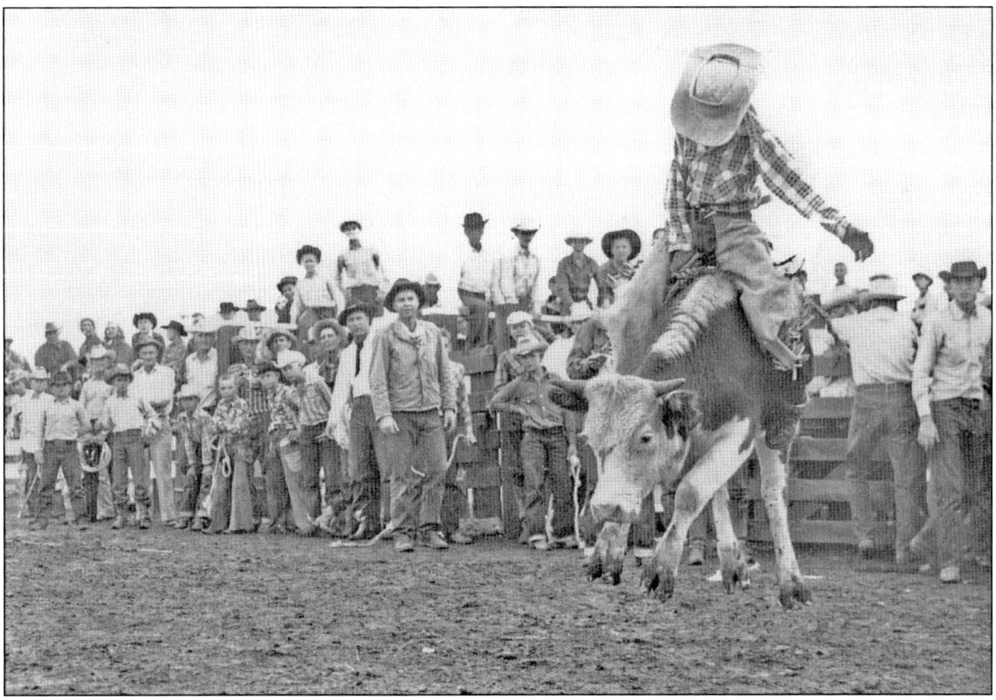

Many of the large ranches, like Three Rivers Ranch, hosted rodeos. Here Ross Coe stays aboard a bull in competition at Three Rivers in 1949. (Courtesy of TBHS.)

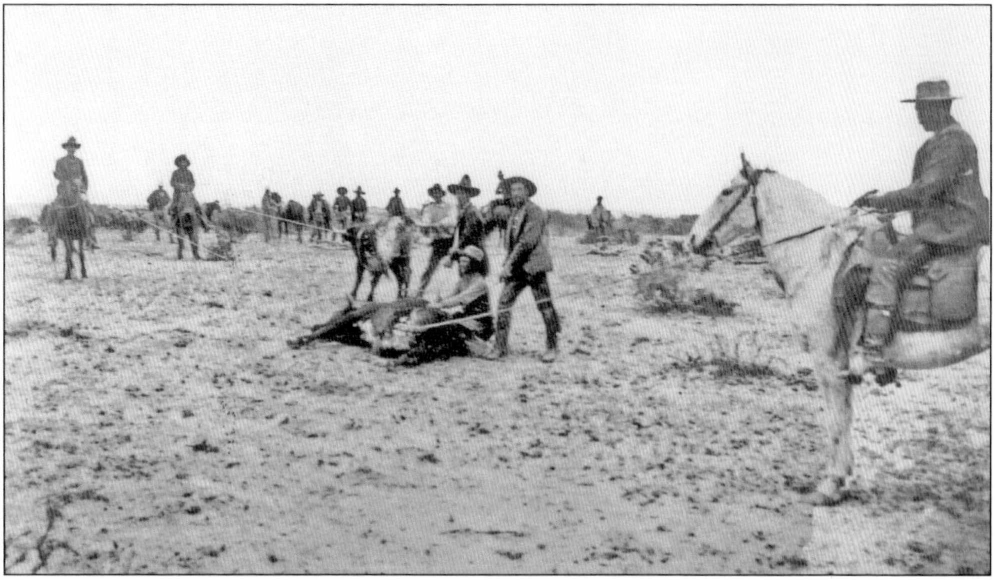

Branding calves and steers during the annual roundup was the only way to assert ownership during the era of the open range. These CA Bar cowhands have roped a steer for branding in this *c.* 1890 photograph. (Courtesy of HCSNM.)

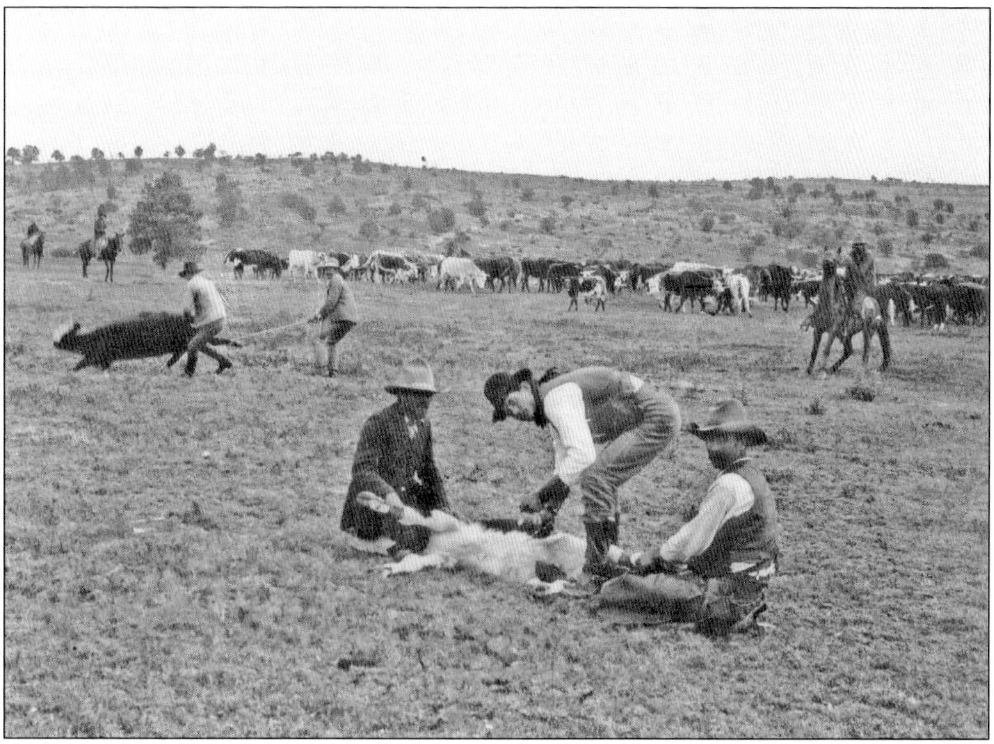

These Sacramento Mountains cowmen were roping and branding stock in Miller's Valley in 1904, when G. E. Miller took their photograph. (Courtesy of Artesia Historical Museum.)

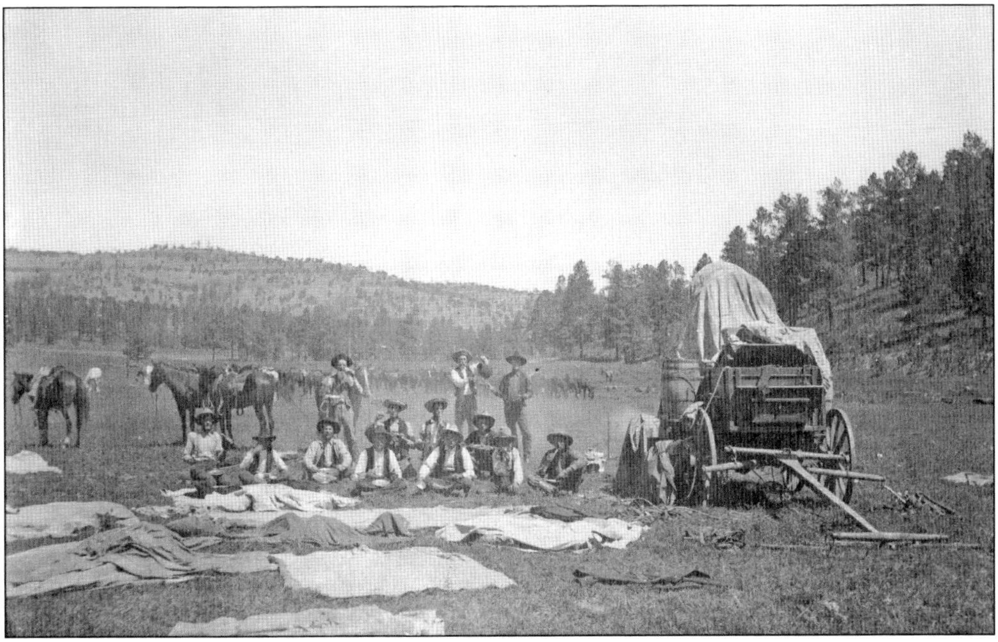

This roundup camp was set up in one of the upland Sacramento Mountains valleys. The only time all the hands gathered was for meals prepared from the chuck wagon, which also carried the bedding seen laid out in the foreground. (Courtesy of TBHS.)

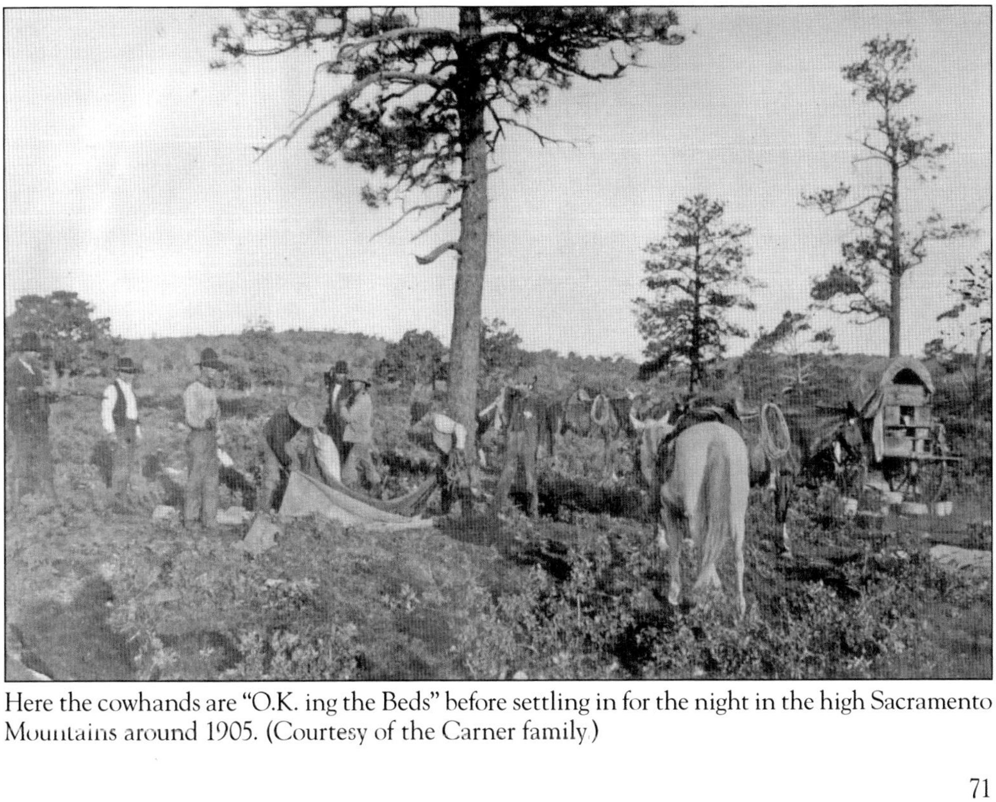

Here the cowhands are "O.K. ing the Beds" before settling in for the night in the high Sacramento Mountains around 1905. (Courtesy of the Carner family.)

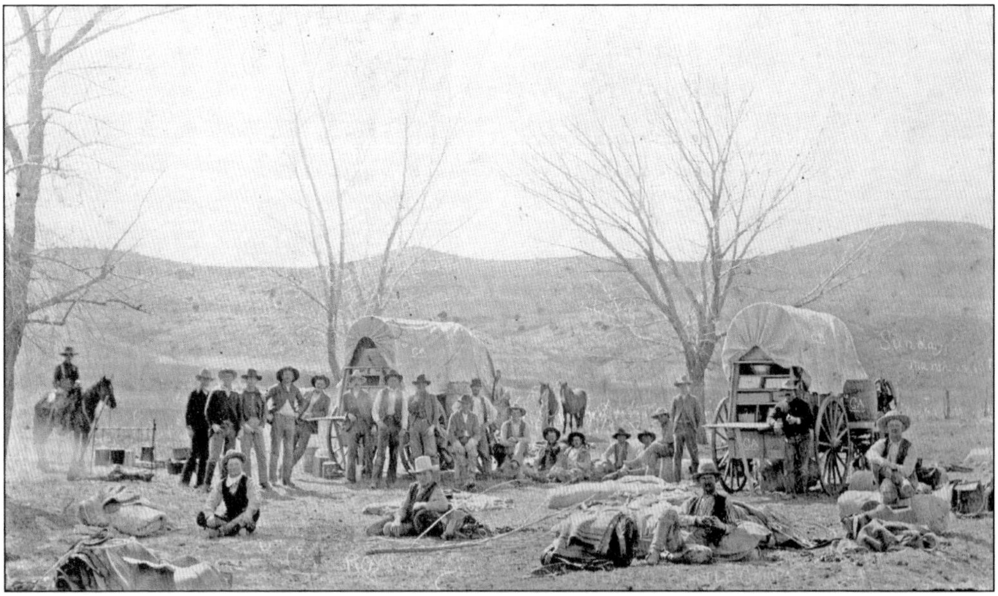

The CA Bar, or the Champion Cattle Company of Texas, established a branch on the Penasco River in 1884. It became the Penasco Cattle Company when the company reorganized in 1891. Here the CA Bar boys gathered for a Sunday portrait in a Sacramento Mountains roundup camp on March 28, 1897. (Courtesy of HCSNM.)

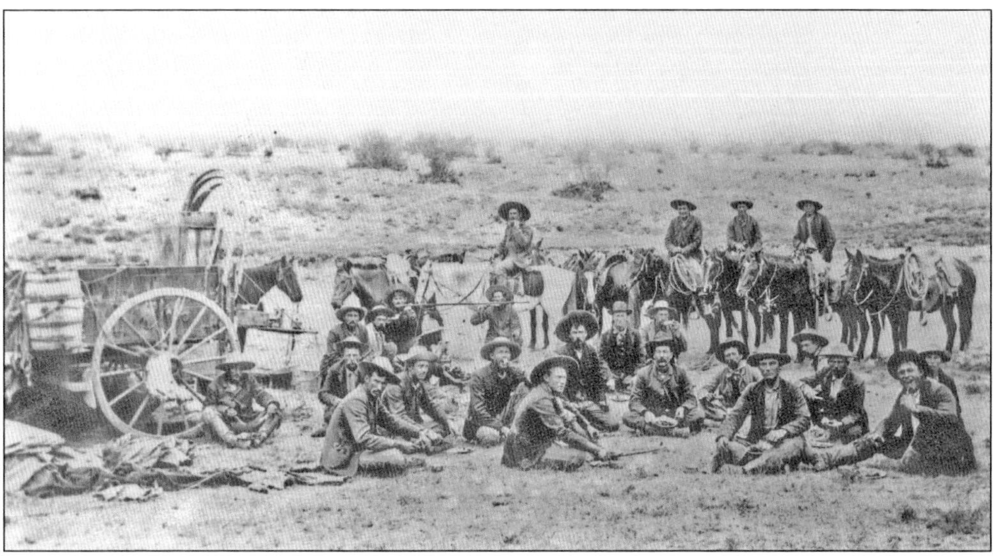

Another CA Bar roundup crew poses for a chuck wagon portrait around 1893. (Courtesy of HCSNM.)

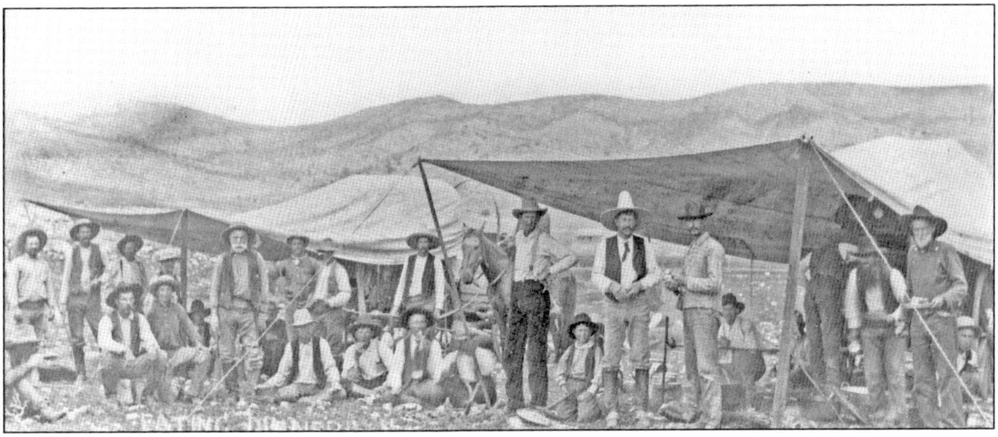

The CA Bar cowboys eat dinner at a more permanent roundup camp in the Sacramentos. (Courtesy of SMHS.)

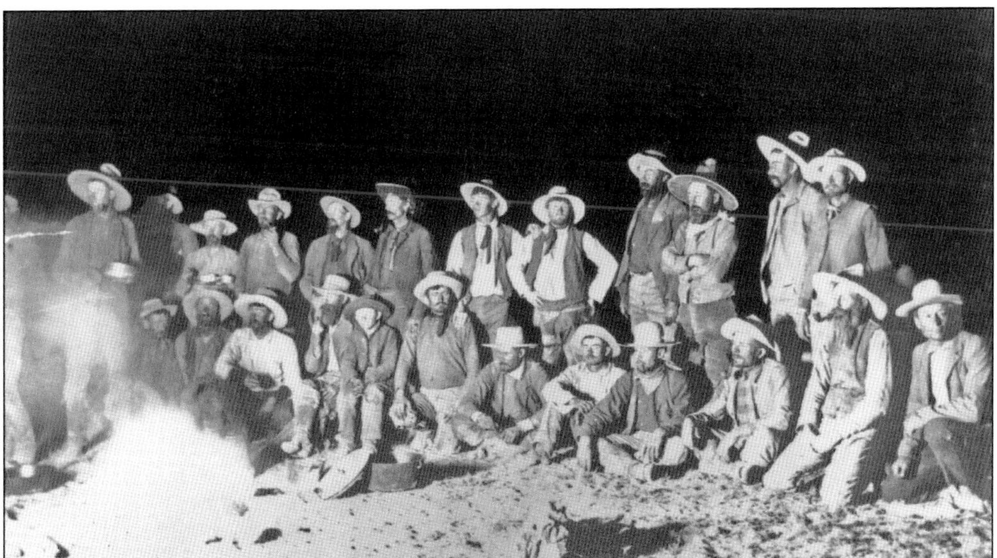

This evening meal of the CA Bar roundup crew was probably the occasion for singing the kind of songs collected by N. Howard "Jack" Thorp and published in 1908 in "Songs of the Cowboys." (Courtesy of HCSNM.)

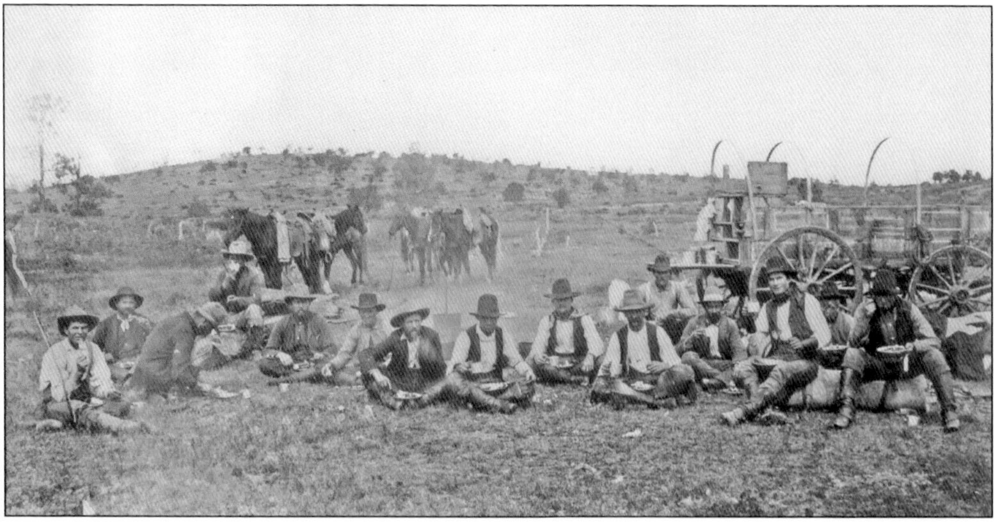

G. E. Miller caught these Sacramento Mountains cowboys eating dinner in Millers Valley in 1904. (Courtesy of the Carner family.)

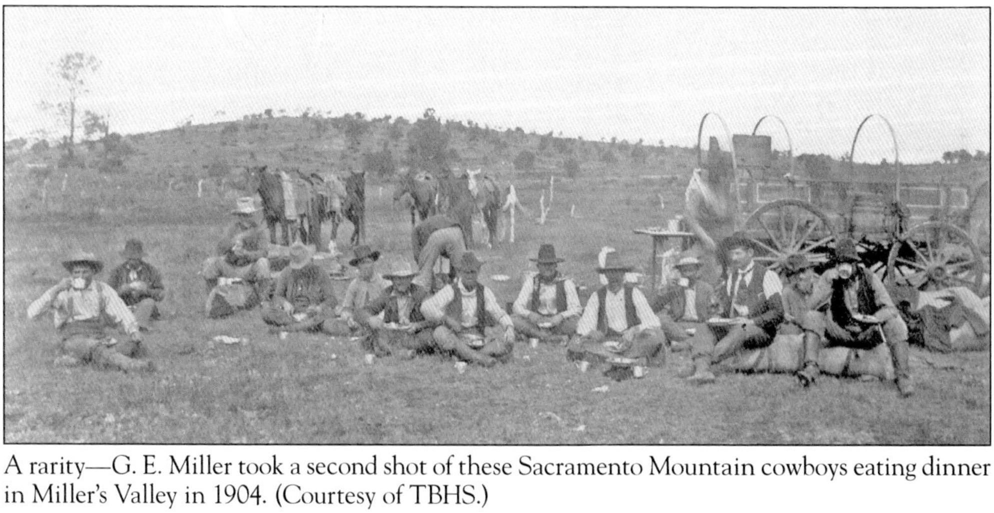

A rarity—G. E. Miller took a second shot of these Sacramento Mountain cowboys eating dinner in Miller's Valley in 1904. (Courtesy of TBHS.)

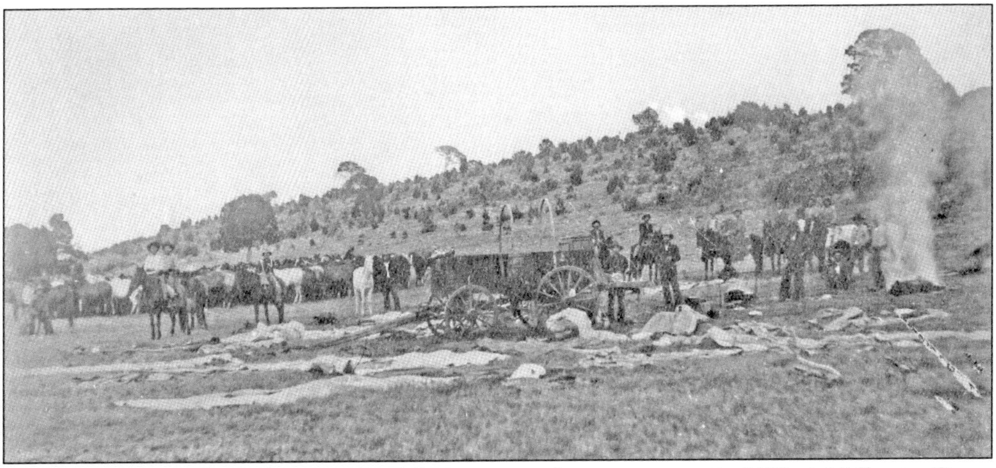

This is perhaps a third photograph of the same cowboys at supper in Miller's Valley in Otero County, New Mexico, in 1904. (Courtesy of the Carner family.)

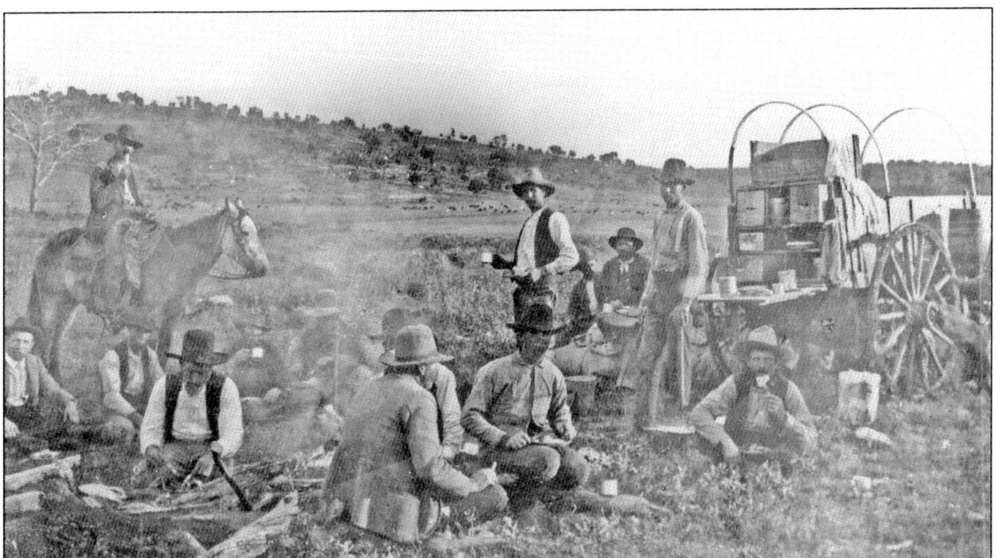

The "Mountain Pool" wagon and hands probably are having breakfast just before starting the day. Bedding is still laid out to dry and air, and the horse remuda has been brought up, so mounts can be cut (chosen) and saddled around 1914 (Courtesy of the Jake Cox family.)

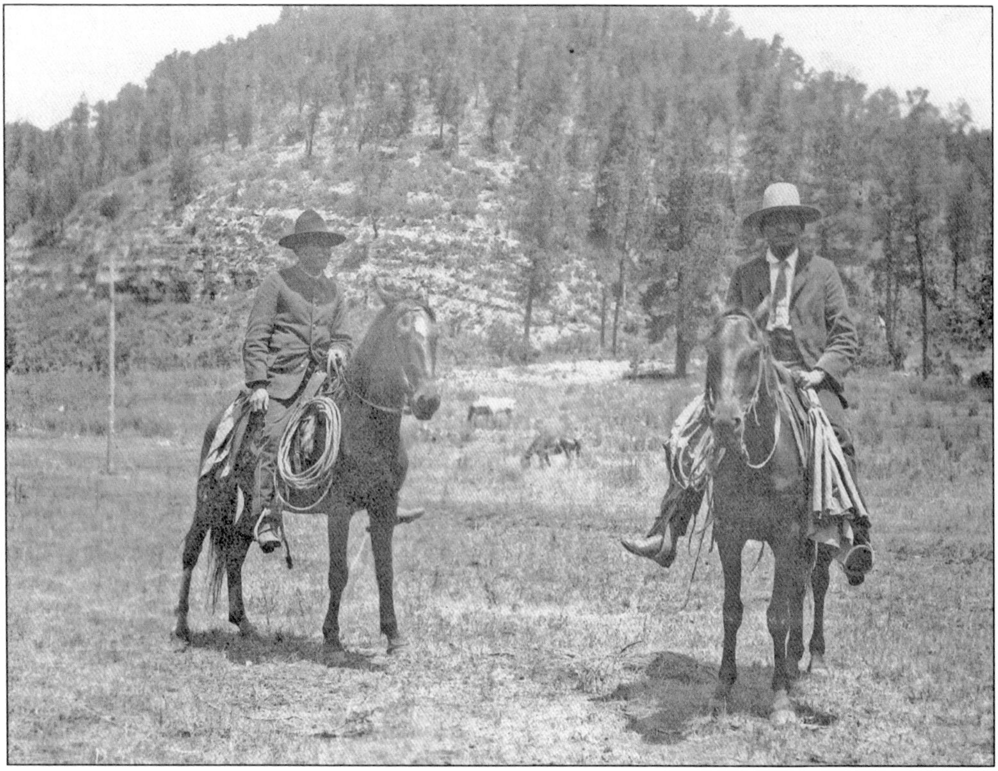

At the turn of the century, the Mescalero Apache adopted cattle ranching, which they had learned from neighboring ranches like the Flying H and the CA Bar. These two Apache cowboys, Jesus and Marion Salazar, are virtually indistinguishable from their non-native contemporaries. (Courtesy of TVHS.)

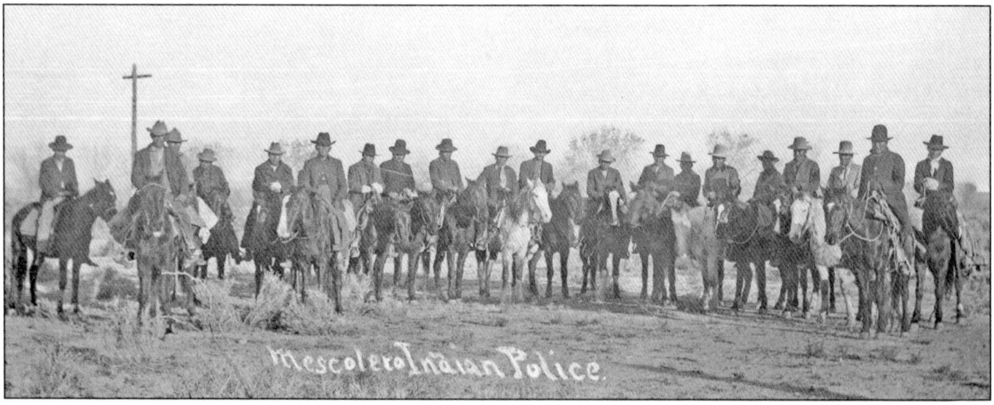

Jim Alexander produced this well-known postcard from a glass photograph plate. Roy McLane, foreman of the Flying H (center), leads a Mescalero Apache posse in 1908 in pursuit of his brother Don McLane's killer, Kit-i-chin. The posse led by subchief San Per consisted of some 20 men, including tribal police Crookneck, Sam Chino, Elmer Wilson, Willie Comanche, Muchacha Negra, Dana Evans, Antonio Joseph, Caje, Charlie Threefingers, Willie Magoosh, Otero County sheriff Henry M. Denney, deputy Gus Ostic, and William Dudley of the New Mexico Territorial Mounted Police. Two days later, the posse found Kit-i-chin in Grapevine Canyon in the southern Sacramentos. He refused to surrender and was killed in the gunfight. (Courtesy of SMHS.)

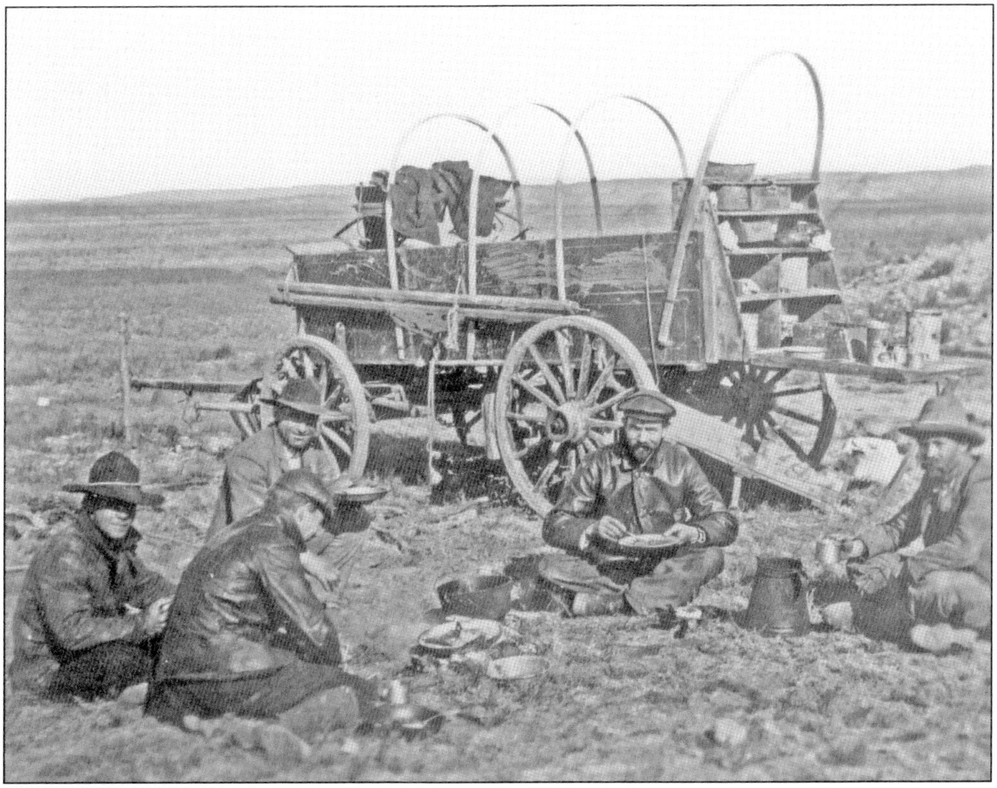

This chuck wagon supper scene was shot near Avis, New Mexico, in the early 20th century. Note the leather jackets and caps worn by two men, who may be visiting surveyors. (Courtesy of SMHS.)

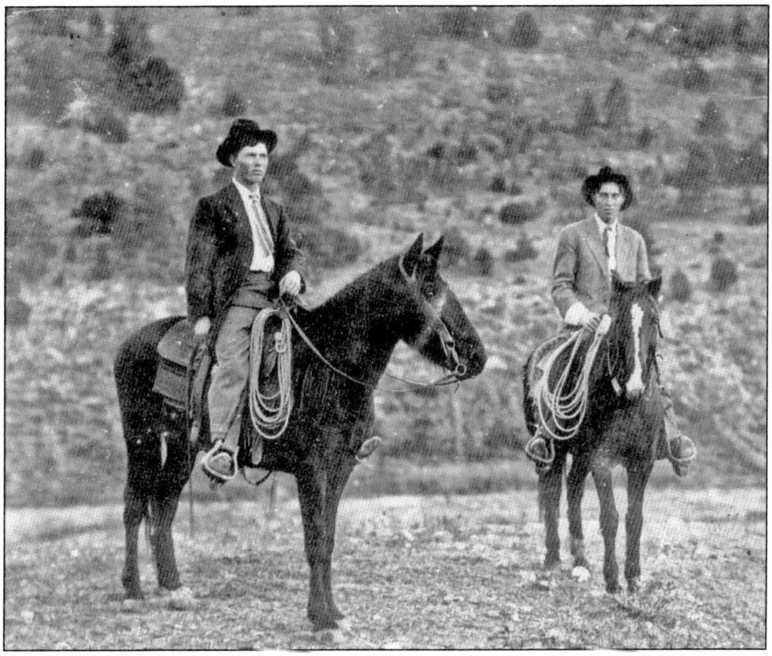

Young cowmen Will Parker and friend Bert Browning pause, probably along the Upper Peñasco River around 1910. Will Parker was a cowman and rancher for more than three decades, working for the Flying H, the CA Bar, and the Circle Diamond. He served as Otero County sheriff from 1939 to 1946. (Courtesy of D. and E. L. Miller.)

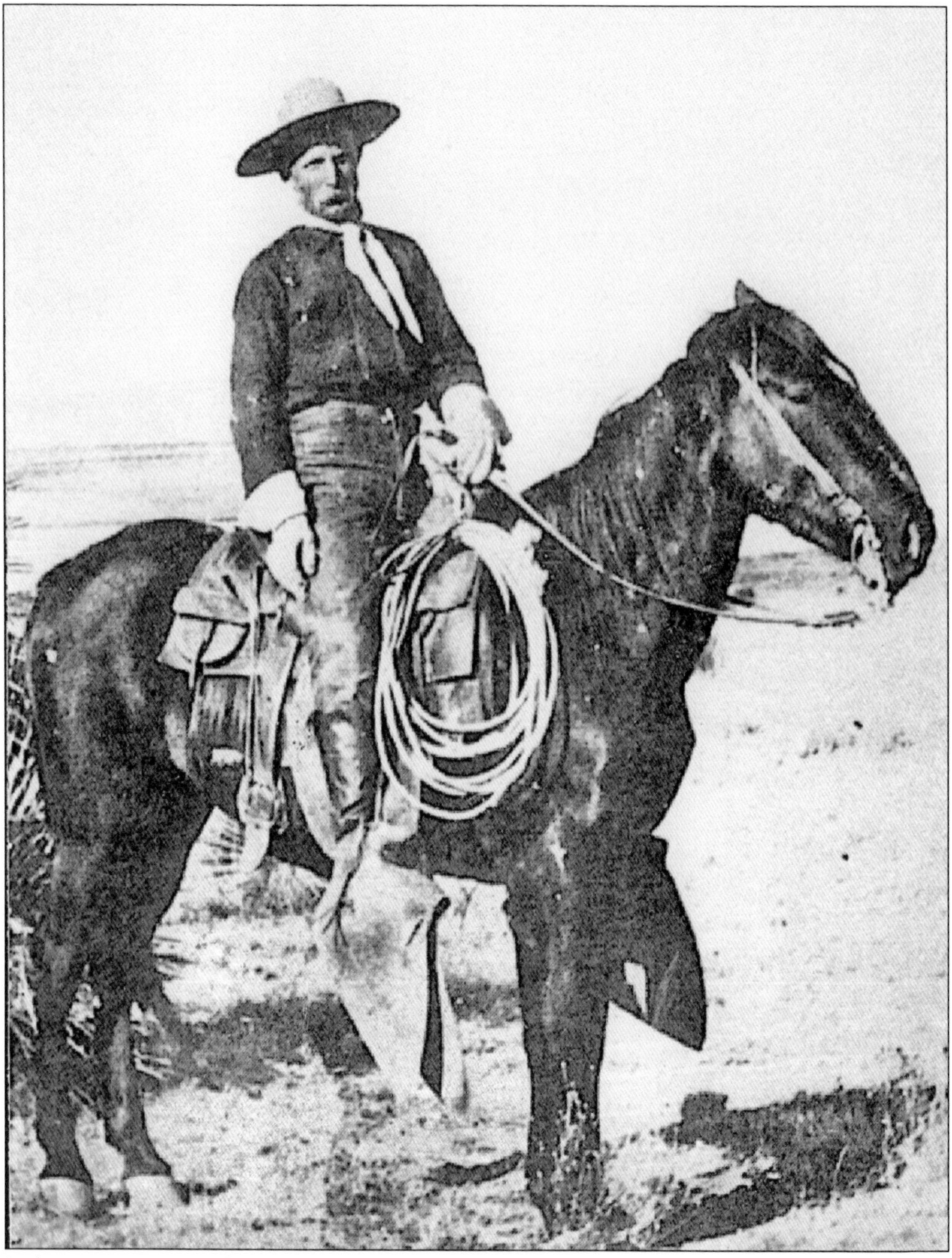

In his prime as a cowboy, Eugene Manlove Rhodes rode for the Bar Cross, headquartered at Aleman, near Engle on the Jornada del Muerto. Gene concluded his dissertation on the cowboy with these words: "And I'll tell you one more thing . . . A large proportion . . . of the cowboys are illiterate, and some of them are grand rascals, but they ain't none of 'em plumb imbeciles. They couldn't stay on the job . . . And they have a chance at 'the education of a gentleman'—to ride, shoot and speak the truth.' They have to ride and shoot—and speakin' the truth comes easier for them than for most folks, 'cause if speaking the aforesaid truth displeases anyone they mostly don't give a damn." (Courtesy of HCSNM.)

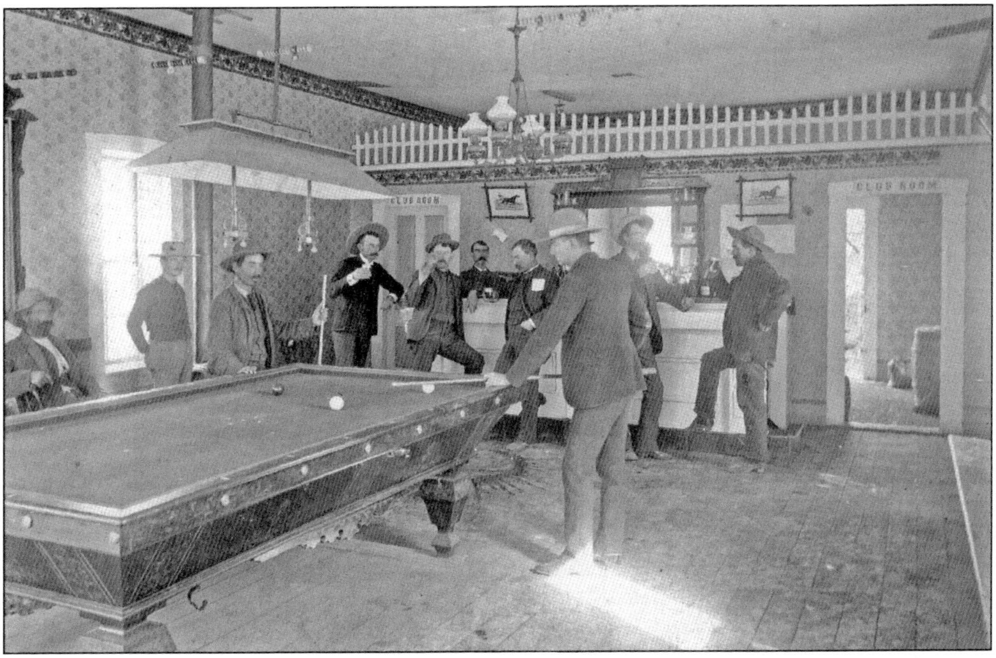

This saloon in Tularosa, photographed about 1890, was reputed to belong to Pat Garrett but was probably Tipton's or Pat Coghlan's and was a favorite spot for local cowboys, with beer, pool, and good companionship. (Courtesy of HCSNM.)

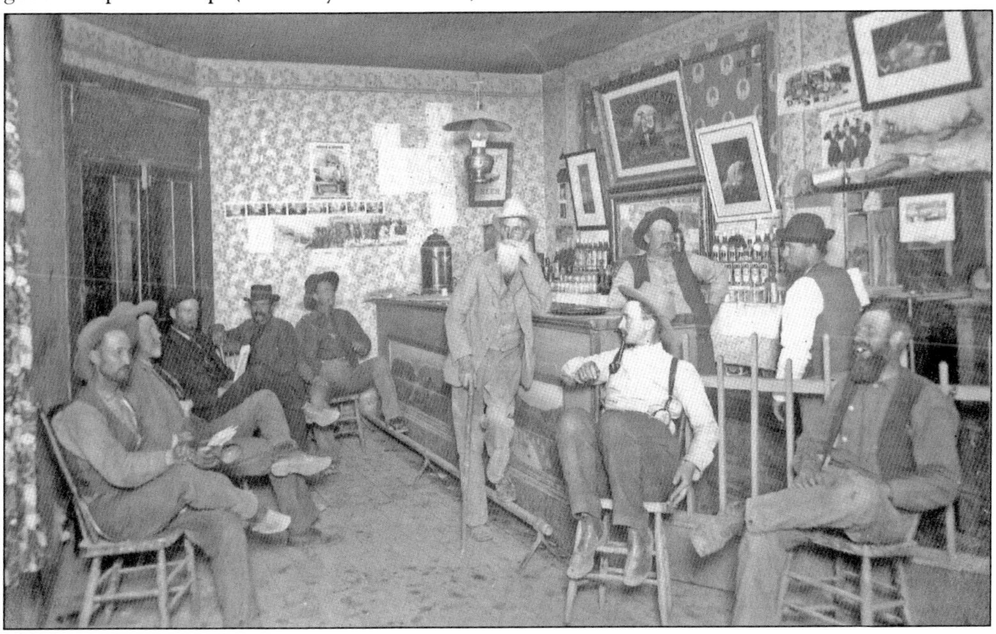

Like so many others, Pat Garrett was many things to many people—possibly a saloon keeper (allegedly in Tularosa, above), cowman, sheriff, Texas Ranger, card player, collector of customs at El Paso, and the man who shot Billy the Kid. Twenty years after Pat was murdered, Eugene Rhodes, who at times was a political opponent, wrote in his defense, "The situation was not of Garrett's making; but he met it in the only possible way . . . It was kill or be killed." (Courtesy of HCSNM.)

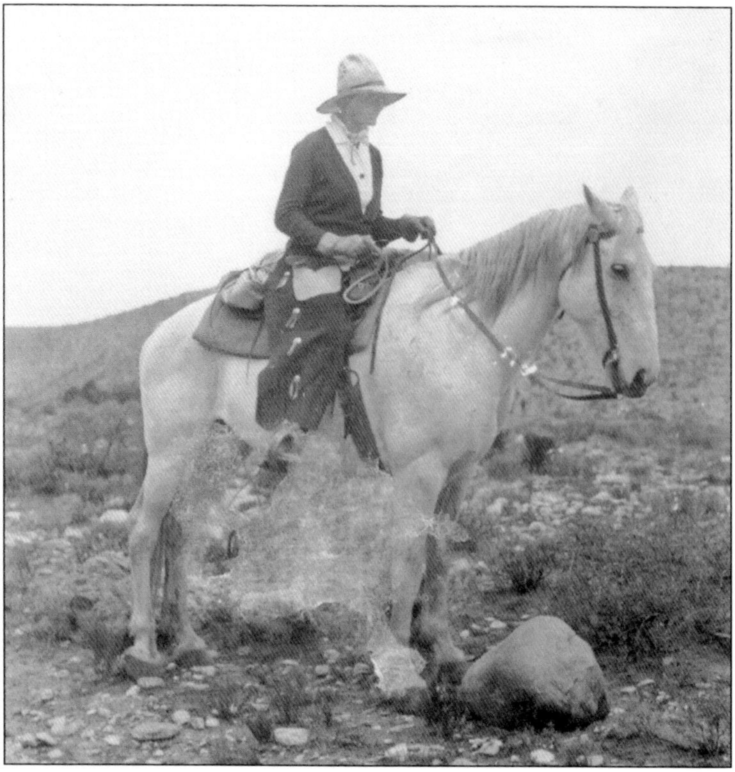

Katherine Cleve, the nurse at the Girl Scout's Camp Mary White, took snapshots of the mounted campers, like this one, during this pack trip to Carlsbad Caverns in 1931. Cleve had been brought up on her family's CA Bar Ranch along the Peñasco. (Courtesy of SMHS.)

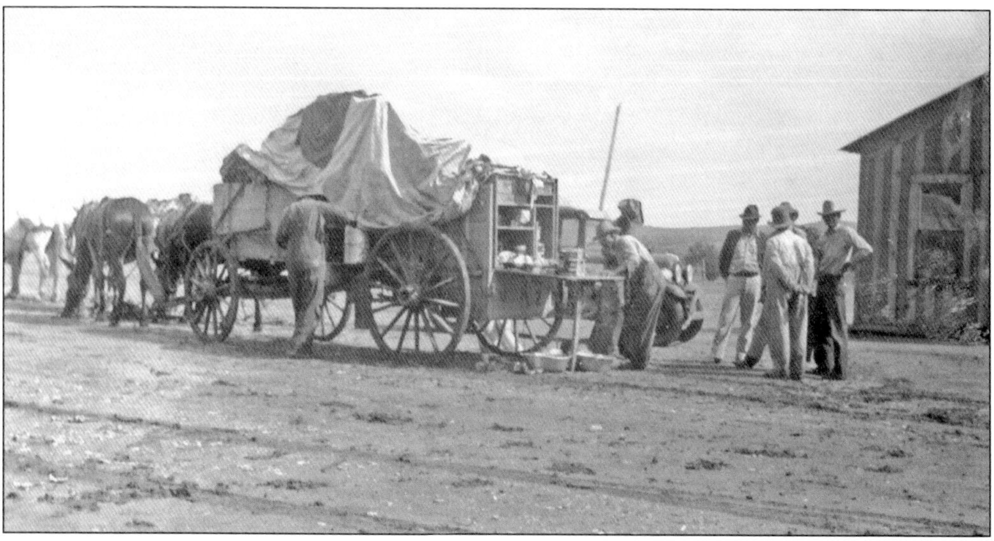

Ranch hands at the CA Bar or the Flying H prepared a complete chuck wagon for the Camp Mary White Carlsbad Caverns pack trip. (Courtesy of SMHS.)

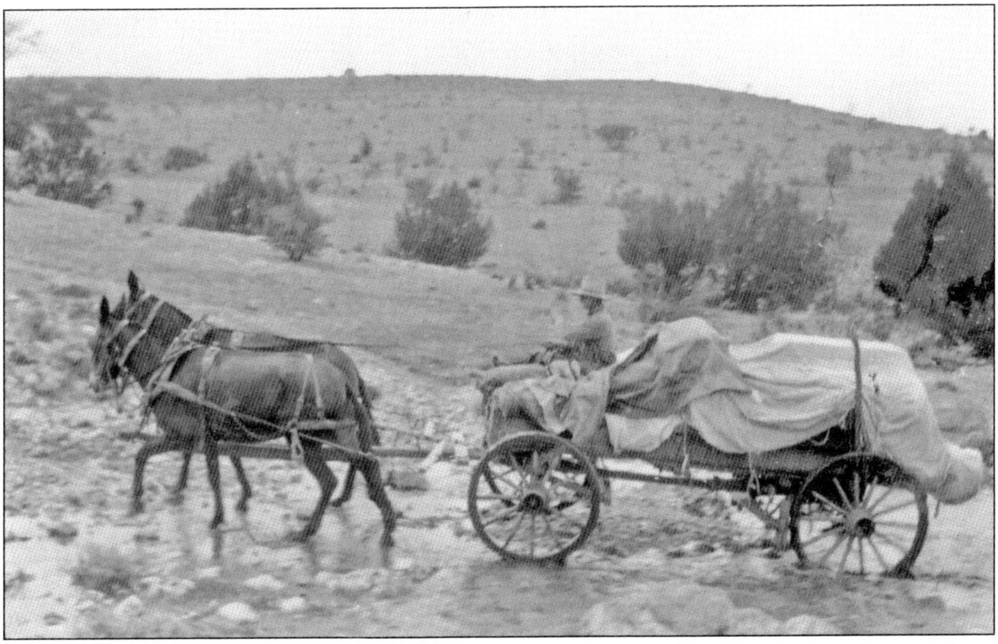

A second wagon was needed to carry Girl Scout campers' gear and bedding during the week-long 100-mile pack trip to Carlsbad Caverns. (Courtesy of SMHS.)

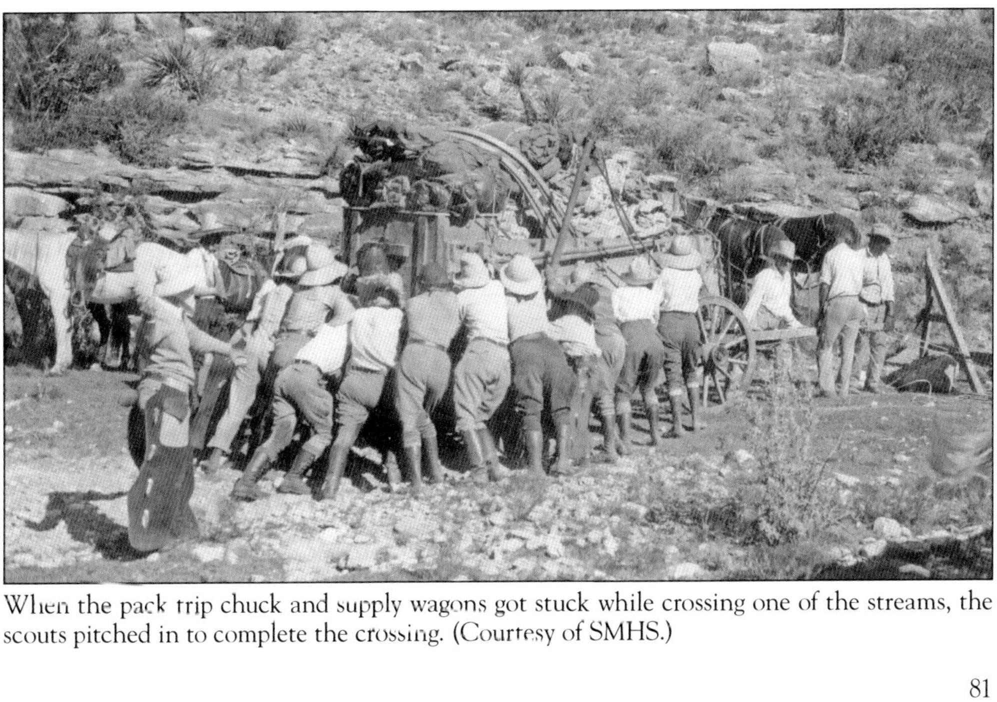

When the pack trip chuck and supply wagons got stuck while crossing one of the streams, the scouts pitched in to complete the crossing. (Courtesy of SMHS.)

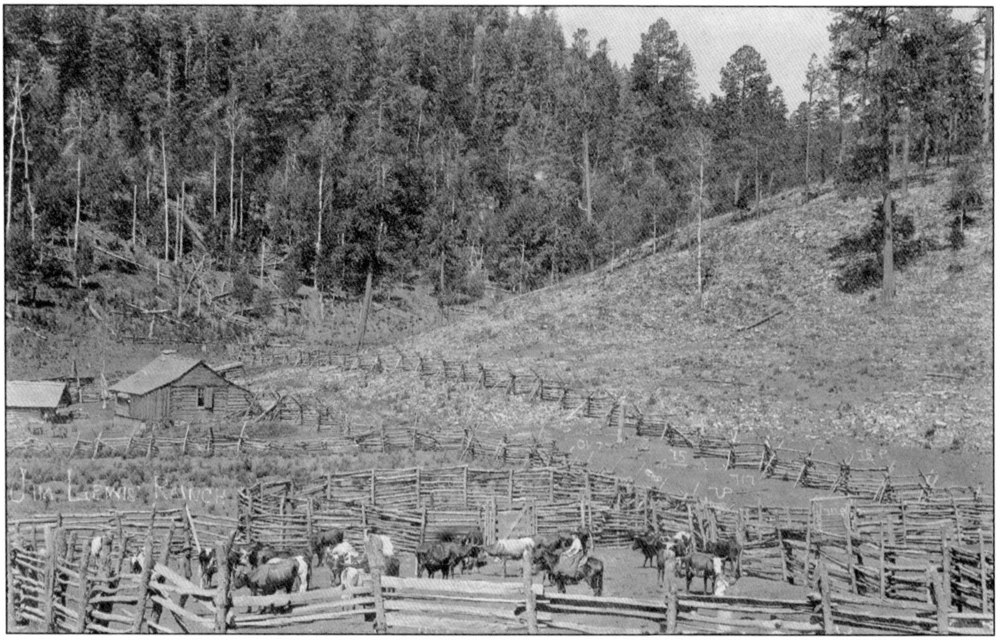

The Jim Lewis Ranch in the high Sacramento Mountains, photographed in 1895, was typical of the smaller family ranches established at the turn of the century. Note the ranch brands written into the picture: OV7, 75 Bar, 7 Bar 7, 7UP, 7 Bar 7P, 75 Bar P. Large brands can be seen on several of the cows in the left forefront. (Courtesy of TBHS.)

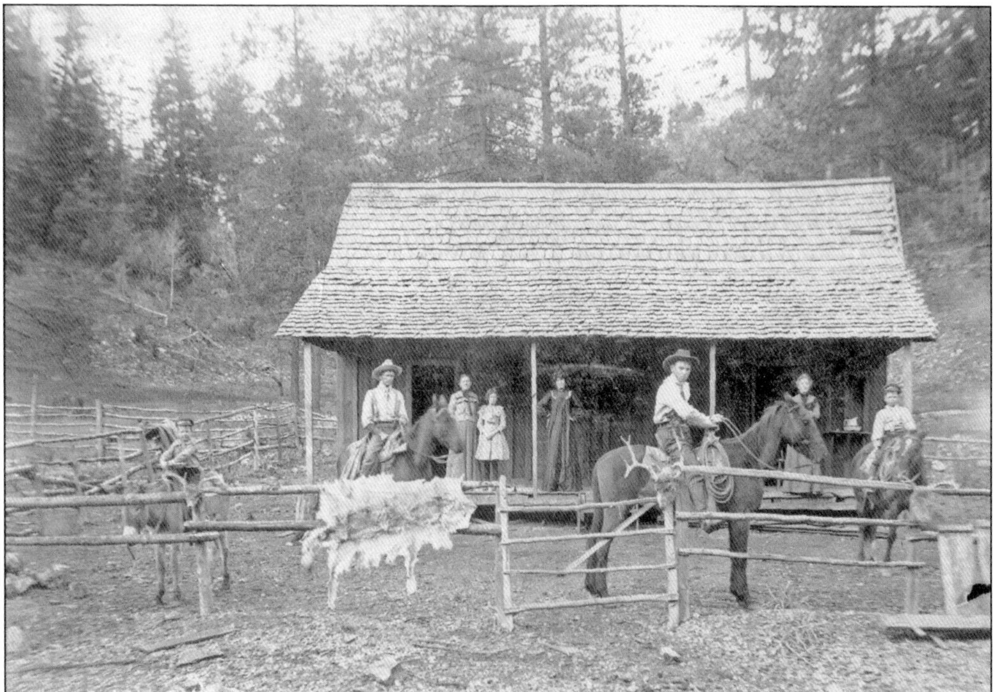

The W. A. Danley family built their small ranch house, shown here in 1904, on the Rio Sacramento. Several sets of antlers indicate that venison was commonly consumed. (Courtesy of TBHS.)

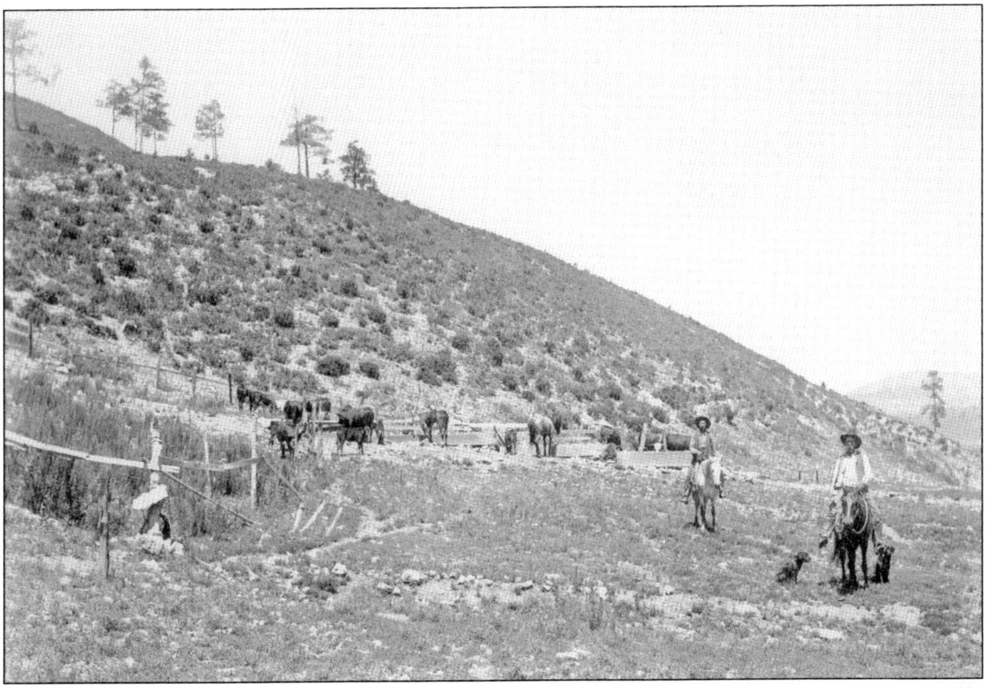

The Tillitson Ranch was located along the Peñasco River. The principal ranch facilities usually included simple rail corrals, board feed, and water troughs like those visible here. (Courtesy of HCSNM.)

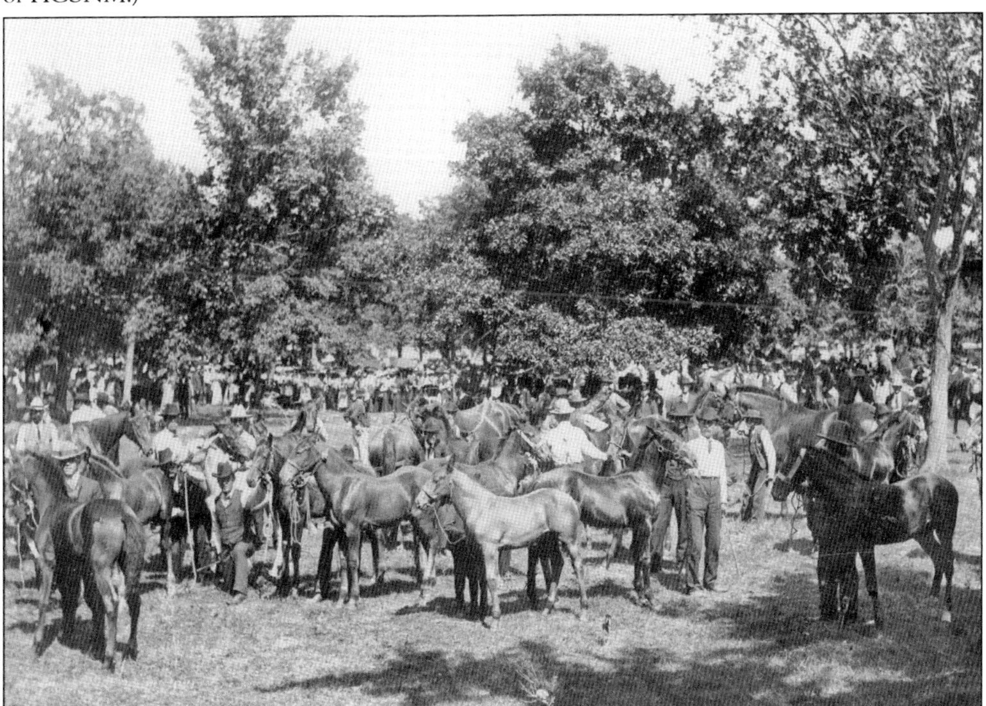

This large horse and mule sale took place in the late 1890s. Tax rolls suggest that horses had an assessed value of about $15 to $20; cows were assessed at about $11. (Courtesy of HCSNM.)

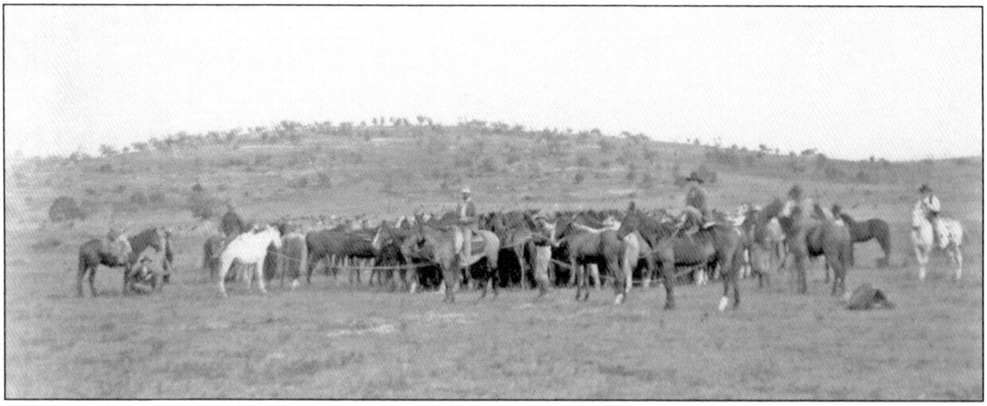

The New Mexico "Pool Outfit," probably consisting of hands from several ranches, is shown gathering the horse remuda to choose horses for night herding guard duty. Each hand rode two horses a day. Two men rode night guard, circling the herd in opposite directions. Night guard was usually divided into two-hour shifts. (Photograph by G. E. Miller; courtesy of Rick Miller.)

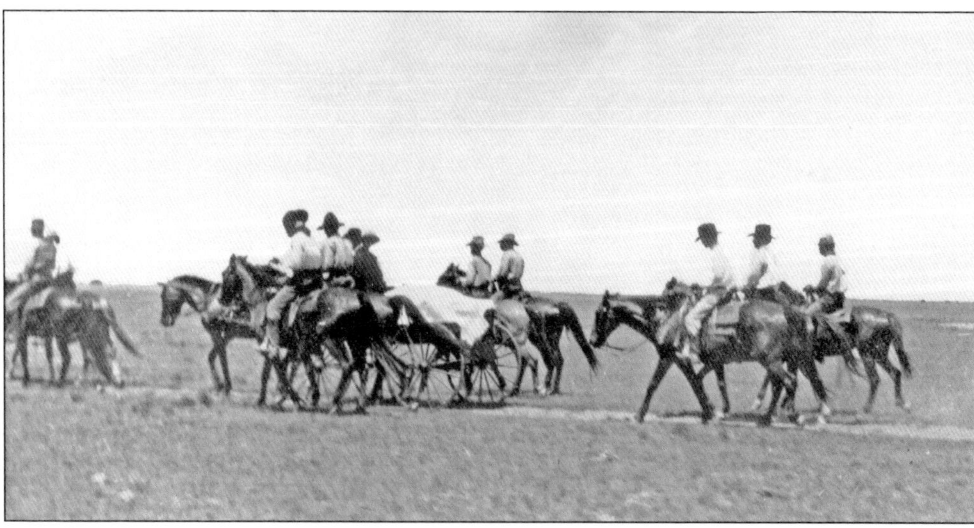

A cowboy's funeral crosses the southeastern New Mexico and Texas plains in this c. 1911 photograph. Perhaps they rode to the tune of "The Cowboy's Lament," first transcribed by "Jack" Thorp in Nebraska in 1886: "Beat the drum slowly and play the fife lowly, play the death march as you bear me along . . . I'm a poor cowboy, and I know I've done wrong." (Courtesy of HCSNM.)

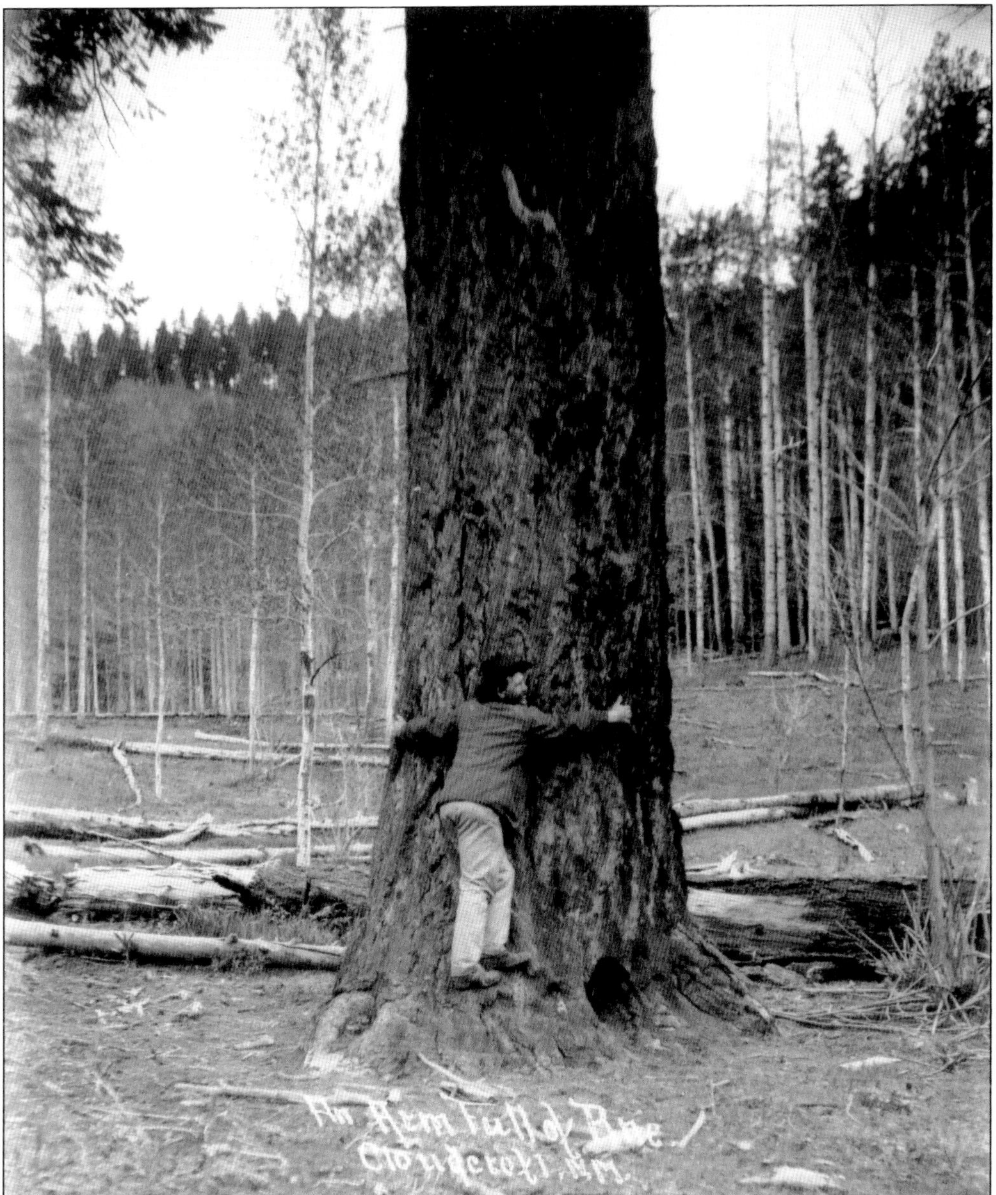

This local lumberjack/cowboy embraces "an armful of pine" near Cloudcroft. This tree was typical of the virgin growth logged at the dawn of the 20th century in the Sacramento Mountains. By the mid-20th century, most of the old growth was gone and smaller, secondary growth trees became the staple crop. (Courtesy of SMHS.)

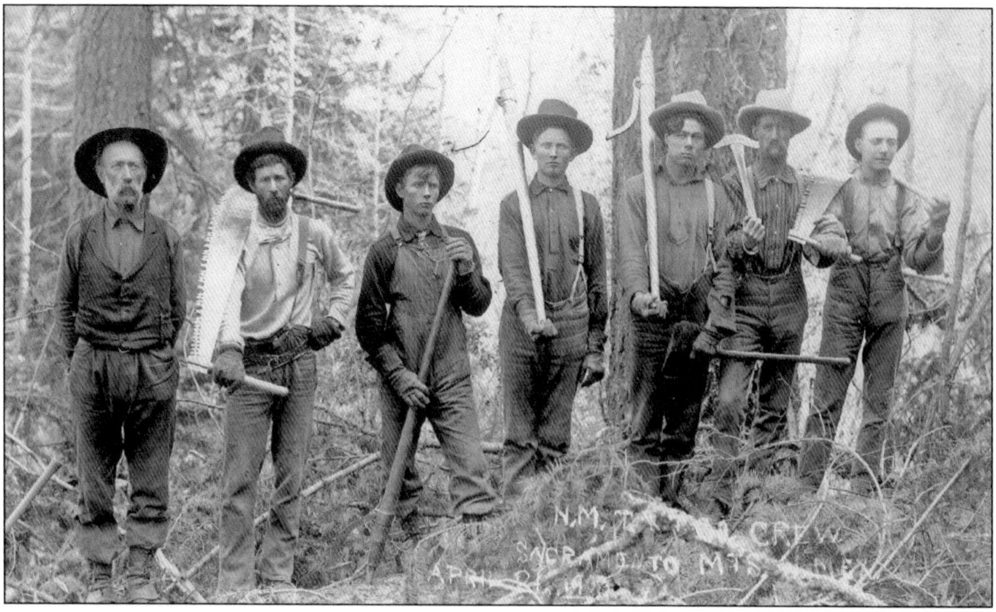

A typical New Mexico Tie and Timber Company logging crew is shown in this *c.* 1900 photograph using simple hand tools to harvest the largest trees. This crew has crosscut saws, double-bitted axes, and peaveys (or peavey hooks) used to turn and position large logs once they were down on the ground. (Courtesy of TBHS.)

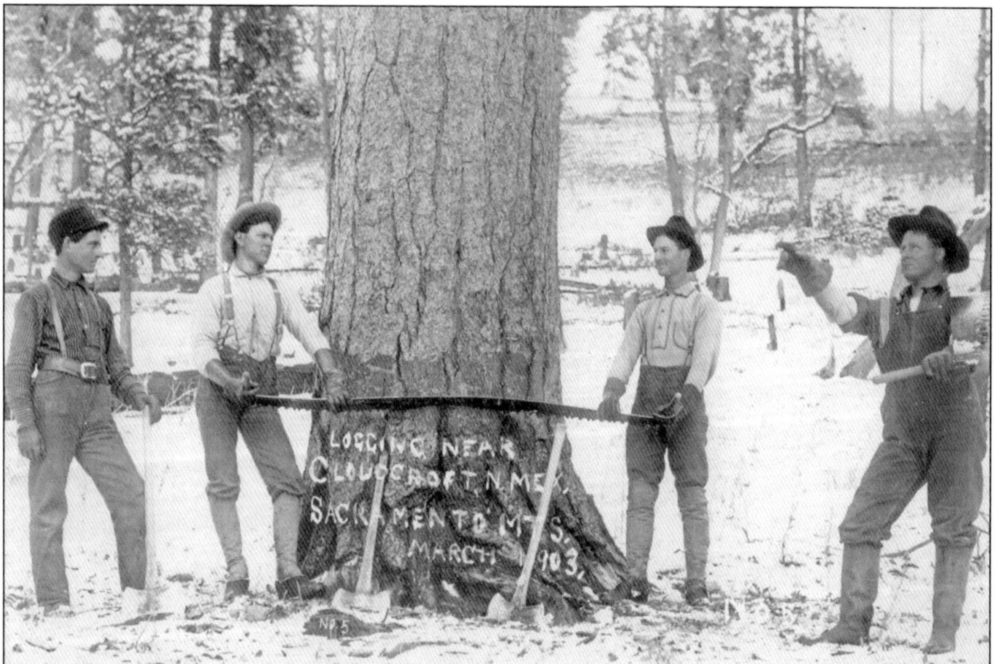

G. E. Miller photographed this crosscut sawyer crew in the snow near Cloudcroft in 1903, as they prepared to begin the main cut to fell this large tree. Before making the cut, the crew used double-bitted axes to cut a fall notch to help direct the tree's fall. (Courtesy of Rick Miller.)

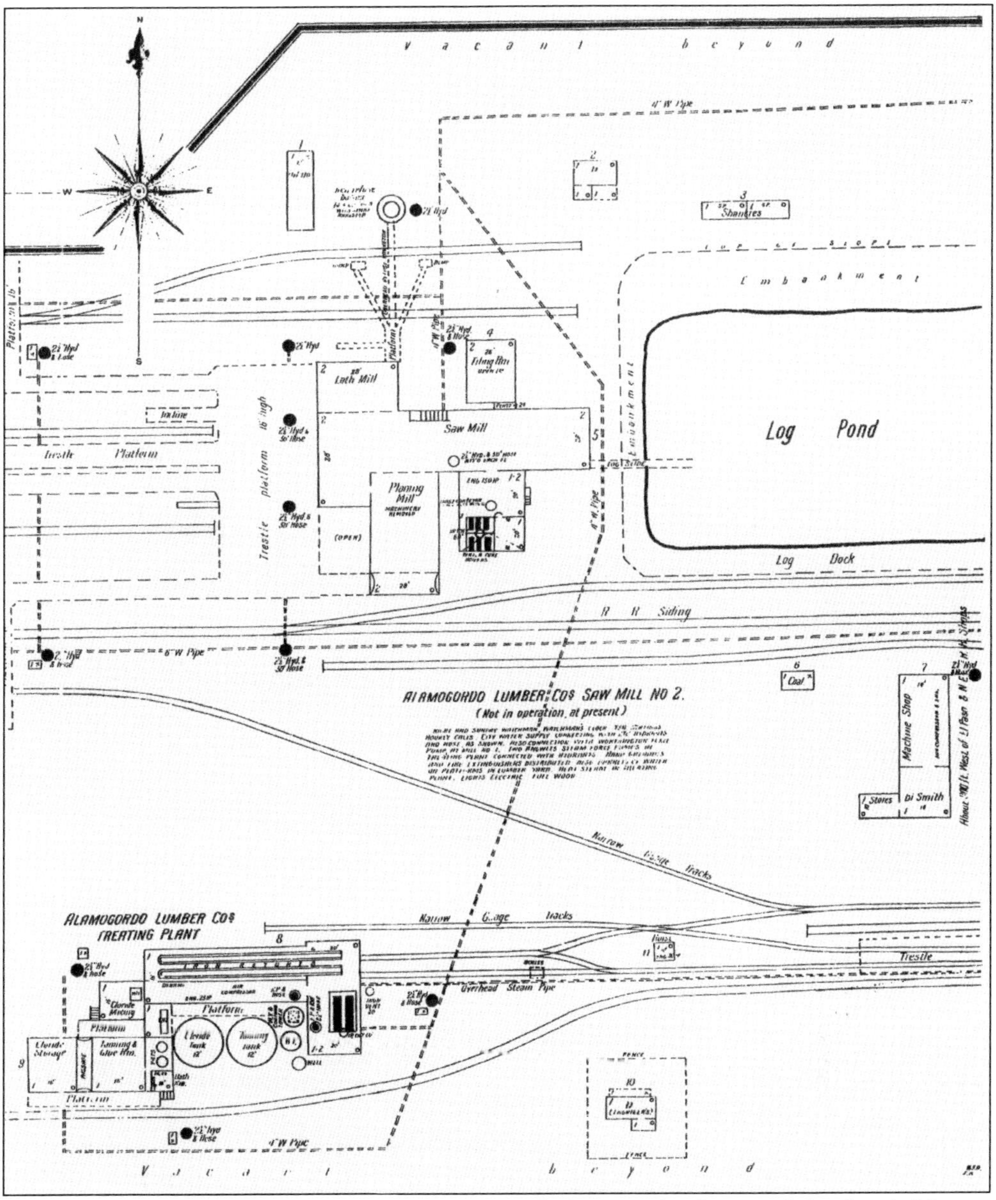

The Sanborn Fire Insurance Company 1905 map of Alamogordo illustrated the detailed layout of one of the two sawmills built to cut ties and timbers for the expansion of the railroad. The timber was cut along the crest of the Sacramento Mountains at 8,600 feet and brought 20 miles down to Alamogordo, at 4,400 feet, on the Alamogordo and Sacramento Mountain Railroad to the mill's log pond. (Courtesy of Library of Congress.)

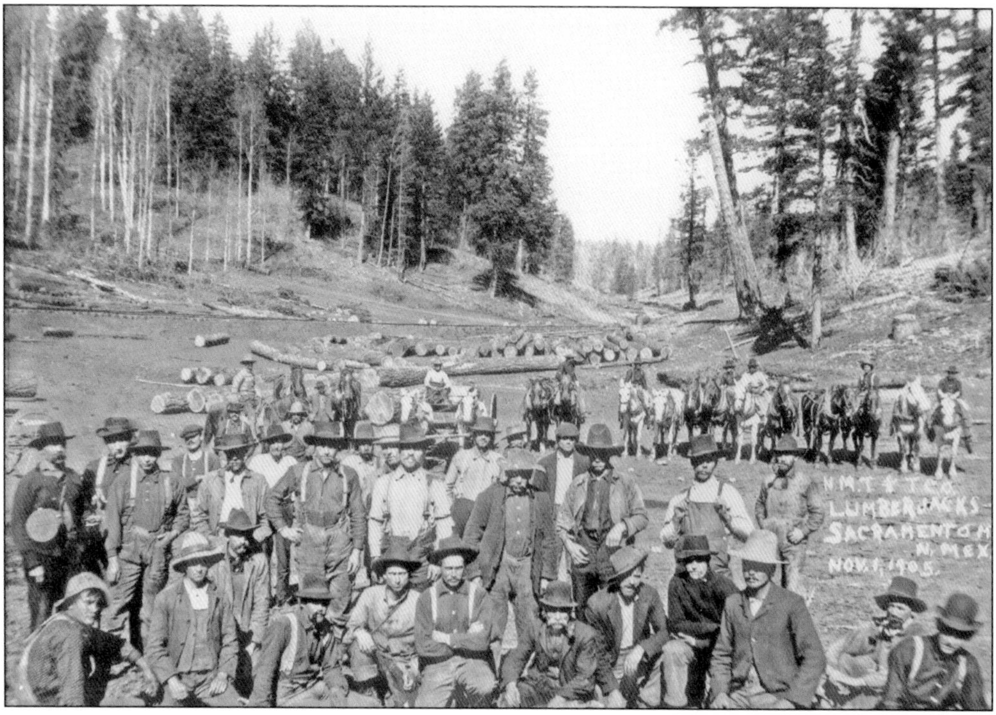

New Mexico Tie and Timber Company lumberjacks and hauling crew gathered in this timber-cut valley near Cloudcroft in 1905 for a portrait by G. E. Miller. (Courtesy of SMHS.)

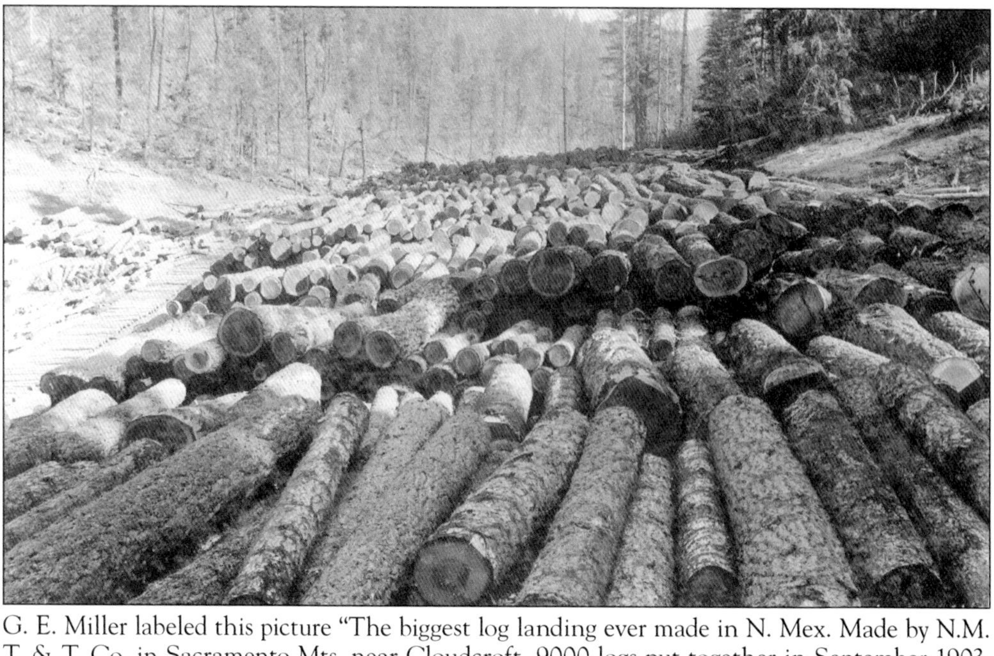

G. E. Miller labeled this picture "The biggest log landing ever made in N. Mex. Made by N.M. T. & T. Co. in Sacramento Mts. near Cloudcroft. 9000 logs put together in September 1903. Altitude 9000 ft." (Courtesy of TBHS.)

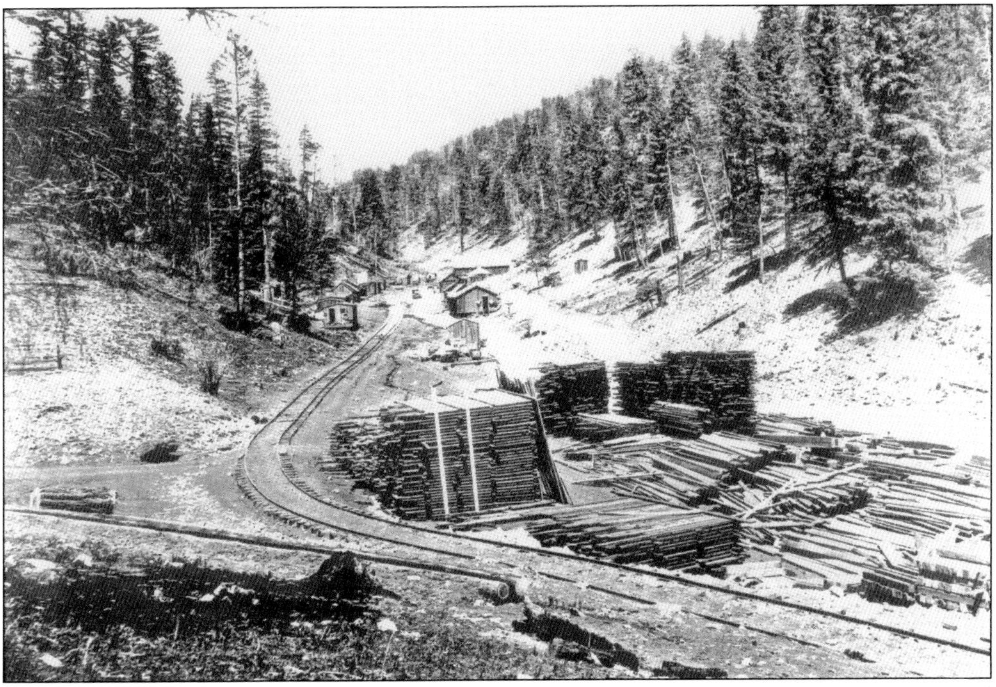

This lumberjack camp borders a single logging railroad track that winds down one of the upland canyons south of Cloudcroft around the turn of the century. Many of these tracks were somewhat temporary, with dirt rather than cinder ballast between ties, and often lacking tie plates to anchor the rails. (Courtesy of Zeke Castro.)

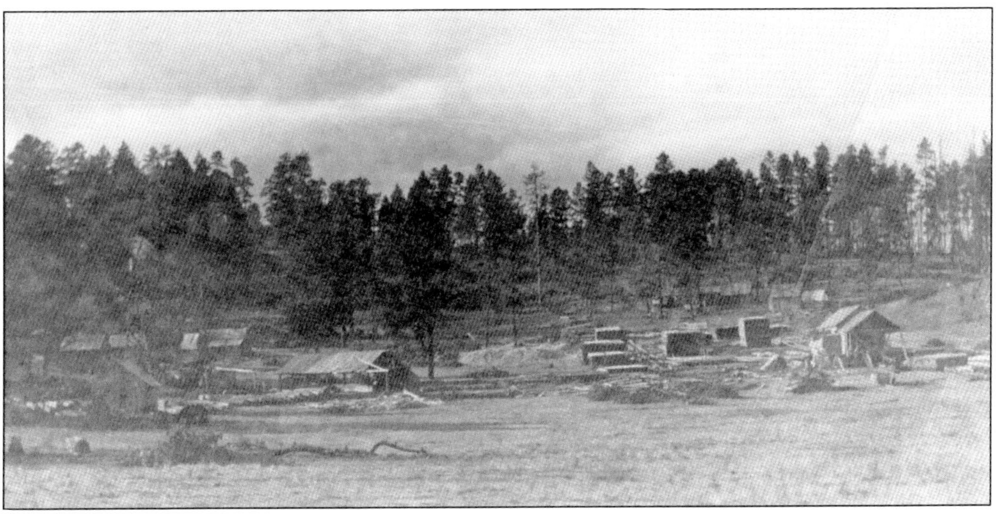

The Mescalero Reservation operated this sawmill near Whitetail around 1913. Throughout the century, there were two distinct lumbering areas: the Mescalero Apache Reservation in the northern Sacramento Mountains and the Alamogordo railroad-based sawmills, generally south and west of Cloudcroft. (Courtesy of R. and R. Buckner.)

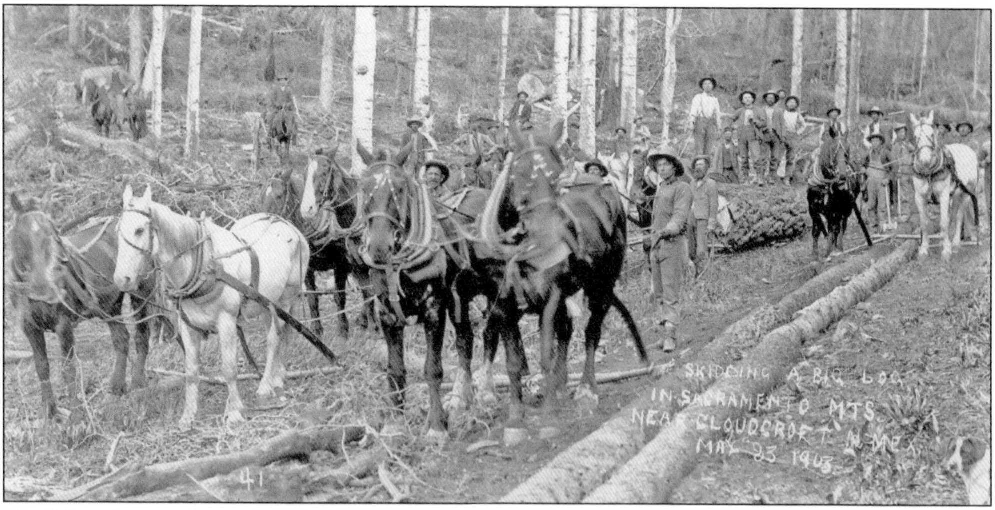

Until logging trucks replaced the railroad, logs were skidded to the nearby railroad track using teams of horses, as seen in G. E. Miller's photograph in the Sacramento Mountains in May 1903. (Courtesy of TBHS.)

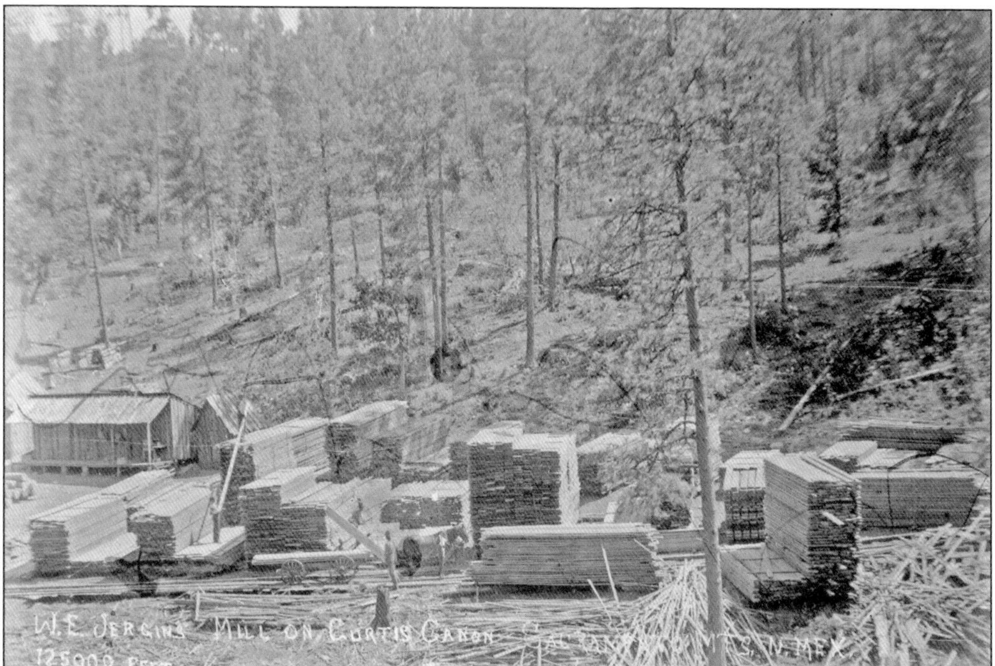

W. E. Jergin operated this sawmill in Curtis Cañón in the Sacramento Mountains and had accumulated 125,000 board feet of lumber by June 3, 1900, when G. E. Miller took this photograph. (Courtesy of Marjorie Curtis.)

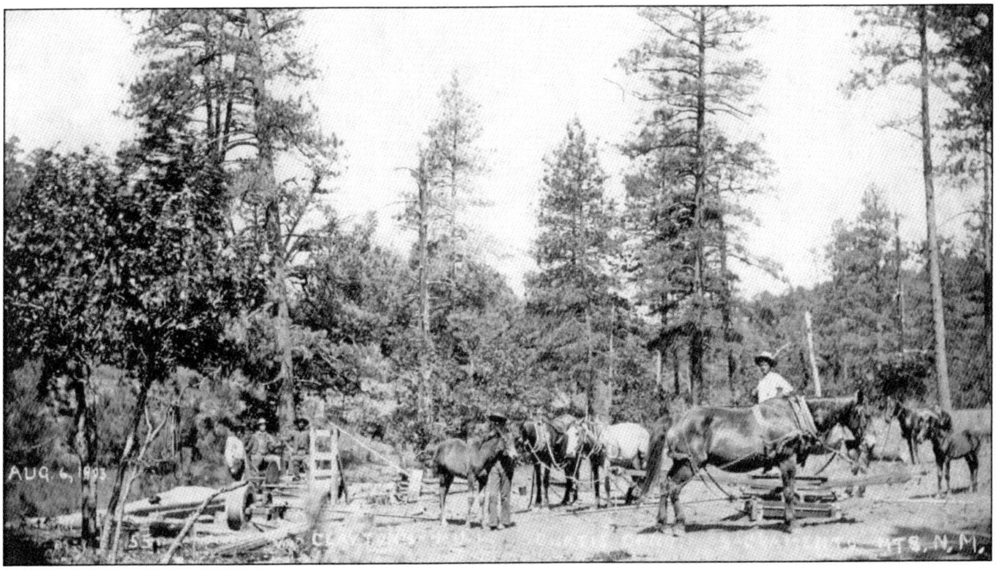

The Clayton's Mill was located in Curtis Canyon in the Sacramento Mountains about 1903. Many of these small mills produced lumber for local consumption by the builders working in nearby communities like Cloudcroft. (Courtesy of Rick Miller.)

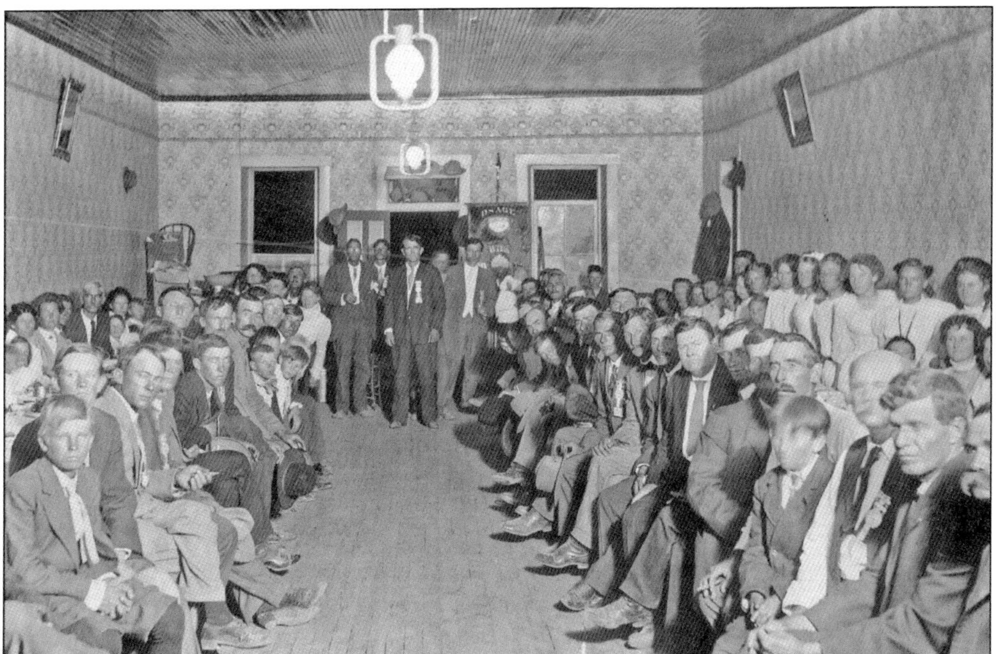

The final supper meeting of the Osage Chapter of the Woodmen of the World (WOW) took place in 1912. The WOW, founded in 1890, provided its members with life insurance, annuities, and distinctive headstones and is active in disaster relief today. (Courtesy of TVHS.)

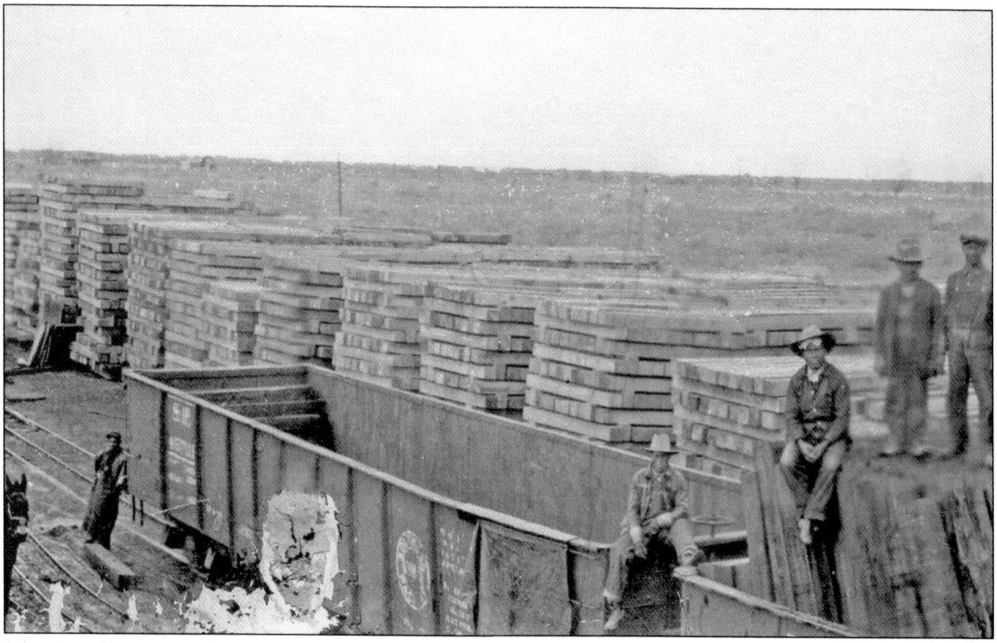

The Southwest Lumber Company, organized by Louis Carr, bought out the interests of the original Sacramento Mountain Lumber Company (SML) in 1920, after its sawmill burned down in 1919. This November 1930 photograph shows the stockpile of railroad ties at the Alamogordo mill. (Courtesy of TBHS.)

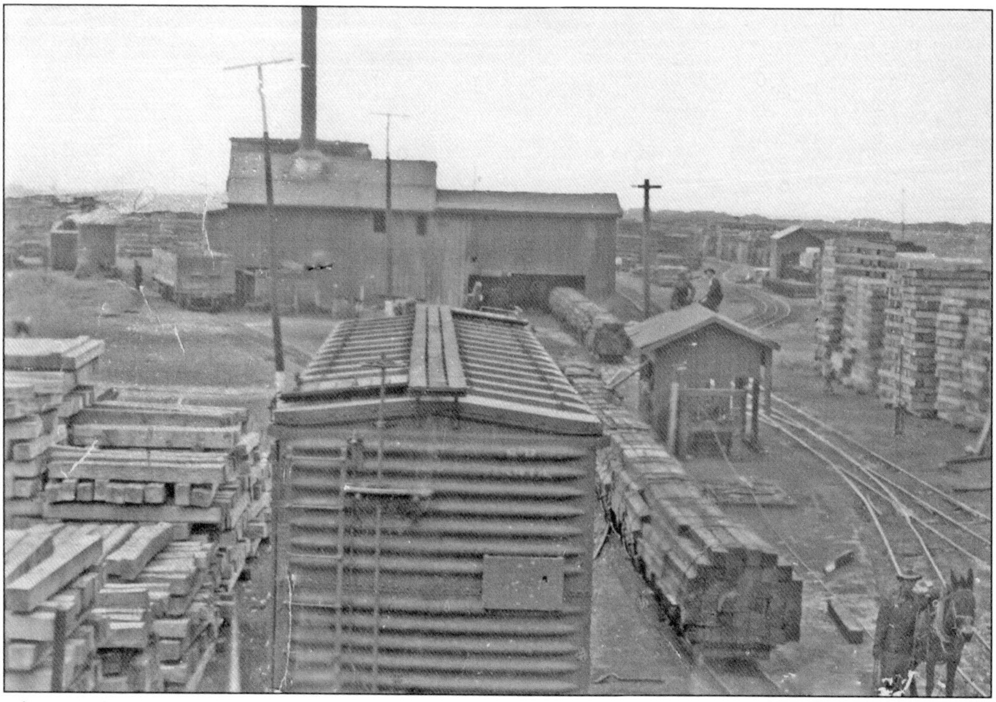

The Southwest Lumber Company Mill relied on large timber cut from its expansion beyond the spur to the small community of Russia into the Peñasco drainage to the south. Here the mill can be seen in the background in November 1930. (Courtesy of TBHS.)

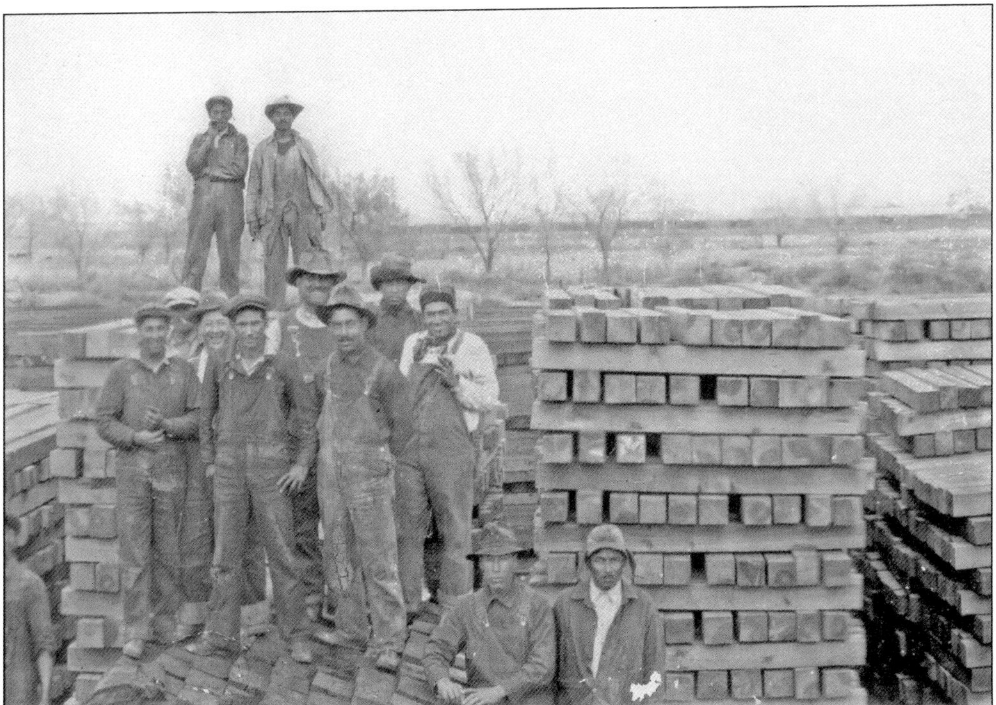

A dozen of the Southwest Lumber Company tie and timber crew pose in November 1930 atop their principal product, the ties that allowed the Phelps, Dodge Corporation's El Paso and Southwestern Railroad and finally, the Southern Pacific, to expand northward to join the Atchison, Topeka, and Santa Fe Railway at Vaughn, New Mexico. (Courtesy of TBHS.)

In 1941, the Prestridge Lumber Company bought the lodge, the timber rights of the railroad company, the Southwest Lumber Company, the Breece Lumber Company, and the mill in Alamogordo, consolidating the timber industry in the Sacramento Mountains. While cutting still relied on the old methods of using axes and saws, by around 1955, transport of logs had shifted to trucks. (Courtesy of TBHS.)

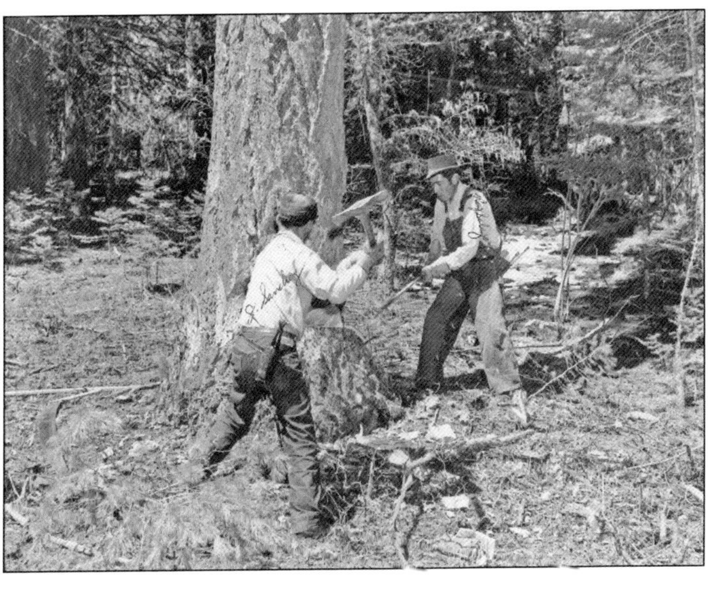

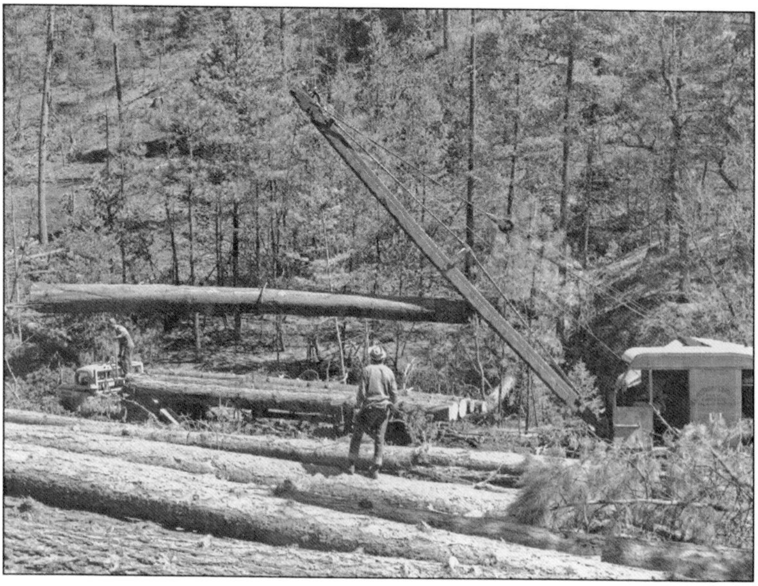

Prestridge Lumber Company shifted to logging trucks, because railroad cars could not carry logs longer than 20 feet. Prestridge wanted to cut logs up to 40 feet, possibly for utility poles, so articulated trucks replaced rail transport, and mobile cranes were used to load logs at the cutting site around 1955. (Courtesy of TBHS.)

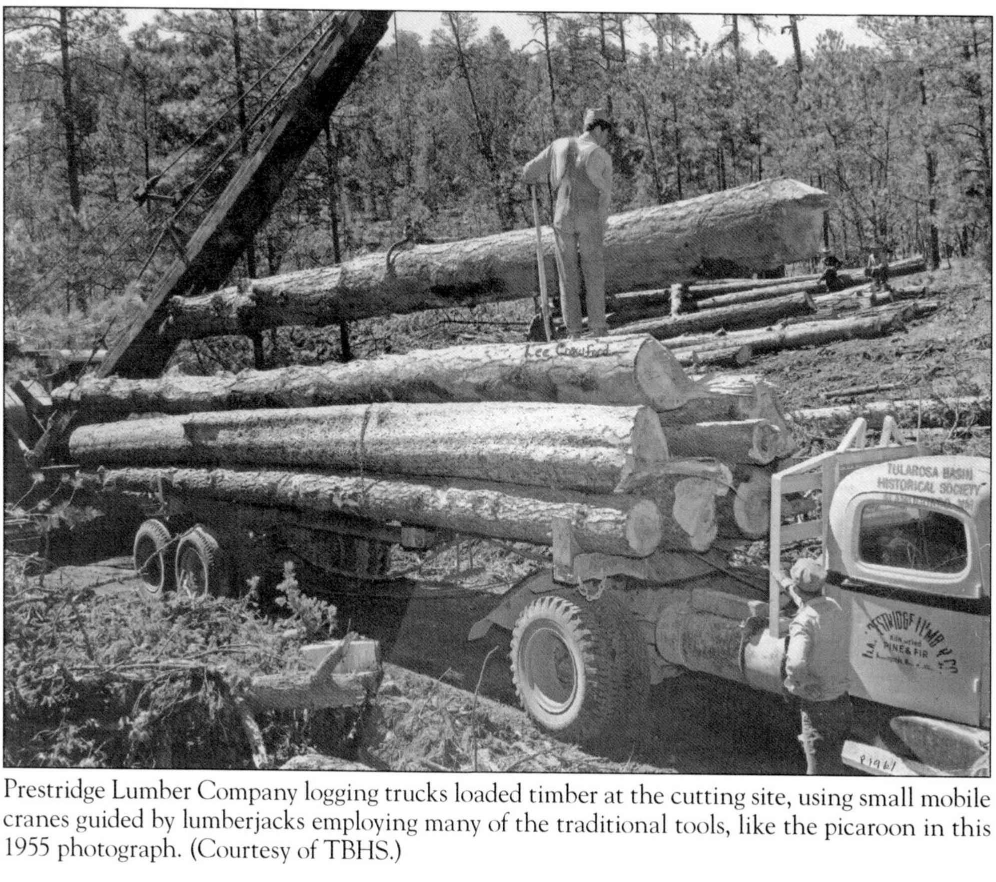

Prestridge Lumber Company logging trucks loaded timber at the cutting site, using small mobile cranes guided by lumberjacks employing many of the traditional tools, like the picaroon in this 1955 photograph. (Courtesy of TBHS.)

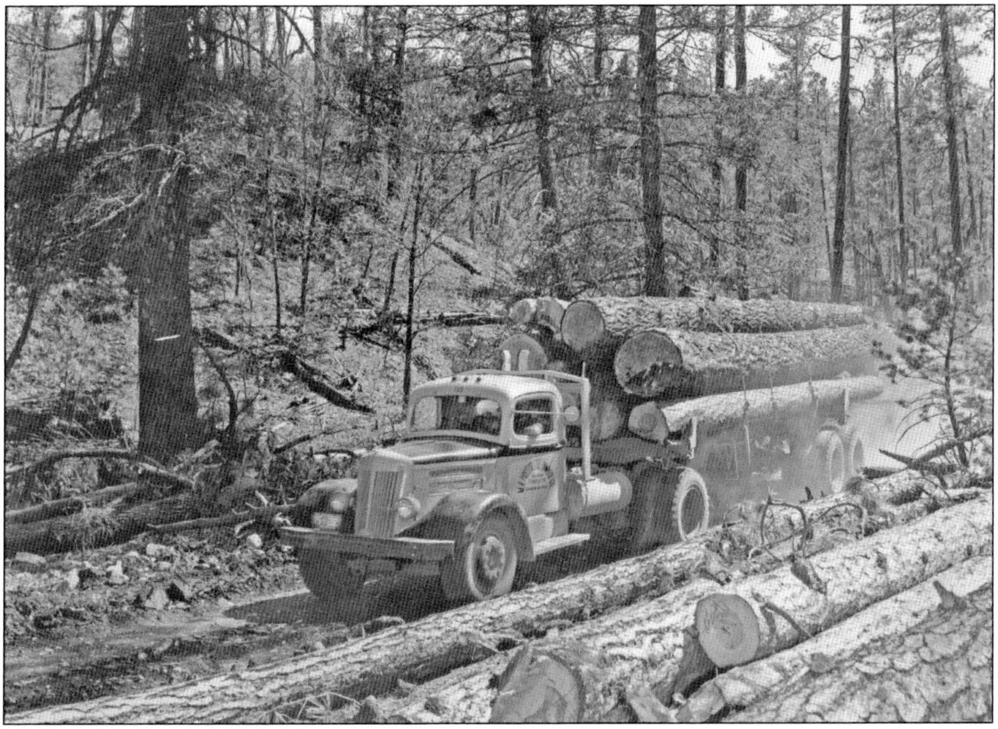

As railroads were completed, demand shifted to finished lumber and utility poles. At the onset of World War II, the U.S. Army Corps of Engineers began the largest construction effort in history. They built mobilization facilities and aircraft hangers at new bases, and airfields, artillery training, and bombing ranges throughout the Southwest. (Courtesy of TBHS.)

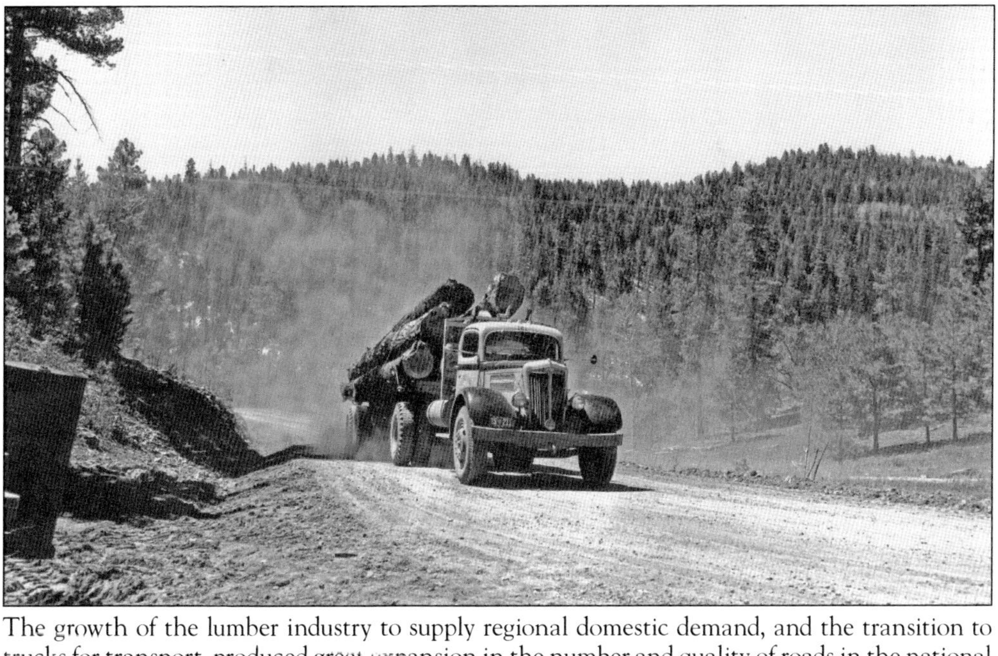

The growth of the lumber industry to supply regional domestic demand, and the transition to trucks for transport, produced great expansion in the number and quality of roads in the national forest, facilitating more extensive public use of forest resources. (Courtesy of TBHS.)

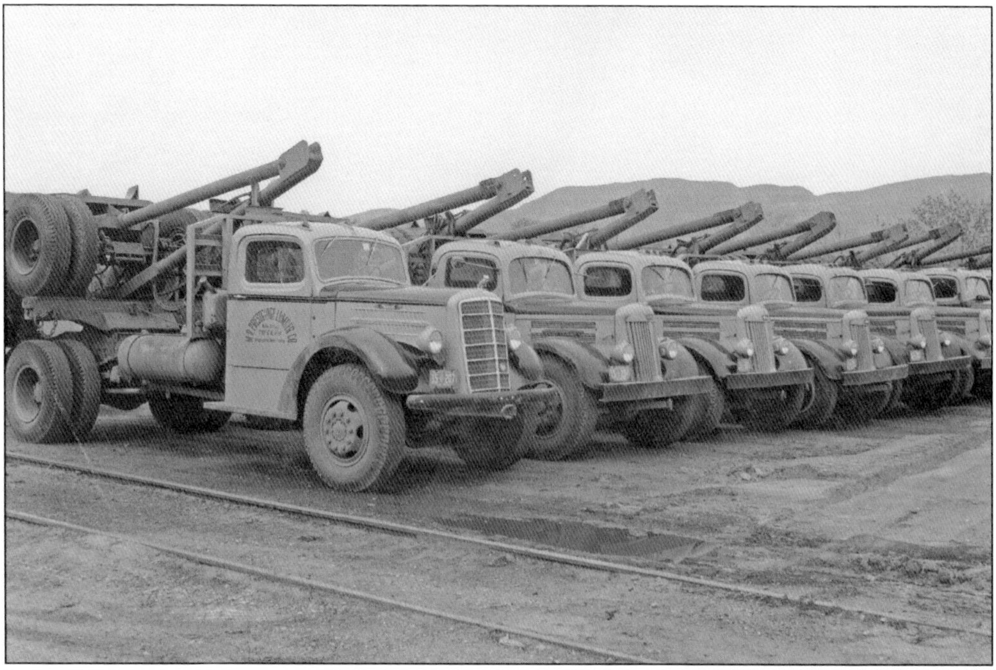

Prestridge Lumber Company used a fleet of new, specialized, articulated logging trucks that could haul the longer logs while retaining greater mobility on the empty return trip back to the logging site. (Courtesy of TBHS.)

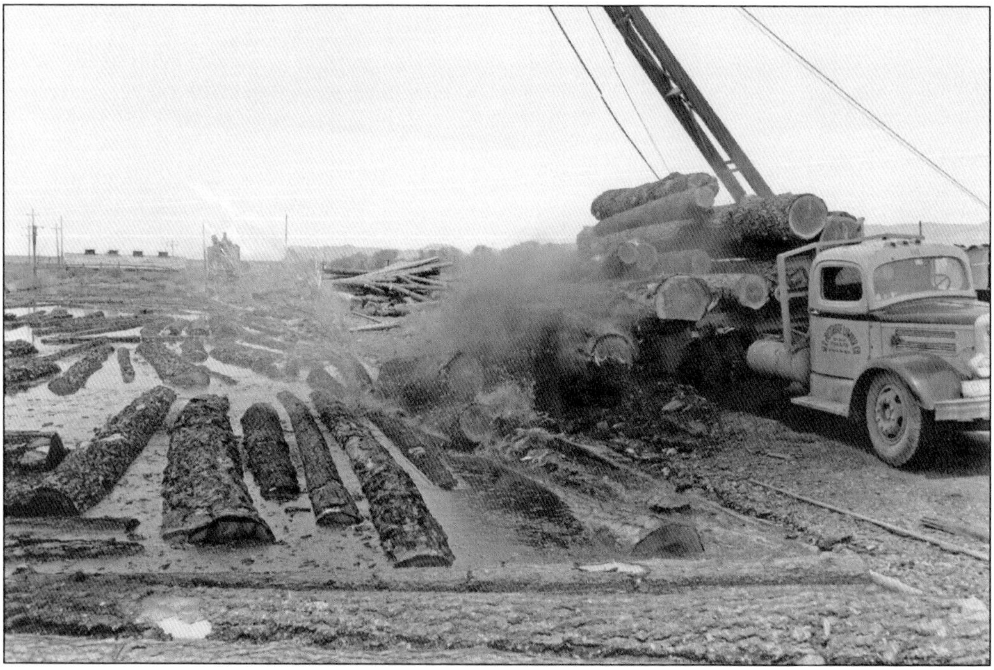

The reorganized Prestridge Lumber Company operation continued to utilize the traditional log pond, where trucks could dump their load, and the floating logs could be more easily selected and managed. (Courtesy of TBHS.)

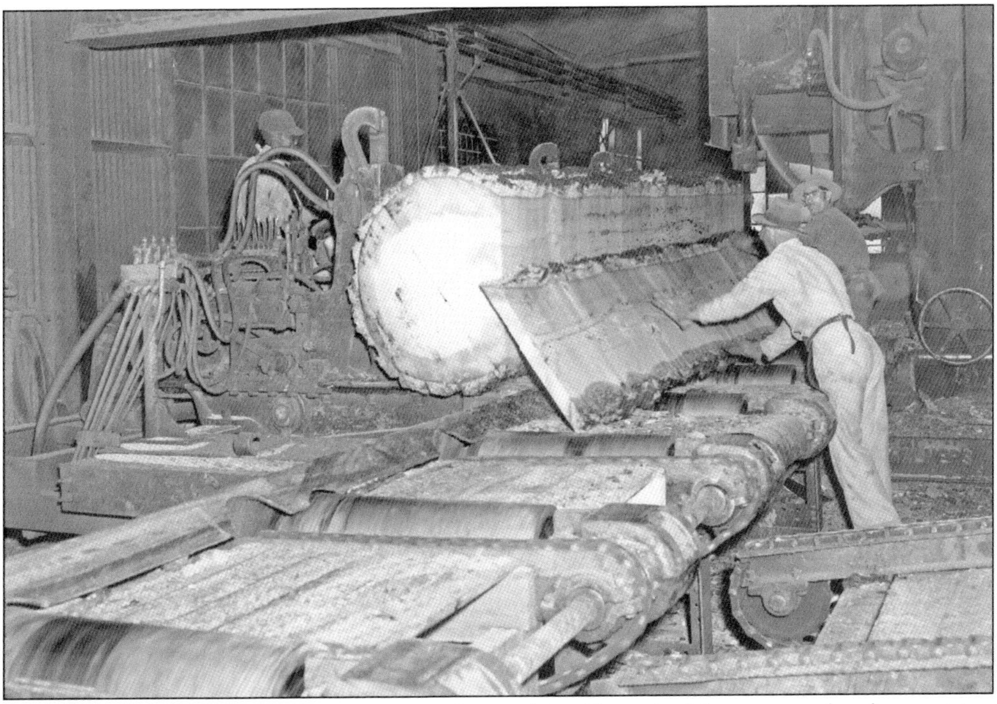

Although sawmill log handling was more mechanized, it still required direct control and supervision of experienced sawyers who could manage the direction and thickness of individual saw cuts. (Courtesy of TBHS.)

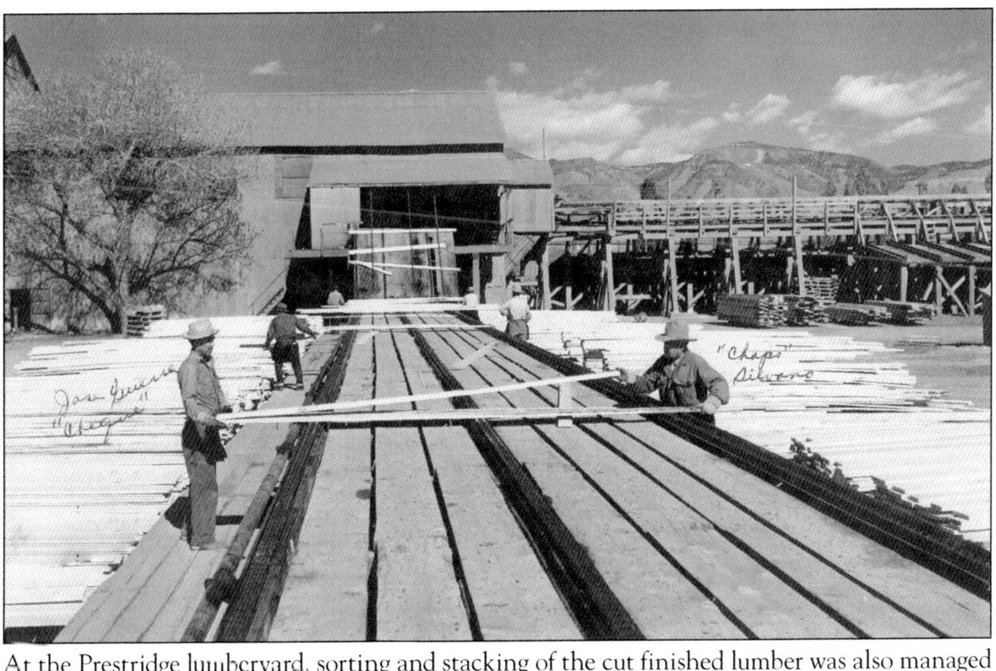

At the Prestridge lumberyard, sorting and stacking of the cut finished lumber was also managed and done by hand by sawyers stationed along a conveyor belt that moved the cut lumber from the sawmill into the yard. (Courtesy of TBHS.)

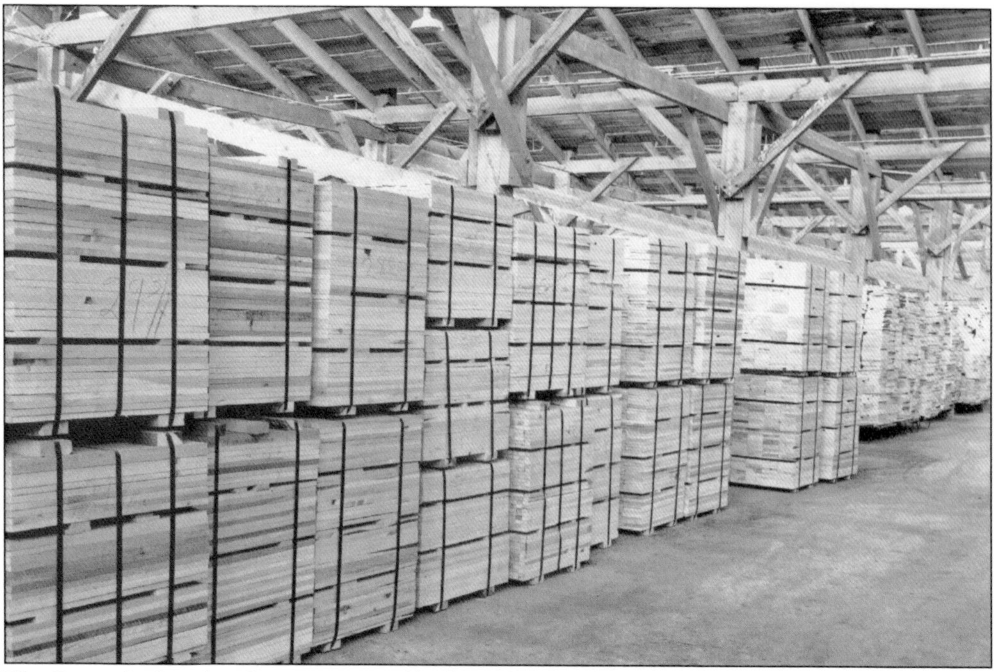

The Prestridge Lumber Company stored high-quality finished lumber inside this warehouse, prior to shipment, to allow the wood to cure slowly out of direct sunlight. (Courtesy of TBHS.)

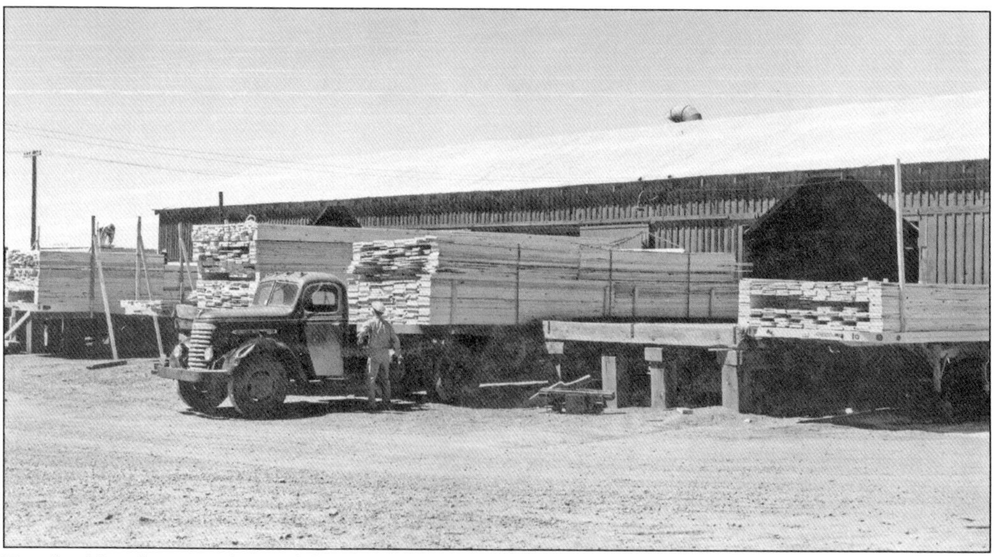

Finished lumber was shipped from Prestridge Lumber Company's Alamogordo warehouse to its commercial markets on another set of flatbed trailer trucks. (Courtesy of TBHS.)

Three

Prohibition, Depression, and Federalization

The "open range" disappeared after the turn of the 20th century, when new public land laws took effect, attracting more farmers and fruit growers to the alluvial fans along the margins of the mountains. The leasing of specific tracts of public lands to individuals brought an end to free grazing and was the first major step in a shift to a cash-based economy. The development of mining and timber industries and construction of railroads and other communication and transportation systems followed rapidly after Alamogordo was established. After an early population decline, Alamogordo had again reached a population of 3,000 by 1930.

After passage of the Volstead Act instituted the prohibition of alcohol, New Mexico's rural border with Mexico became a favorite smuggler's route. In 1920, Howard Beacham was elected Otero County sheriff and began a strong campaign against smugglers, bootleggers, and sellers of spirits. He collaborated with young undercover customs enforcement officer Juanita McDaniels, achieving a noteworthy record, sufficient to ensure he was not reelected until 1935. In the interim, Beacham was federally appointed to enforce Prohibition throughout Southeastern New Mexico.

The Depression and the drought years of the 1930s combined to further disturb the early ranching, mining, and timbering settlement pattern. WPA and CCC programs were initiated to improve power and transportation infrastructure, and new businesses began to develop, including the Continental Oil Company Warehouse and Roland Hazard's nationally famous La Luz Pottery.

In the 1930s, the U.S. government began to set aside vast tracts of land in the central and western portions of the basin. White Sands National Monument was established in 1933. By the 1940s, these and many other tracts were designated for artillery and bomber training in the Alamogordo Bombing Range. On July 16, 1945, the world was changed forever with the first atomic explosion at the Trinity Site at the northwest corner of the bombing range. At the close of World War II, these federalized lands were adopted for defense systems testing as part of present-day White Sands Missile Range.

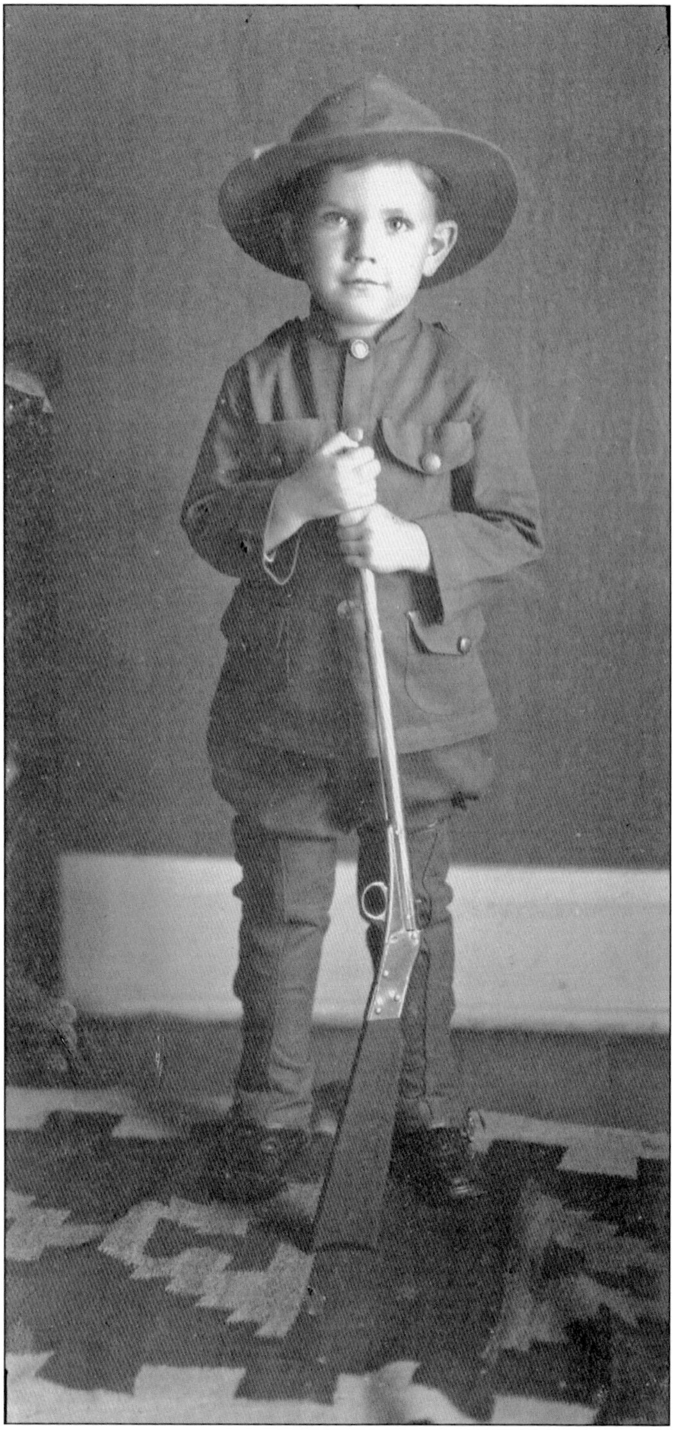

Pancho Villa's raid on Columbus, New Mexico, helped mobilize the new state's first National Guard units, which served under Gen. John Pershing, first in the Mexico campaign, and later in Europe. Military service became a popular occupation in New Mexico, paralleling and partially replacing the cowboy life. (Courtesy of Frances Evans.)

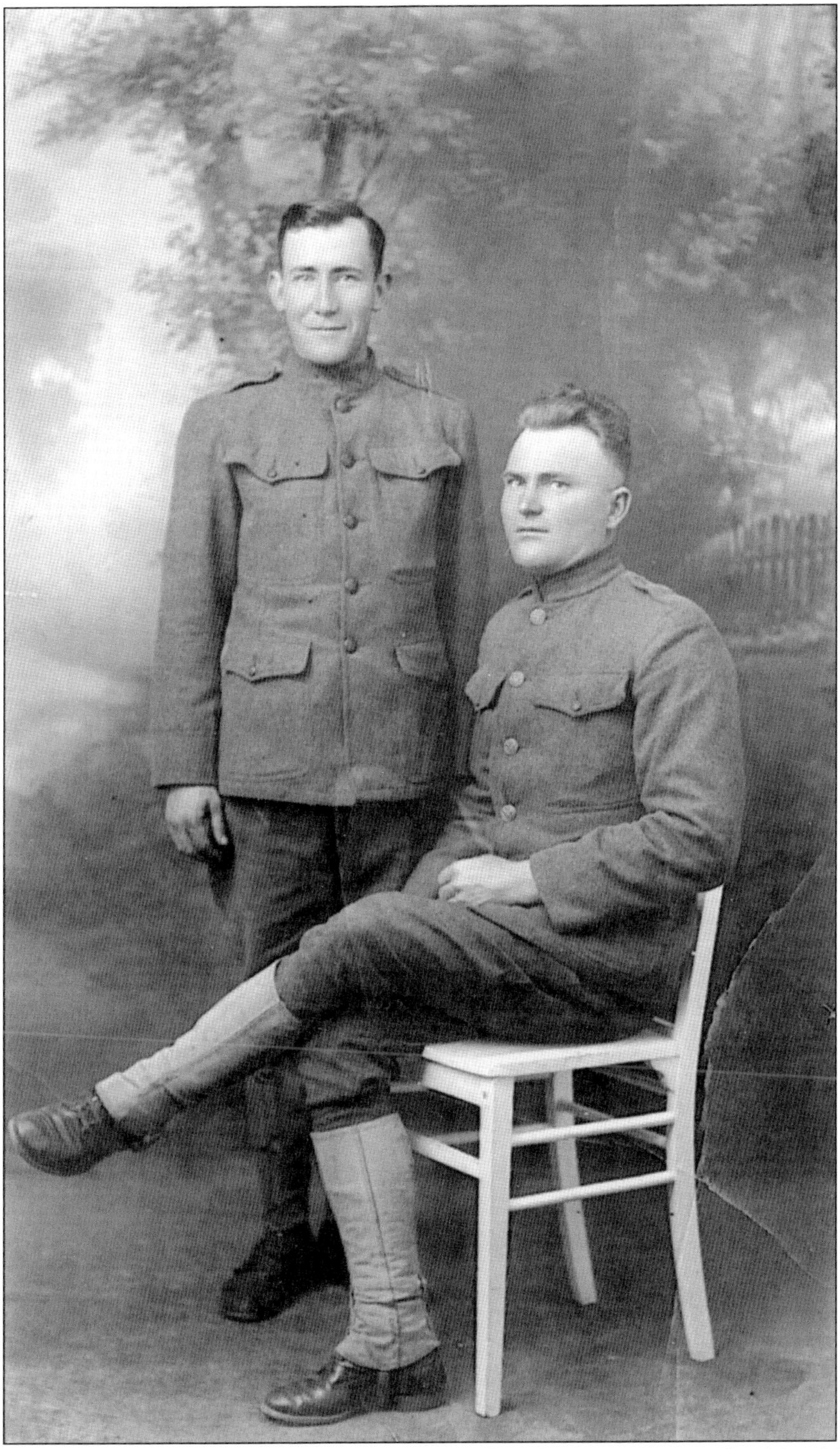

The sons of many local families, like Bob Carr (seated) and Lee Reves, served in New Mexico's first military units: the 1st Field Artillery and the 1st Infantry Regiment New Mexico National Guard, which fought in the Battle of the Marne. (Courtesy of Bob Carr.)

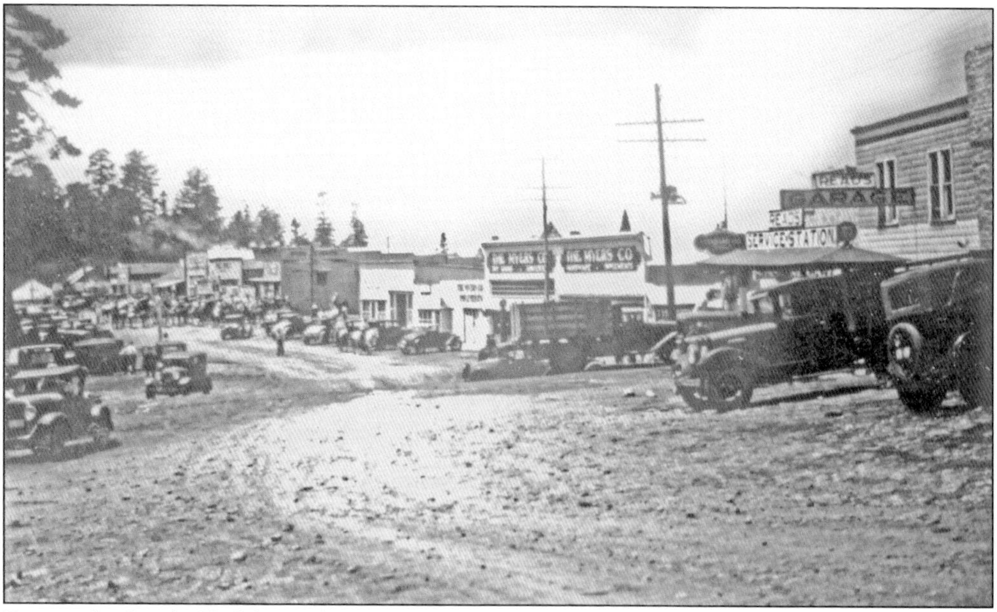

During the first half of the 20th century, Cloudcroft remained much the same as it had been at its founding. Tourism increased with the popularity of automobiles and new, larger mercantile businesses appeared as the summer population grew. (Courtesy of Emily Watson.)

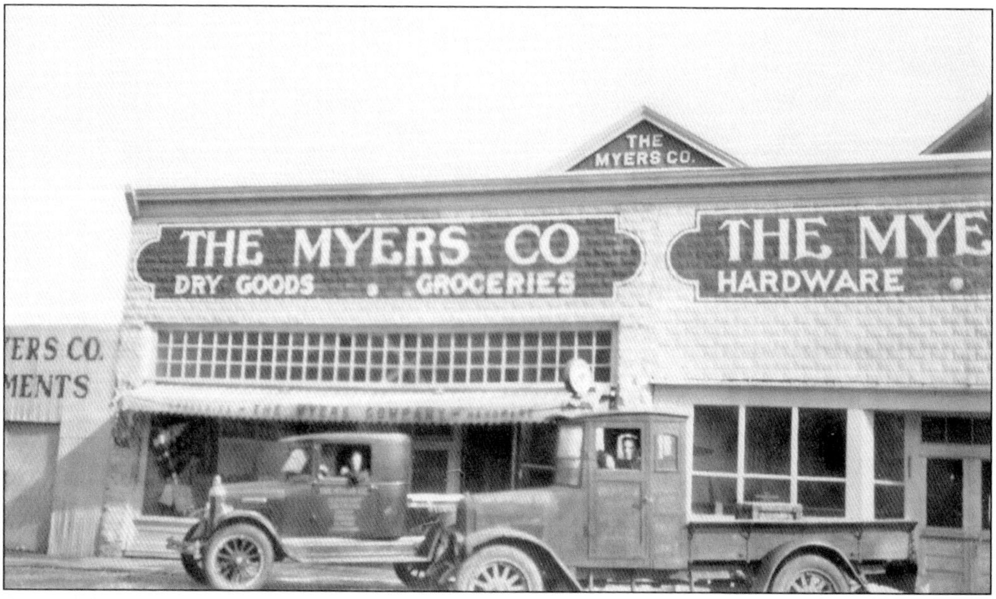

One of the larger, new Cloudcroft businesses in the growing community was Meyers Company, which represented the new, modern trend toward mercantile consolidation. Meyers combined farm implements, hardware, dry goods, and groceries under one roof, photographed about 1927. (Courtesy of SMHS.)

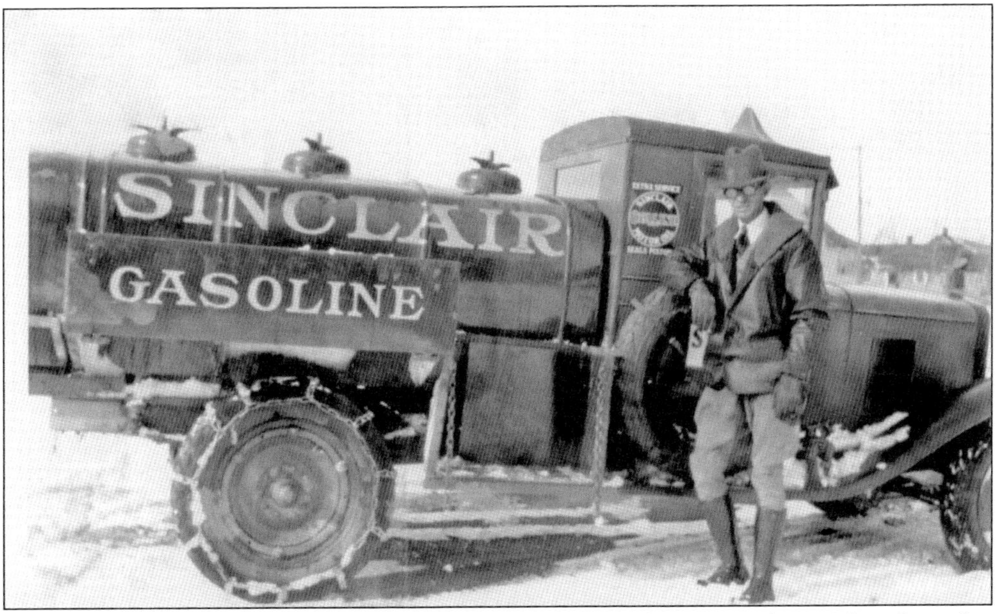

Automotive gasoline distribution also became common during the 1920s. Sidney Nelson drove this (all-weather) delivery truck for Edgar Dodds's Sinclair Oil distribution business in the Sacramento Mountains. (Courtesy of Bob Carr.)

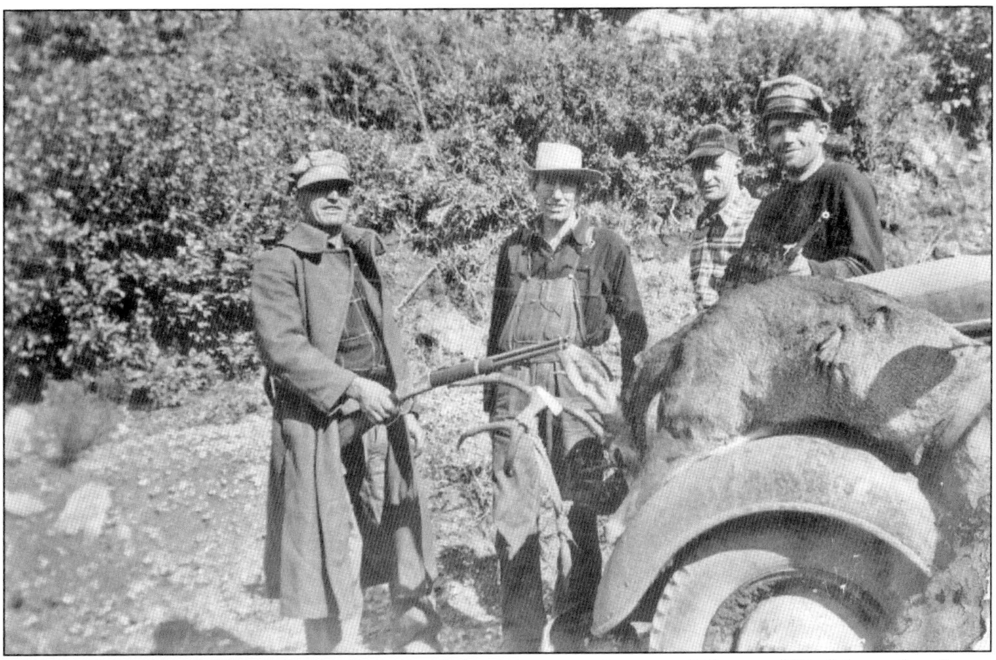

The growth of roads through the forest and the increase of automobiles modified forest land use, offering easier access. Here Frosty Bellows, who worked driving a logging truck for Prestridge, and friends pose with a buck over the fender in this c. 1942 photograph. (Courtesy of the Bellows family.)

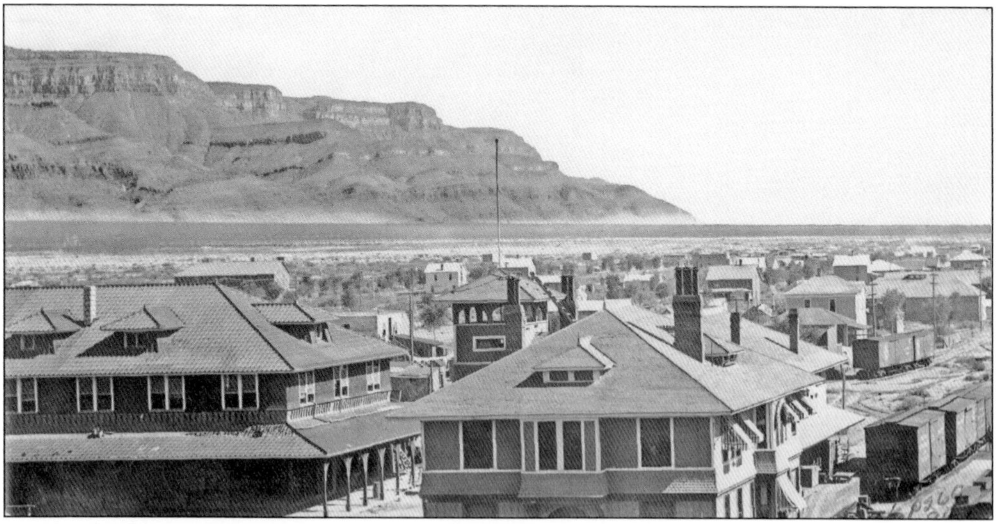

Much of Alamogordo's early commercial growth paralleled the railroad and Pennsylvania Avenue (modern White Sands Boulevard). Looking south over the tops of the depot and Southwestern Hotel, the main highway on Pennsylvania Avenue can be seen lined with trees. (Courtesy of TBHS.)

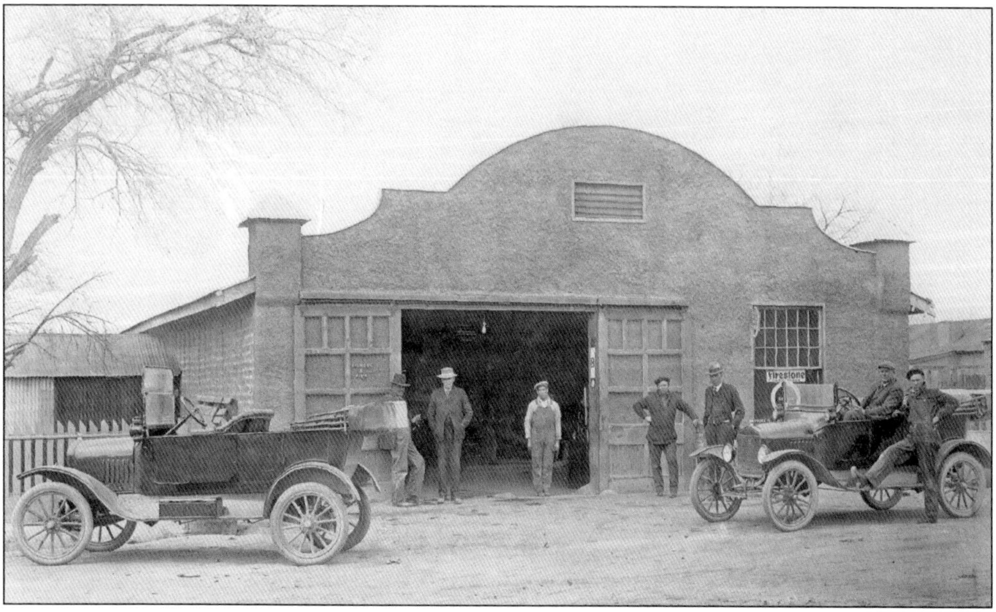

The 20th century brought a new commercial structure to the urban landscape—the garage, which rapidly evolved into the modern "service station." Tularosa's Gilmore Garage provided Firestone tires as well as gasoline. (Courtesy of Erma Tully.)

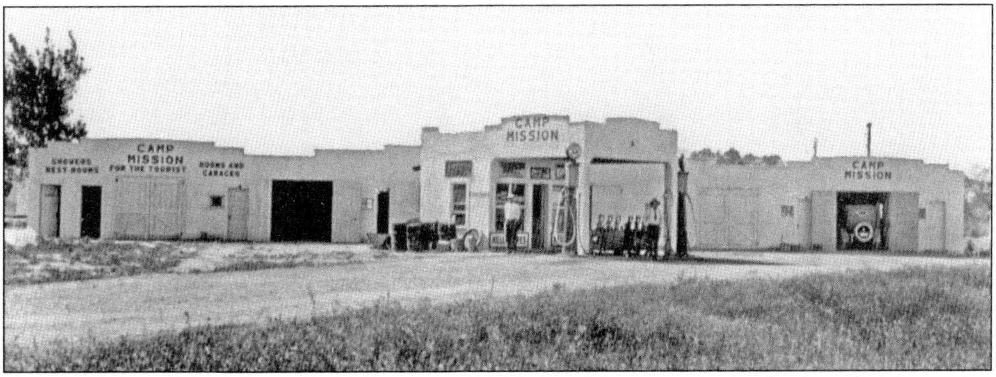

The Camp Mission garage "motel" was one of the first "motor courts" in Alamogordo. Located at the northwest corner of Sixteenth Street and Florida Avenue, it provided fuel, auto repair, and rooms with showers "for the tourist" as early as 1923. (Courtesy of TBHS.)

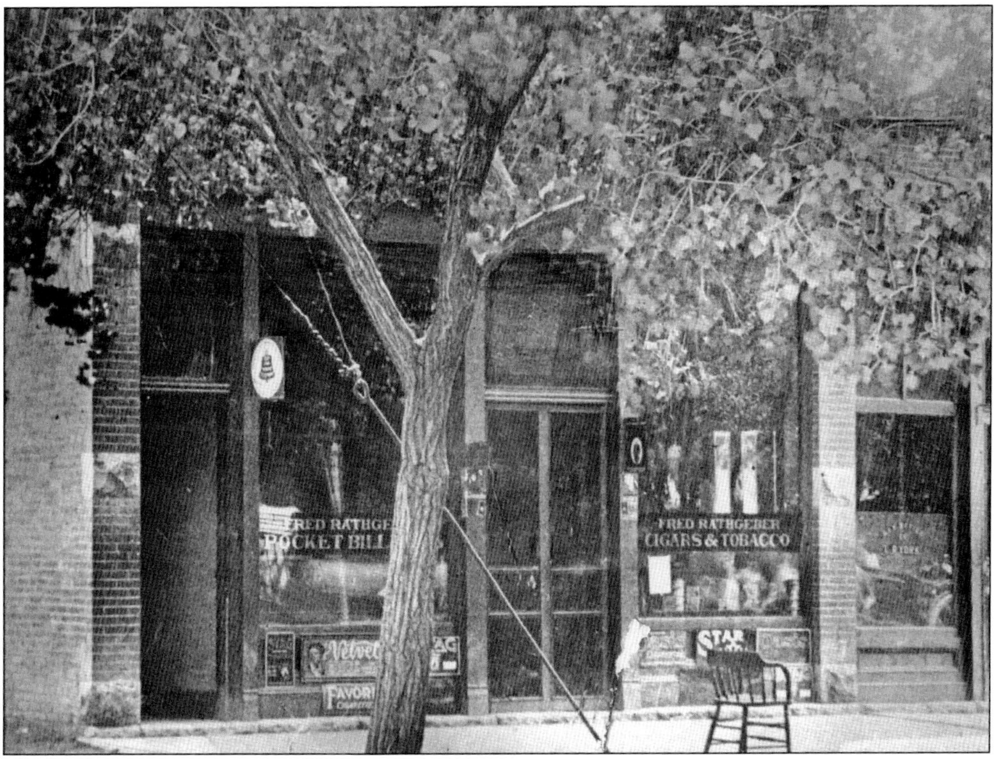

Fred Rathgeber's billiard hall and smoke shop provided sundries, recreation, and a public Bell telephone in downtown Alamogordo. (Courtesy of TBHS.)

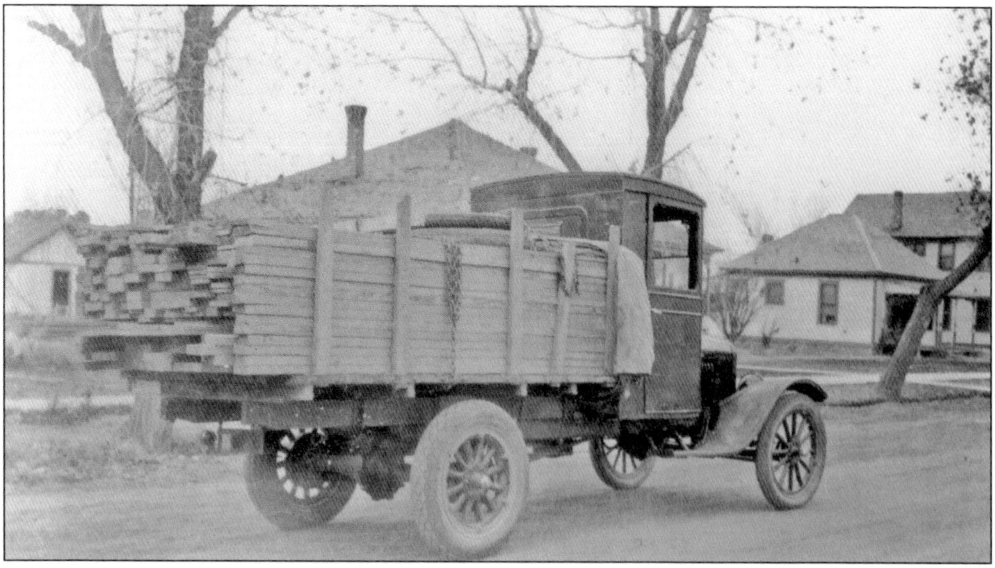

Prohibition officer Howard Beacham spotted his famous "catch" right outside his front door on Indiana Avenue in 1928, when he noticed this load of high-quality, but dusty, lumber pass by headed toward the mountains instead of into town and bypassing the main road, Pennsylvania Avenue. Suspicious, Beacham followed the truck to La Luz. (Courtesy of TBHS.)

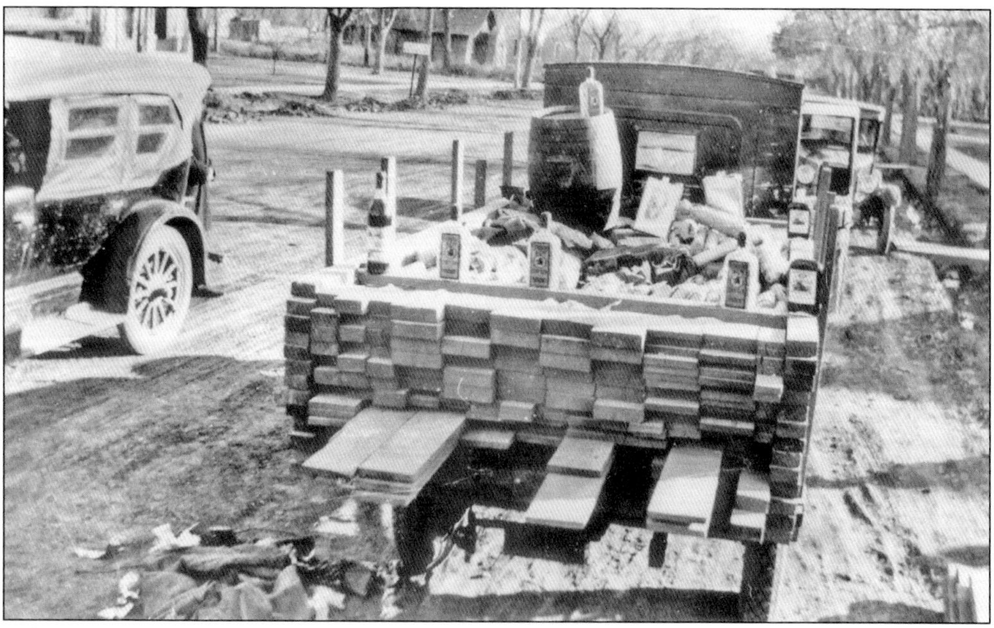

When Beacham stopped D. E. Sherry in this lumber truck, he discovered more than 170 gallons of alcohol, including Gordon's gin, American whiskey, tequila, cognac, and pure alcohol. Sherry, who was smuggling his load out of Mexico, had heard about Beacham and avoided the main road to try and escape scrutiny. (Courtesy of TBHS.)

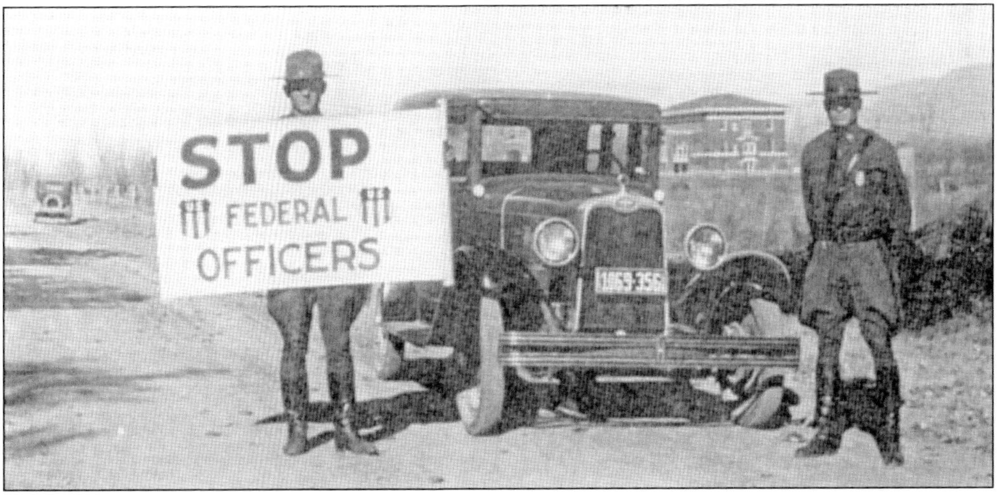

Prohibition officer Howard Beacham was innovative as well as persistent. He designed this roll-up stop sign for himself and colleagues who were stopping vehicles along Pennsylvania Avenue several blocks south of the New Mexico Institute for the Blind, whose main building can be seen in the background. (Courtesy of TBHS.)

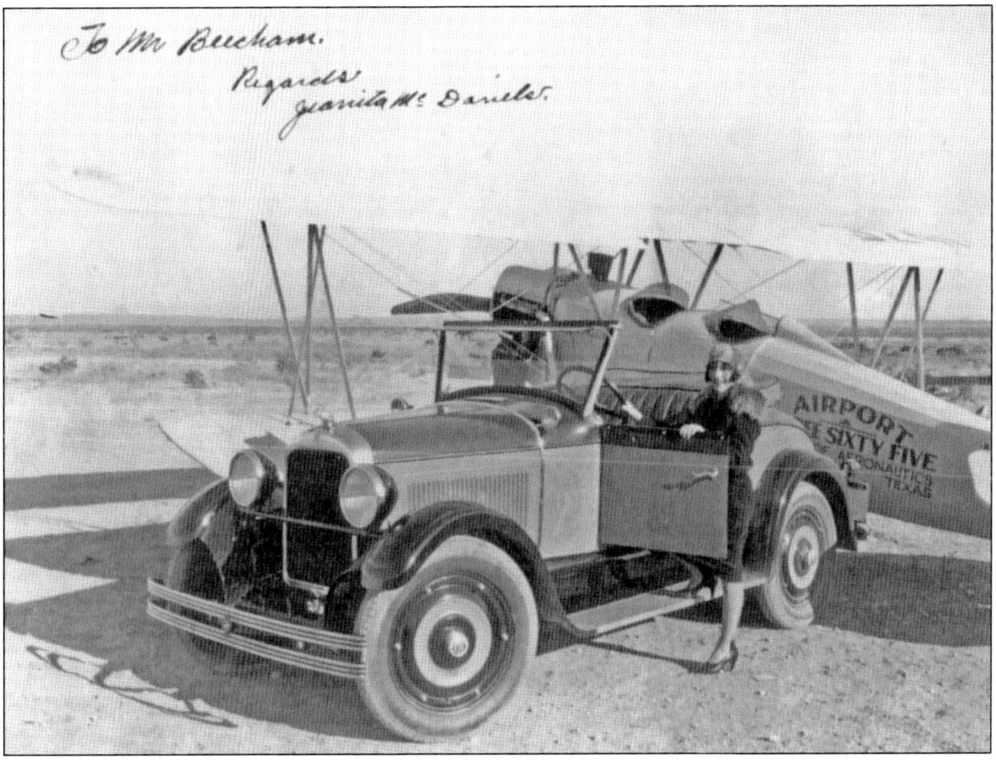

Customs enforcement agent Juanita McDaniels, a skilled aviatrix, a crack shot, and an expert auto pursuit driver, gave Howard Beacham this personally autographed photograph for his Prohibition scrapbook. McDaniels, who posed as a high school student to gather undercover intelligence in El Paso/Juarez, once shot a bootlegger's airplane out of the sky and collaborated with Beacham in finding and seizing the numerous illegal "stills" hidden in southern New Mexico. (Courtesy of TBHS.)

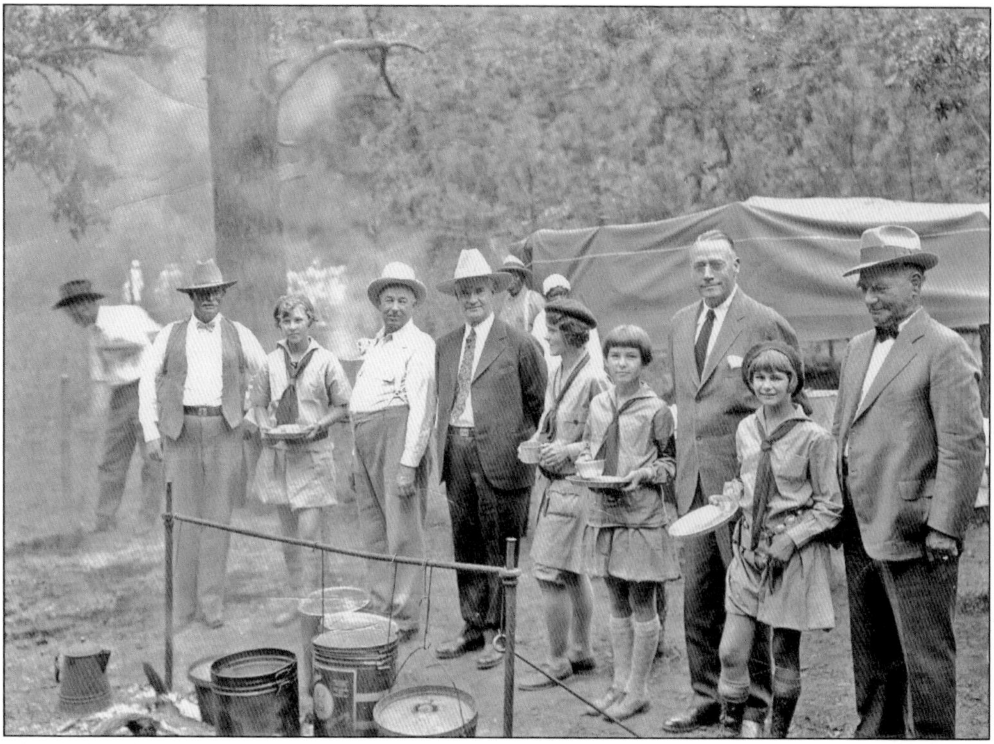

This father-daughter cookout was held at Camp Mary White near Mayhill in the Sacramento Mountains. The camp property was donated by Mary's father, Elzy (in the white shirt with no vest, facing the camera), in 1927, while Mary was commissioner of the Roswell Girl Scout troops. (Courtesy of TBHS.)

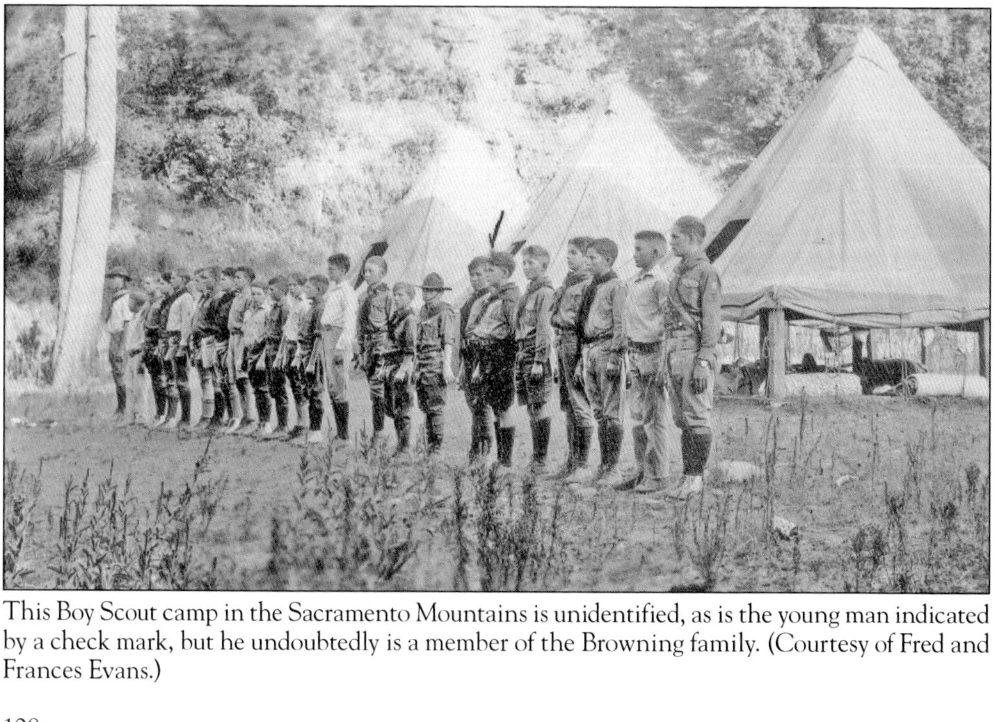

This Boy Scout camp in the Sacramento Mountains is unidentified, as is the young man indicated by a check mark, but he undoubtedly is a member of the Browning family. (Courtesy of Fred and Frances Evans.)

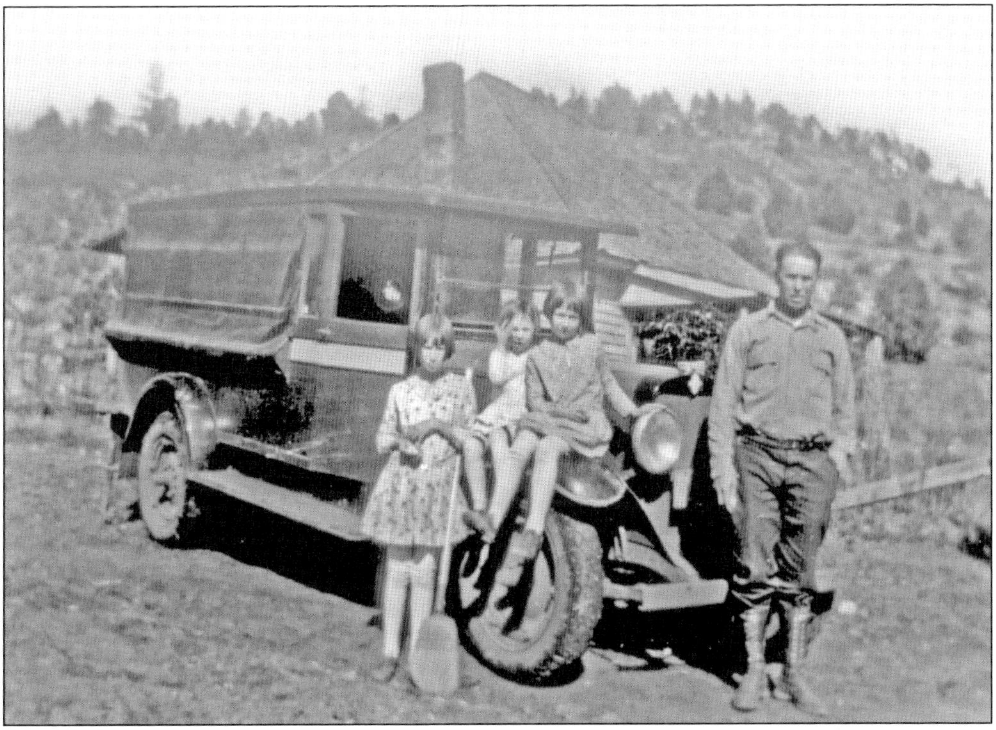

Clevie Dockray and his three daughters, Mable, Glynn, and Lanelle, are prepared to take a trip to Cloudcroft on the bus from Cox Canyon. While rural buses were probably commonly used, little historical information about these buses is extant. (Courtesy of Emily Watson.)

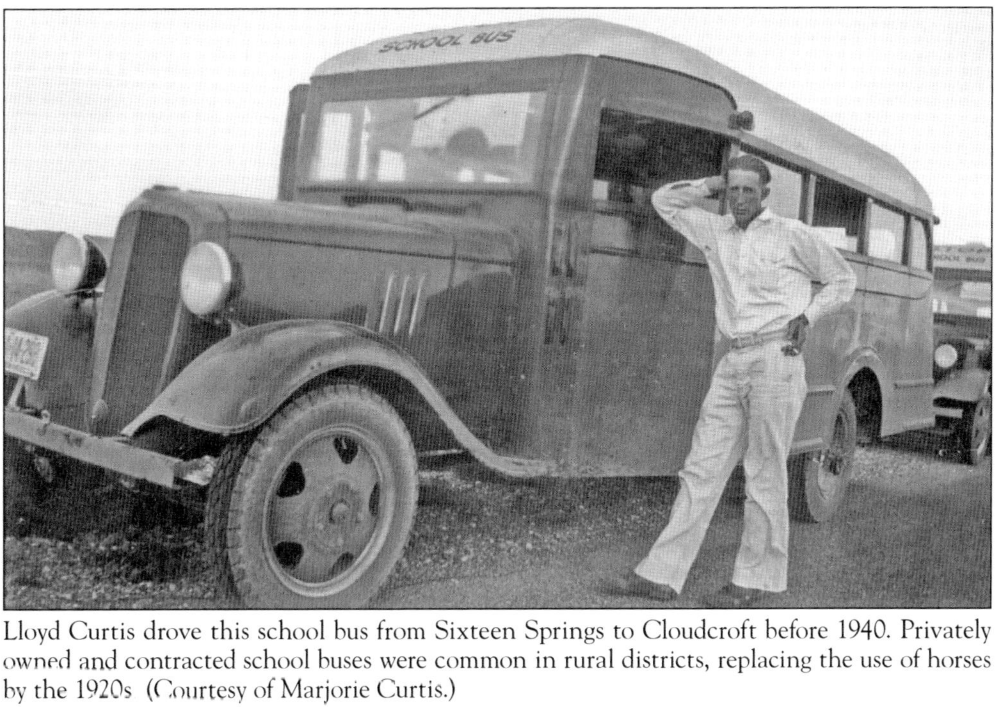

Lloyd Curtis drove this school bus from Sixteen Springs to Cloudcroft before 1940. Privately owned and contracted school buses were common in rural districts, replacing the use of horses by the 1920s. (Courtesy of Marjorie Curtis.)

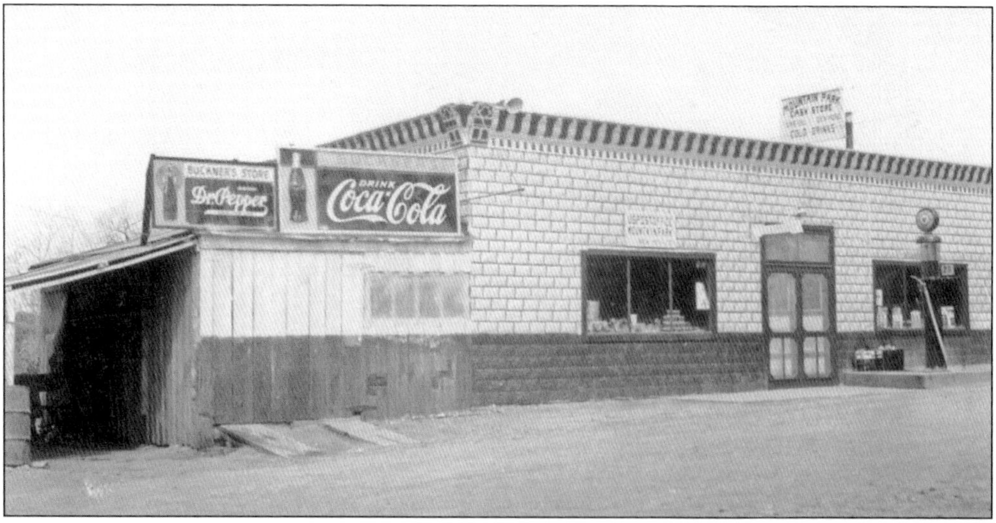

As rural communities like High Rolls-Mountain Park continued to grow and attract motor traffic, new commercial stores like Buckner's opened along the roads into the mountains. Buckner's Mountain Park Store was the local post office, and also sold gasoline, general merchandise, snacks, and cold drinks to travelers. Buckner's exterior was clad with ornamental pressed-tin shingles made to resemble cut stone. (Courtesy of Ray and Ruby Buckner.)

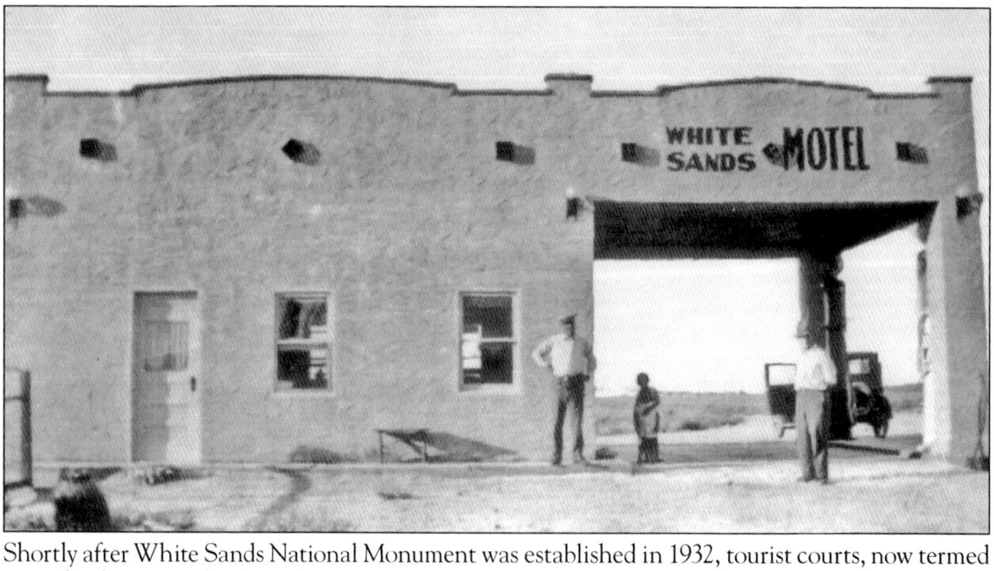

Shortly after White Sands National Monument was established in 1932, tourist courts, now termed "motels," began to develop along its periphery. (Courtesy of Clif McDonald.)

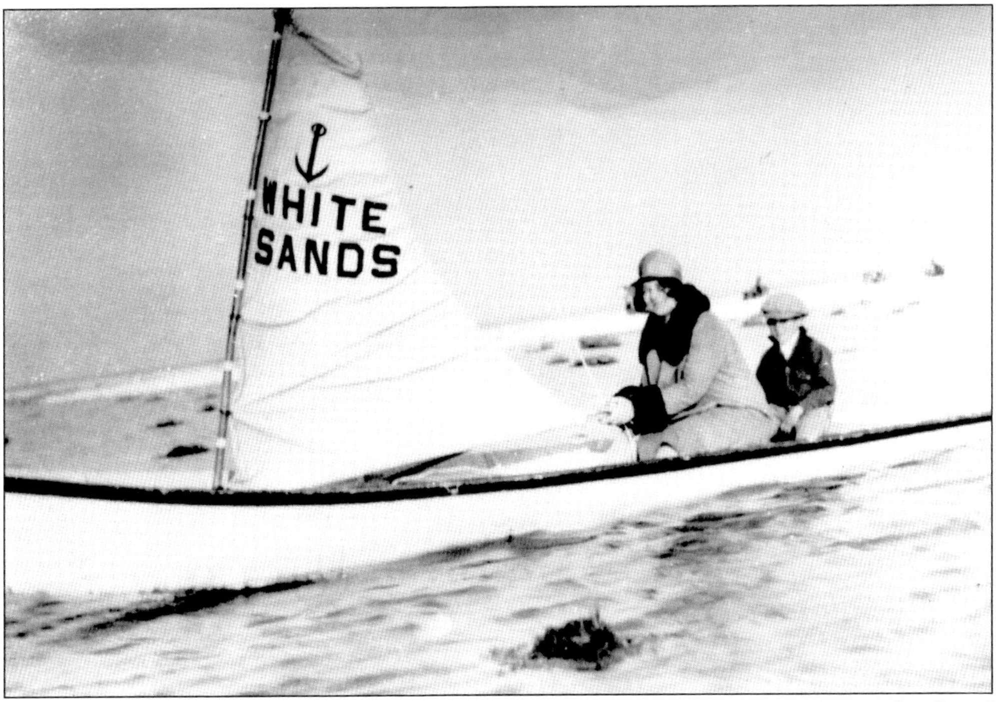

Before White Sands National Monument was established, entrepreneur L. L. Garton developed the "Pools of Siloam" spa on 1,200 acres south of today's monument. Using mineralized, hot (94 degrees) artesian water, he experimented with raising oysters and rented small sailboats like this one for local recreation. (Courtesy of TBHS.)

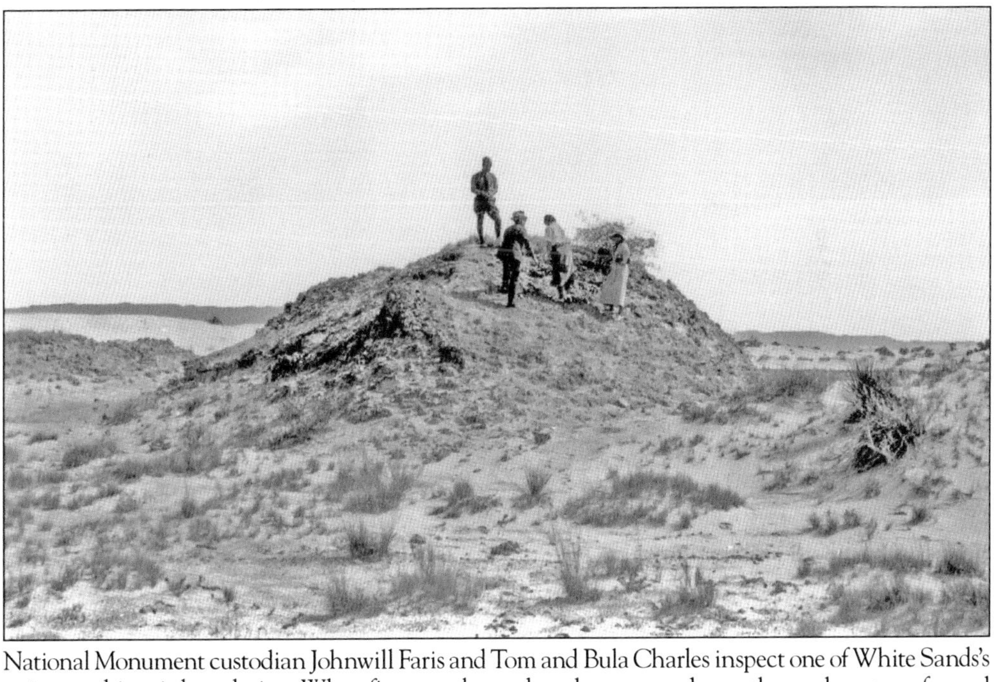

National Monument custodian Johnwill Faris and Tom and Bula Charles inspect one of White Sands's unique prehistoric hearth sites. When fires were burned on the gypsum dunes, the sand was transformed into plaster of paris, which would set after moistened by rainfall. (Courtesy of TBHS.)

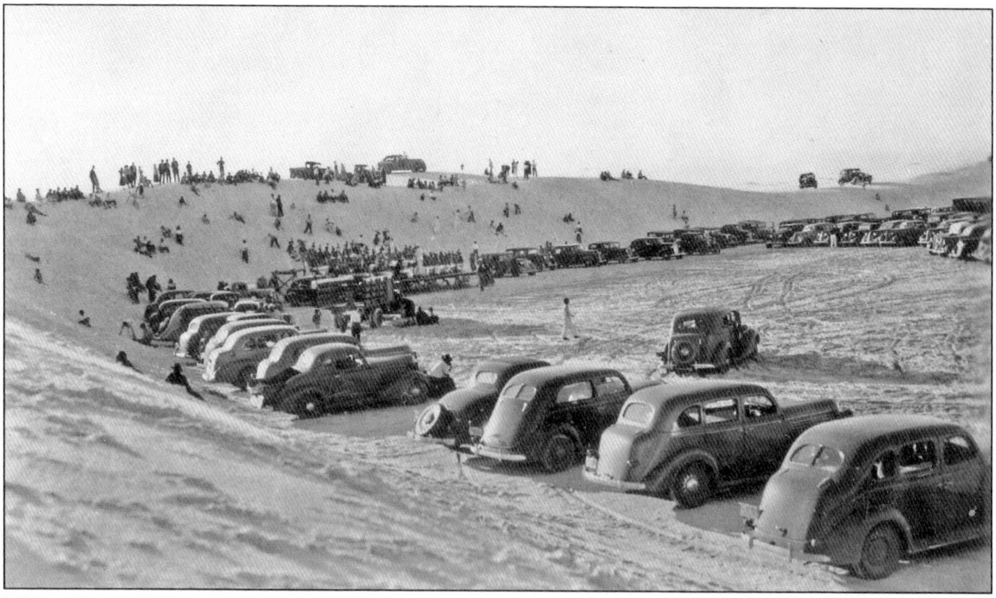

The official "Play Days" of White Sands became common shortly after the monument was established. Play Days like this one in 1935 often had organized entertainment events, parades, Native American dancing, and later, missile exhibits. (Courtesy of TBHS.)

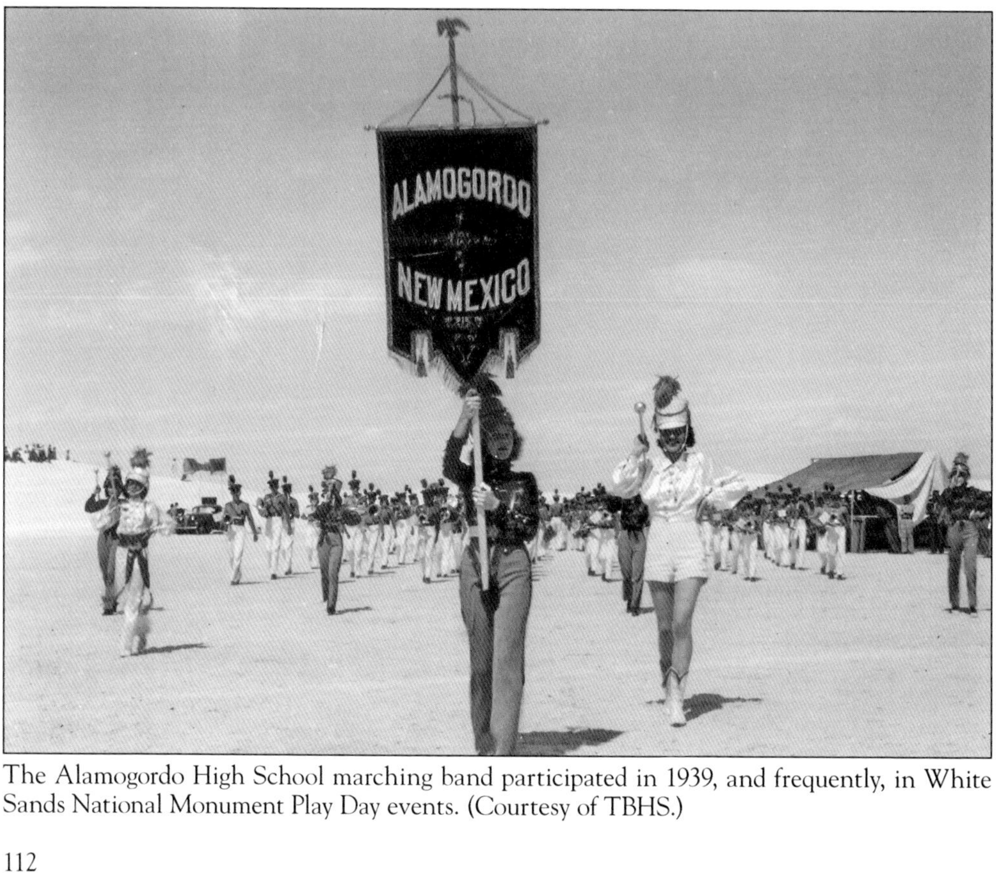

The Alamogordo High School marching band participated in 1939, and frequently, in White Sands National Monument Play Day events. (Courtesy of TBHS.)

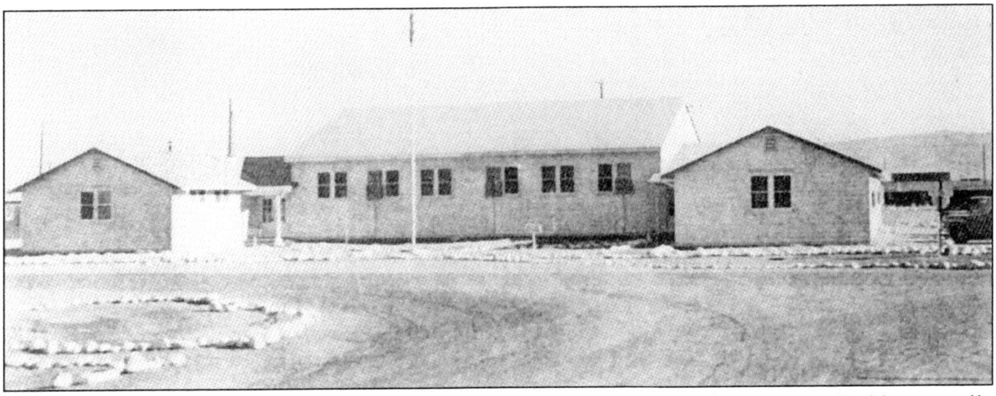

In 1941, the U.S. Army Air Force (USAAF) established the Alamogordo Army Air Field, originally intended for overseas British Royal Air Force training. When Britain declined, the USAAF began American bomber and gunnery training here. This first headquarters building was later replaced, and the air force base was renamed Holloman AFB in 1948, becoming the Air Force's main missile development center. (Courtesy of TBHS.)

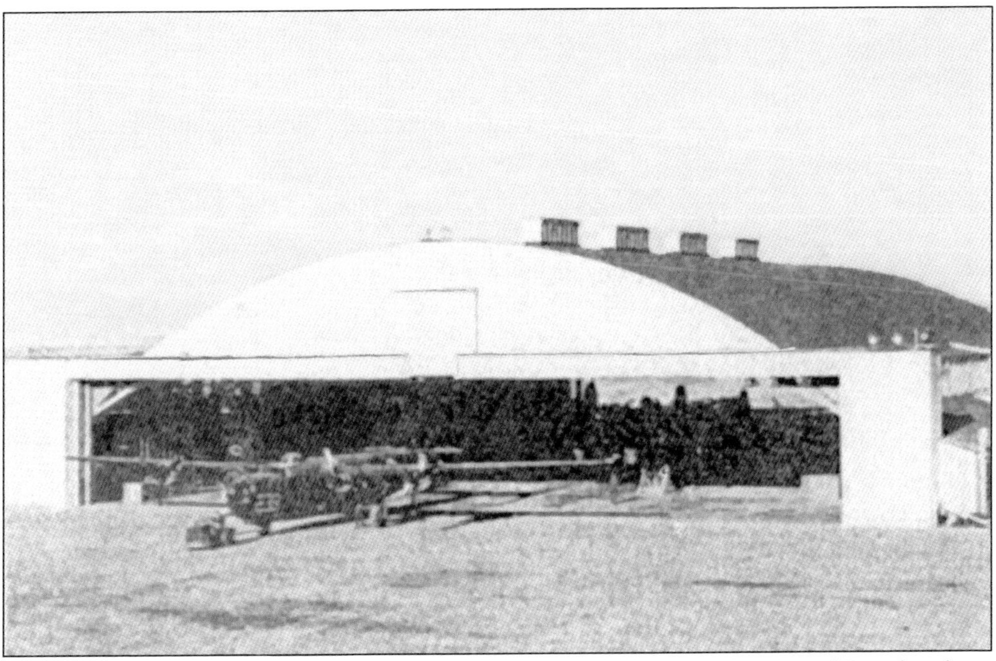

The several heavy aircraft hangers, like this one built to accommodate B-24 and B-29 bombers, used an innovative roofing system. Laminated, curved wood trusses spanning as much as 202 feet were built from locally cut lumber. (Courtesy of TBHS.)

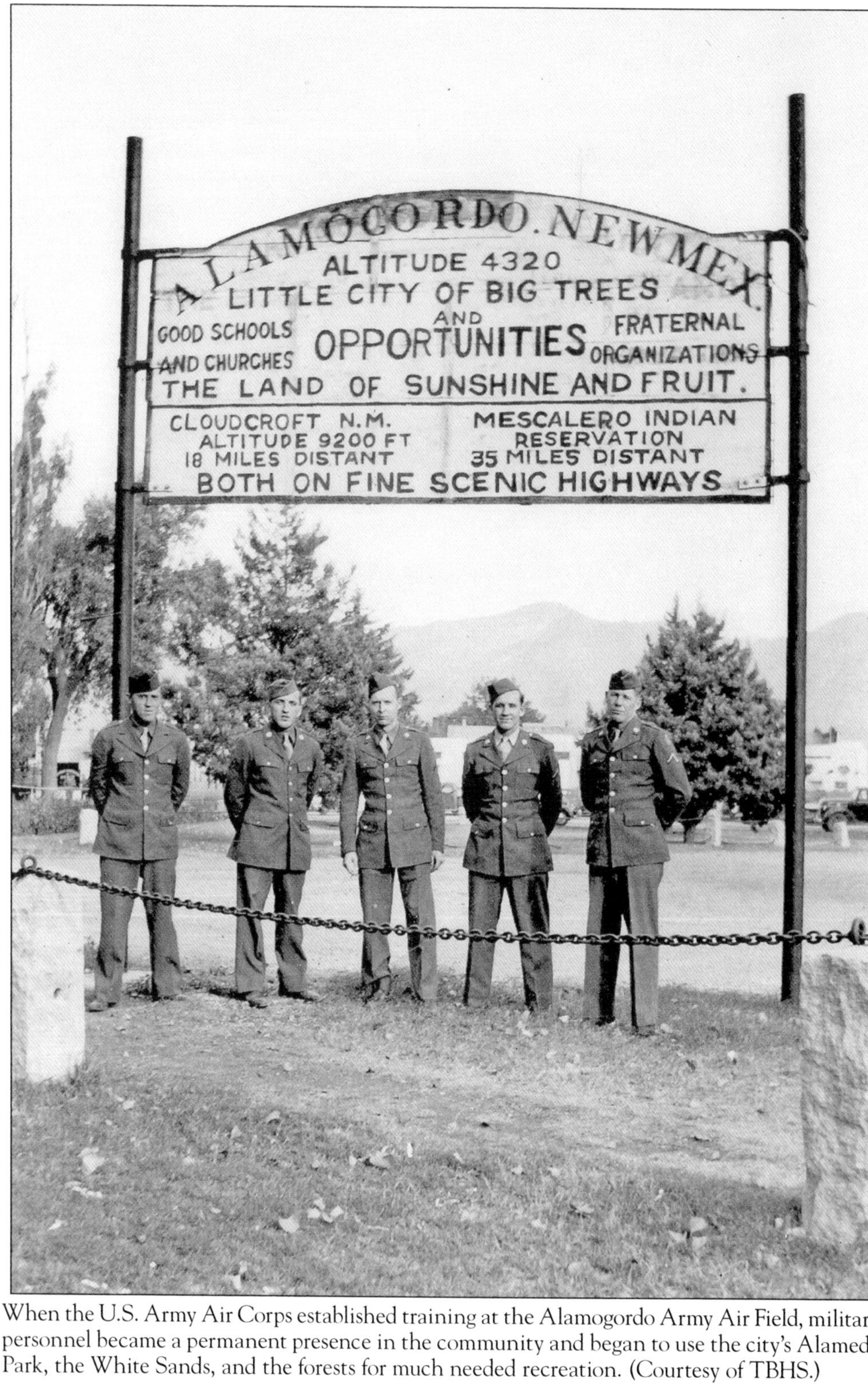

When the U.S. Army Air Corps established training at the Alamogordo Army Air Field, military personnel became a permanent presence in the community and began to use the city's Alameda Park, the White Sands, and the forests for much needed recreation. (Courtesy of TBHS.)

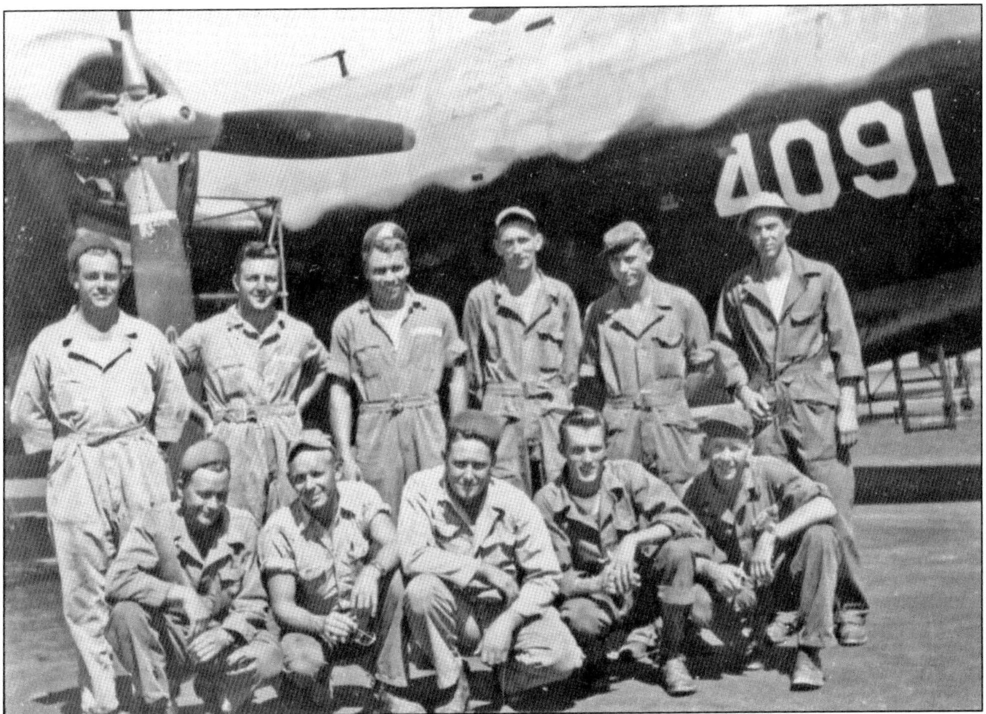

Alamogordo Army Air Field was one of 14 heavy bomber training bases in the southwest, one of 5 in New Mexico, 5 in Texas, and one each in California, Colorado, Arizona, and Louisiana. (Courtesy of TBHS.)

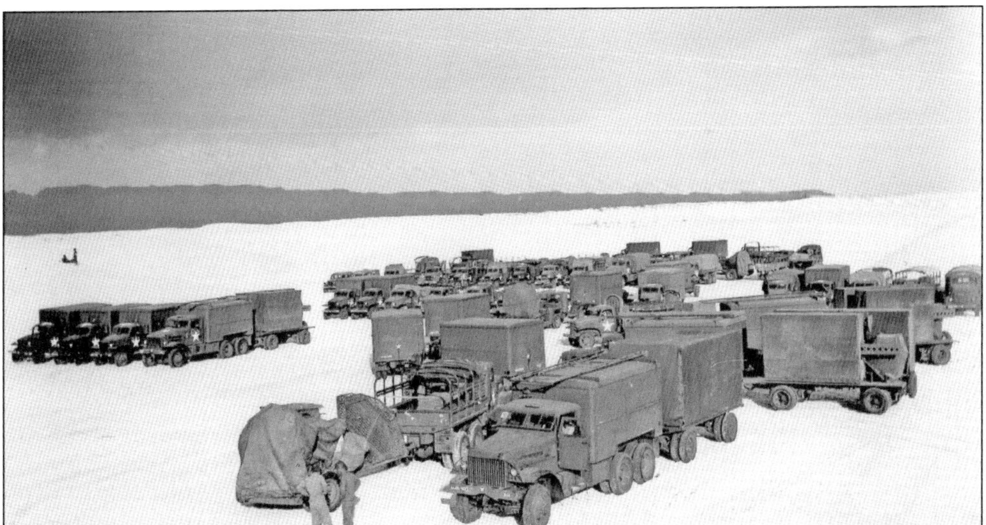

Army troops from Fort Bliss in El Paso, Texas, to the south used the southern parts of the Alamogordo Range for gunnery and maneuver training. Here the 737th Battalion, 32nd Brigade, Antiaircraft Artillery set up camp on the White Sands for an overnight bivouac in 1943. (Courtesy of TBHS.)

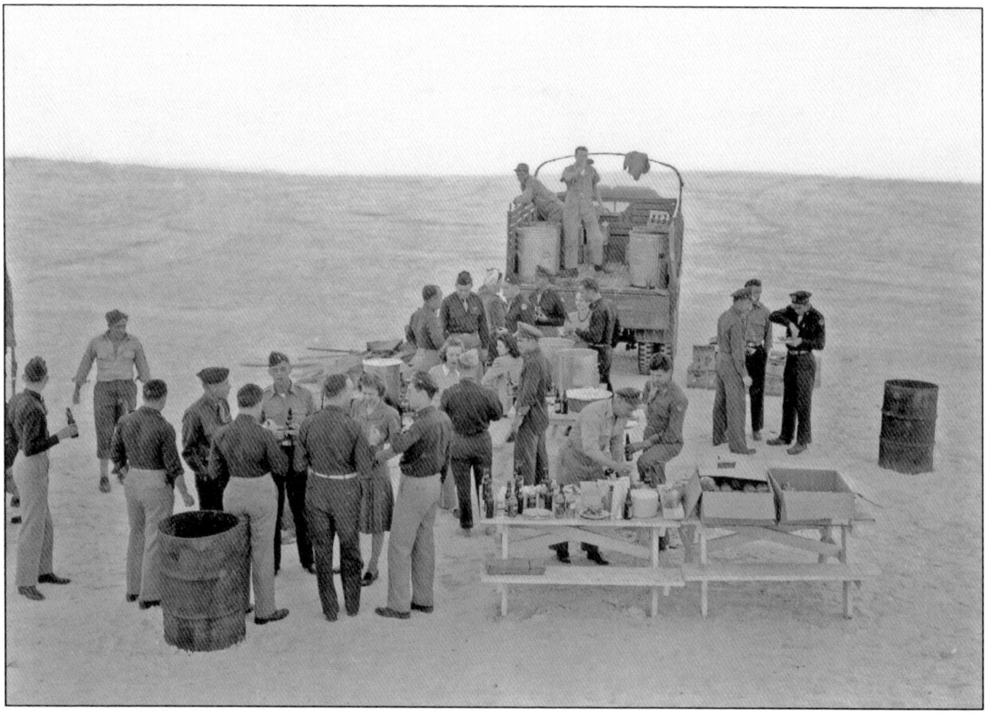

White Sands National Monument became popular among air base personnel for family recreation. Here the officers and their wives, 22nd and 36th Pursuit Squadrons, pause for a Sunday afternoon picnic on the sands in 1943. (Courtesy of TBHS.)

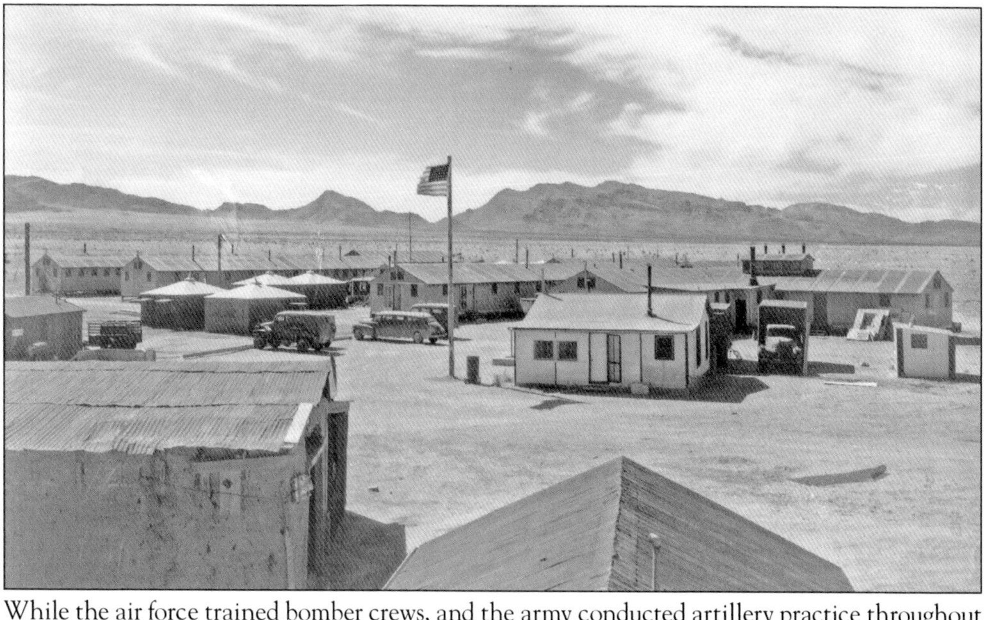

While the air force trained bomber crews, and the army conducted artillery practice throughout the central Tularosa Basin, the Manhattan Project prepared a small area just across Mockingbird Gap northwest of the basin for a secret experiment. The army set up its secret base camp here at the McDonald Brothers Ranch in 1944 and assembled the "device" just to the north at the George McDonald Ranch. (Courtesy of U.S. Army.)

Four

The Military Mission Transforms the Frontier

World War II transformed Alamogordo and the Tularosa Basin. The establishment of Alamogordo Army Air Field (AAAF) and the Bombing and Gunnery Range dispossessed rural ranching families from a vast area almost the size of the state of Delaware. By 1942, the population of Alamogordo had almost doubled from 3,000 in 1930 to 5,000 in 1942. The local economy became dominated by the U.S. military, a trend that increased with the expansion of the bombing range to accommodate missile development at White Sands Proving Ground. Early on a July morning in 1945, the world was transformed when the first nuclear explosion was detonated at Trinity Site, 75 miles northwest of Alamogordo.

The AAAF expanded, became the home of the Air Force missile program, and was rechristened Holloman AFB. Col. John Paul Stapp began America's first aeromedical program at the Holloman Test Track, pioneering seatbelts and the technologies for our entry into space. White Sands Proving Ground developed U.S. space and missile programs, starting from captured German technology and scientists beginning with the V-2 rocket. White Sands V-2s took the first photographs of the earth from space and launched the first living creatures beyond the atmosphere. Finally, man reached the edges of space when Lt. Clifton McClure, Lt. Col. Dave Simons and Capt. Joe Kittenger rode Holloman balloons to 100,000 feet, followed by Kittenger's parachute jump from 76,000 feet.

Alamogordo's growth kept pace with the expansion of military research and training. The Air Force established the Sacramento Peak Solar Observatory to study solar radio interference, and the Proving Ground expanded into the 4,000 square mile missile range. Soon a local community college, New Mexico State University at Alamogordo, followed, and finally the New Mexico Museum of Space History. Alamogordo had become world famous as the birthplace of America's space and missile program.

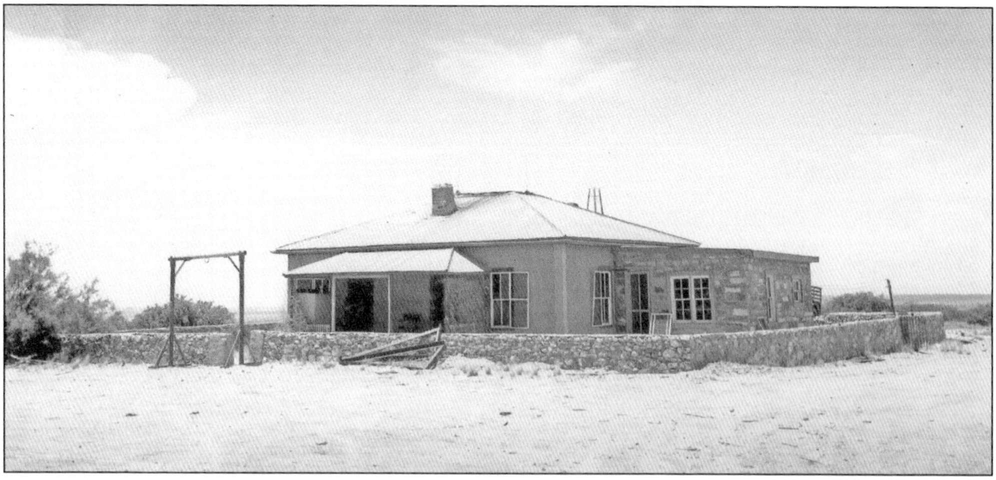

The George McDonald Ranch house where the first atomic device was assembled had a deep history. The location was originally homesteaded by outlaw Billy Mitchell (aka Baldy Russell), who sold the ranch to the Schmidt brothers, who later sold it to the McDonald family. The McDonald family still disputes their compensation for dispossession of what is now part of a National Historic Landmark. (Courtesy of U.S. Army.)

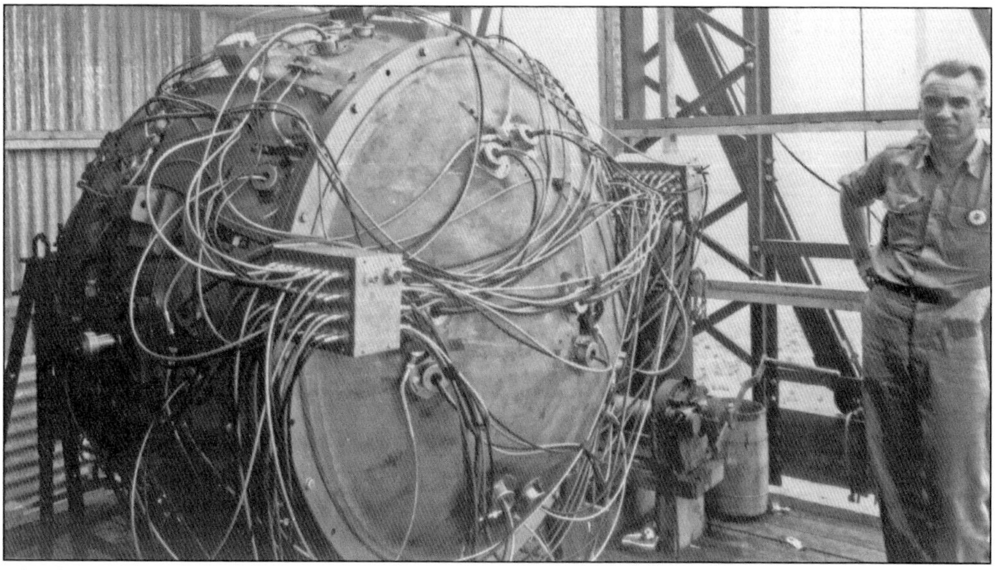

The first atomic device, nicknamed "the gadget," being mounted at the top of its 100-foot tower was a plutonium implosion design, the first of its kind. The scientific observers had a betting pool to predict the explosive yield, which ranged from zero to destruction of the whole state of New Mexico. (Courtesy of U.S. Army.)

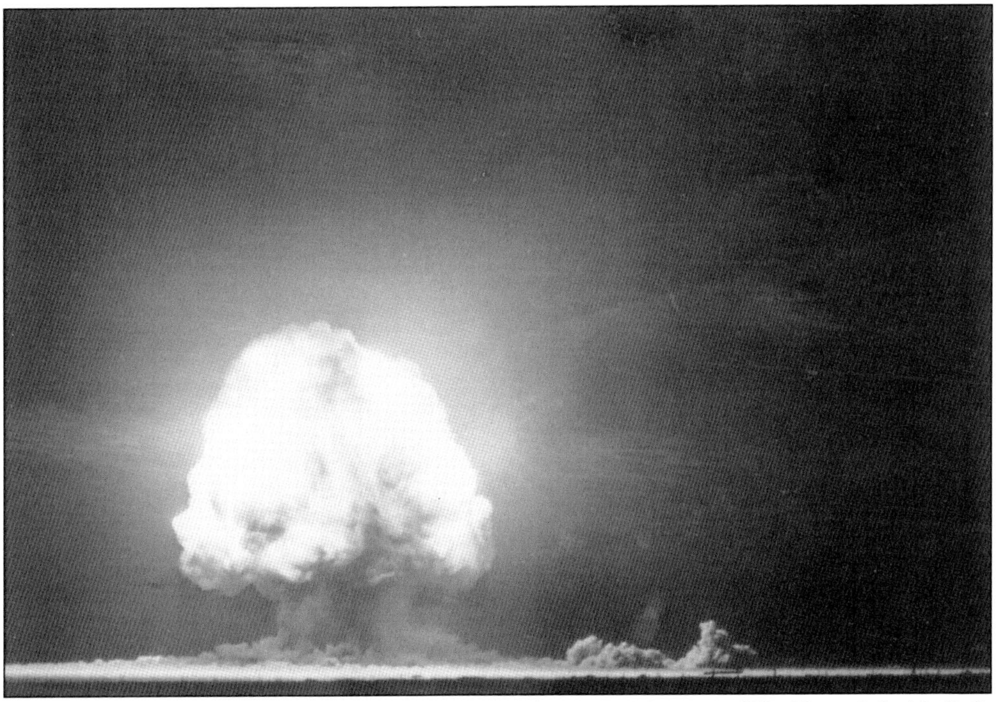

The Trinity explosion, 15 seconds after ignition at 5:29 a.m., Mountain War Time, July 16, 1945, produced a flash seen by people in local communities, a shock wave felt up to 100 miles away, and an explosion equivalent to about 19 kilotons of TNT. It produced a mushroom cloud 7.5 miles high and a crater in the sand that fused into glass, known as "trinitite." (Courtesy of U.S. Army.)

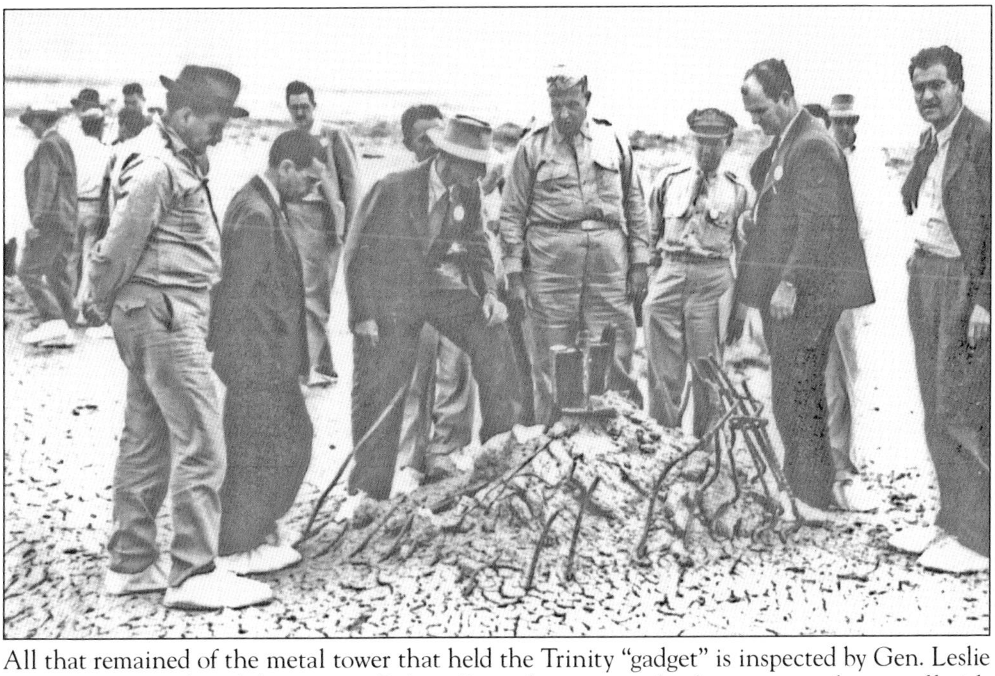

All that remained of the metal tower that held the Trinity "gadget" is inspected by Gen. Leslie Groves, commander of the project; Robert Oppenheimer, its chief scientist; and test staff with little thought to potential radiation hazards. (Courtesy of U.S. Army.)

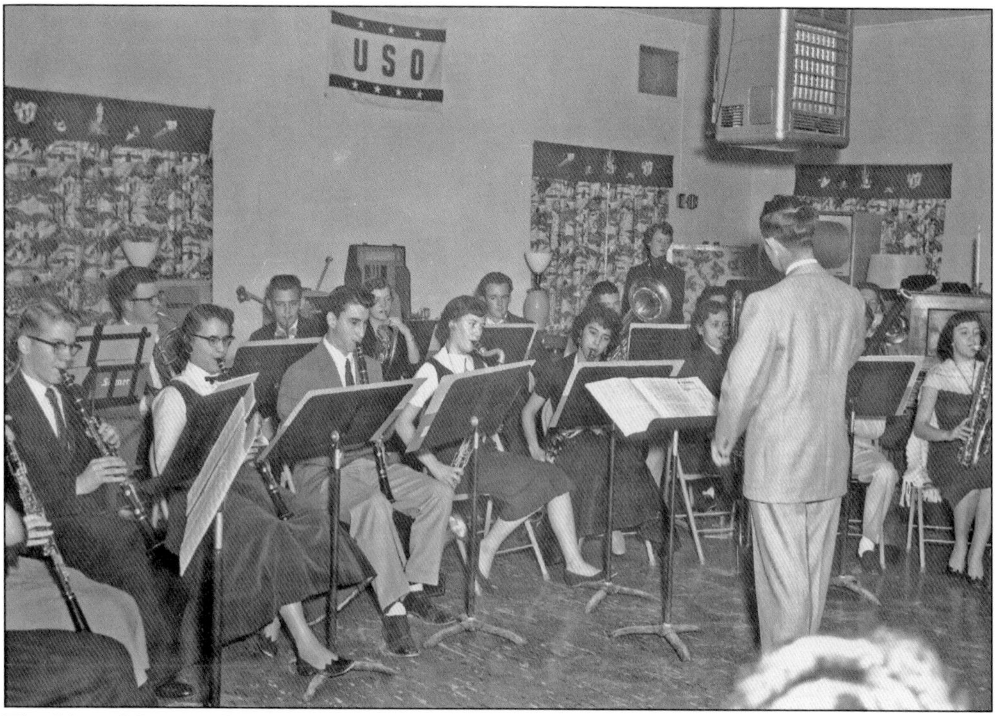

The United Service Organizations (USO) provided recreational and morale-support services at more than 3,000 clubs throughout the nation during the war in communities large and small. At these events, famous entertainment personalities as well as local entertainers, like this local high school band, provided a variety of shows for servicemen. (Courtesy of TBHS.)

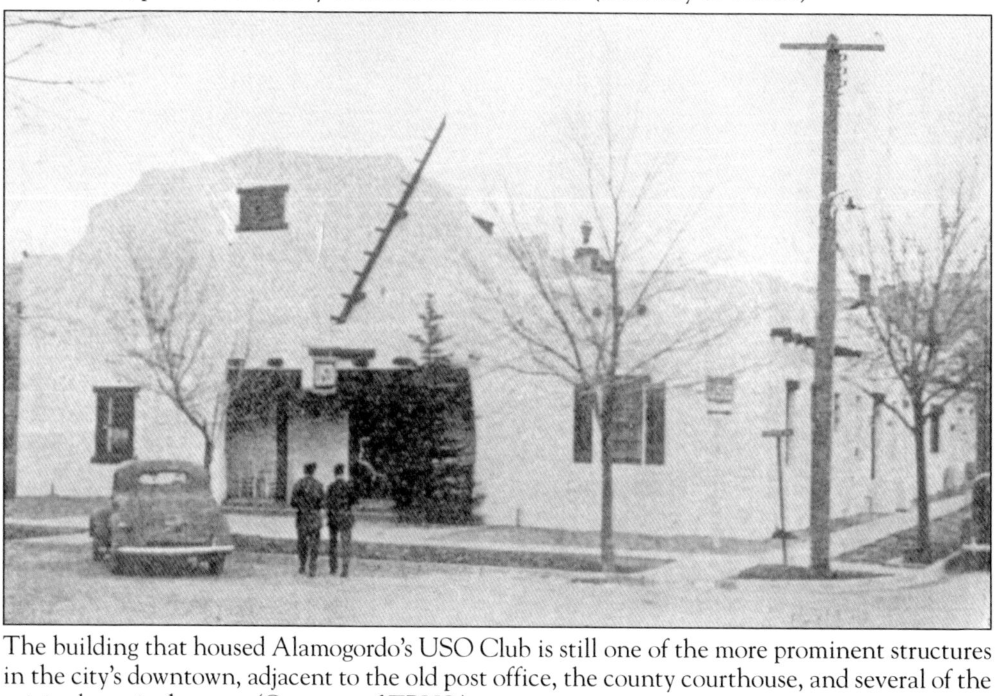

The building that housed Alamogordo's USO Club is still one of the more prominent structures in the city's downtown, adjacent to the old post office, the county courthouse, and several of the original movie theaters. (Courtesy of TBHS.)

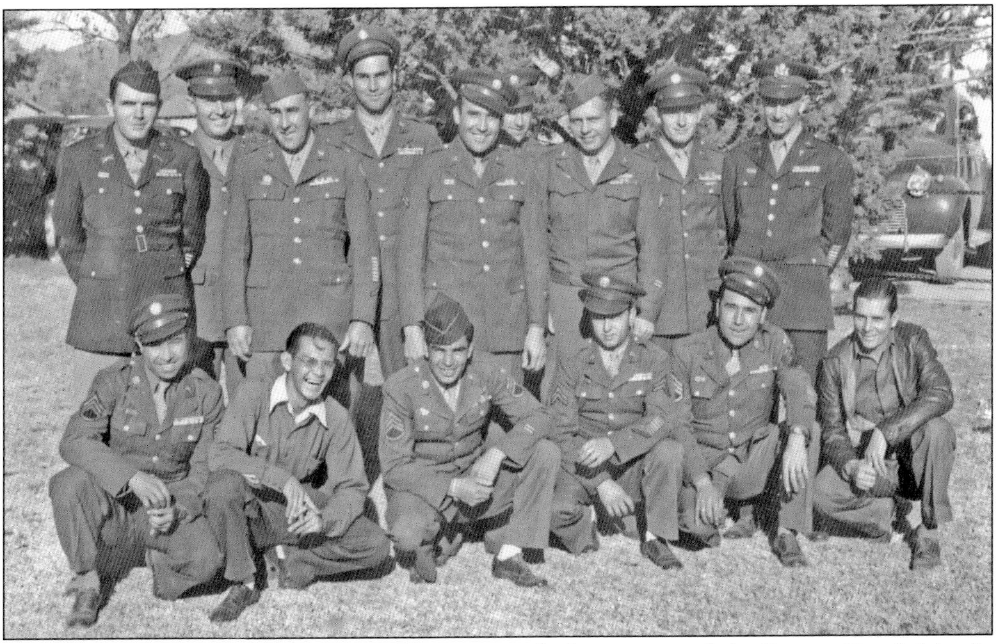

Otero County's returning prisoners of war, some of whom survived the Bataan Death March, included from left to right (first row) S.Sgt. Teofilo "Chito" Sanchez, Rudolph Cadorna, S.Sgt. Frank Madrid, Cpl. Benny Daugherty, S.Sgt. Juan Baldonada, and Pfc. Floyd Brunson; (second row) Capt. Fred B. Evans, S.Sgt. Luther Ragsdale, Cpl. Leslie G. Fleming, S.Sgt. Albert Rowland, Cpl. Jose M. Baldonado, Cpl. Albert M. Gonzales, Cpl. Earl H. Holcomb, S.Sgt. Norbert R. Roessler, and Chaplain Albert W. Braun. (Courtesy of Fred and Frances Evans.)

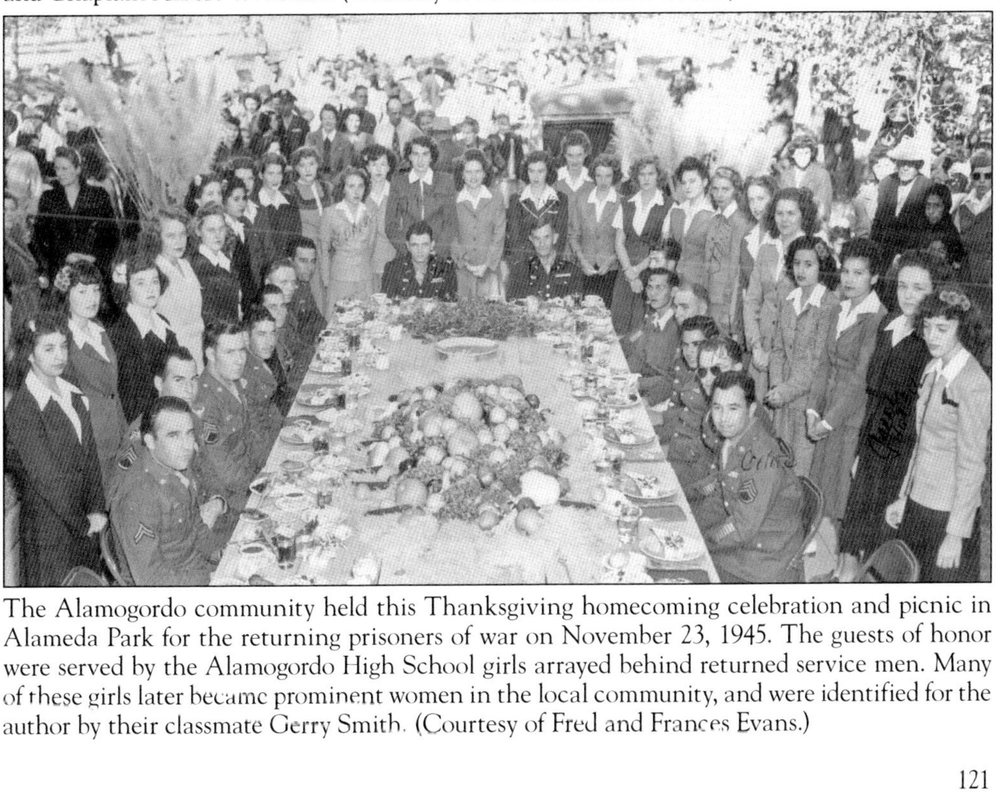

The Alamogordo community held this Thanksgiving homecoming celebration and picnic in Alameda Park for the returning prisoners of war on November 23, 1945. The guests of honor were served by the Alamogordo High School girls arrayed behind returned service men. Many of these girls later became prominent women in the local community, and were identified for the author by their classmate Gerry Smith. (Courtesy of Fred and Frances Evans.)

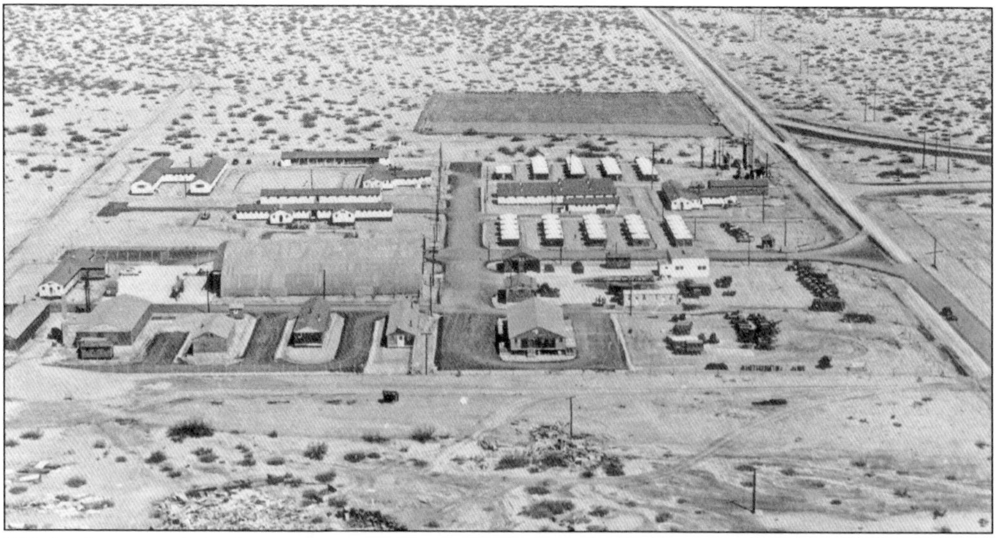

While the secret Manhattan project was preparing for the Trinity test, the army was searching for a suitable location for testing its second missile research and development project, Hermes. The site for White Sands Proving Ground (WSPG) in the Tularosa Basin was approved the day after the last German V-2 missile was fired in Europe. The original cantonment was photographed from a light airplane by Signal Corps T.Sgt. Martin Sauber in 1946. (Courtesy of U.S. Army.)

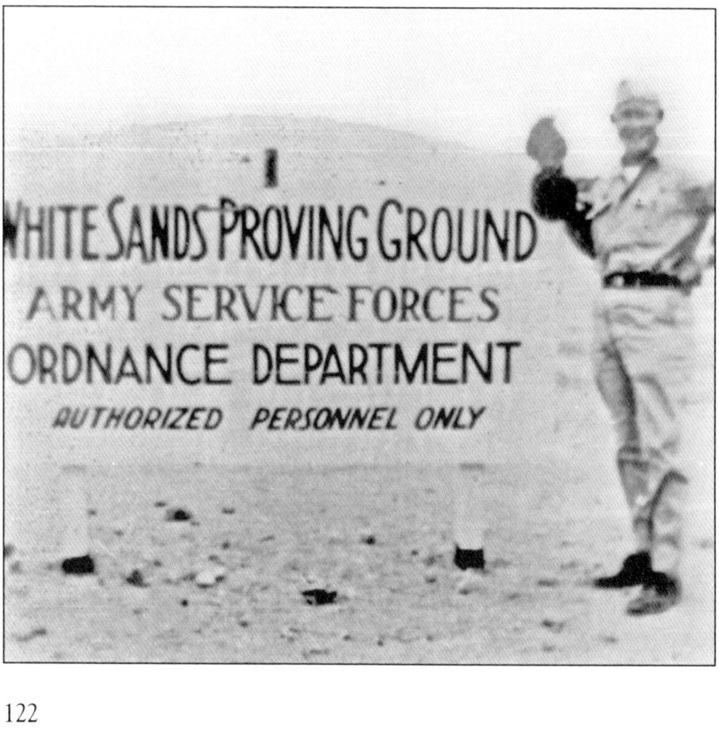

This original White Sands Proving Ground sign identified WSPG, the headquarters of the army's 1st Guided Missile Battalion, with the flaming cannonball logo of the U.S. Army Ordnance Department. (Courtesy of U.S. Army.)

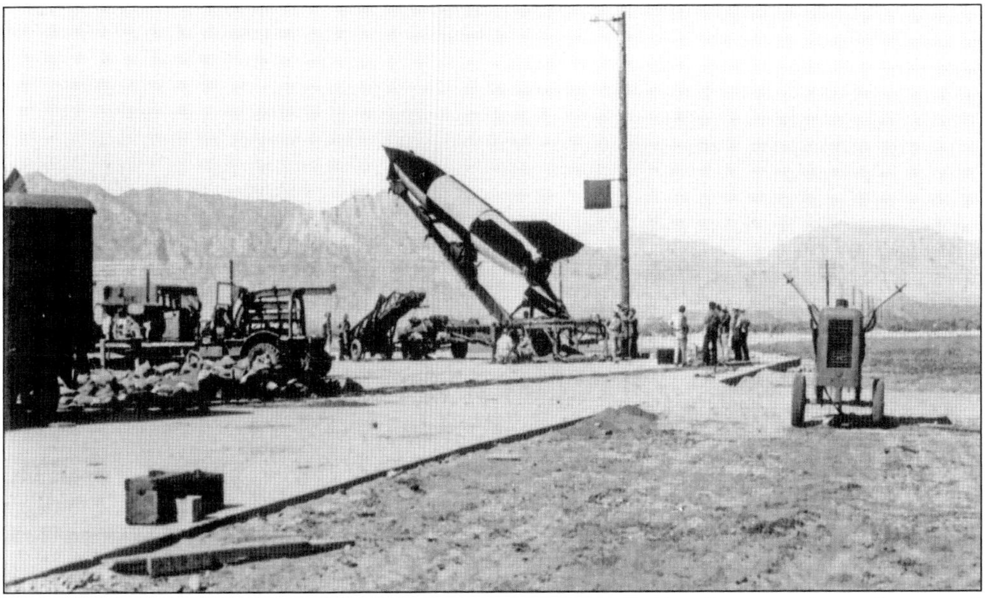

In 1945, Special Mission V-2 had captured German military hardware at the underground Mittelwerk factory in Nordhausen, Germany. Werner von Braun and his scientific staff from Pennemunde had surrendered. The 144th Ordnance Company marshaled the missile hardware, von Braun's "Paperclip" scientists, and a wealth of technical documents recovered at Dorten for shipment to WSPG where General Electric began to test the captured V-2 missiles. (Courtesy of U.S. Army.)

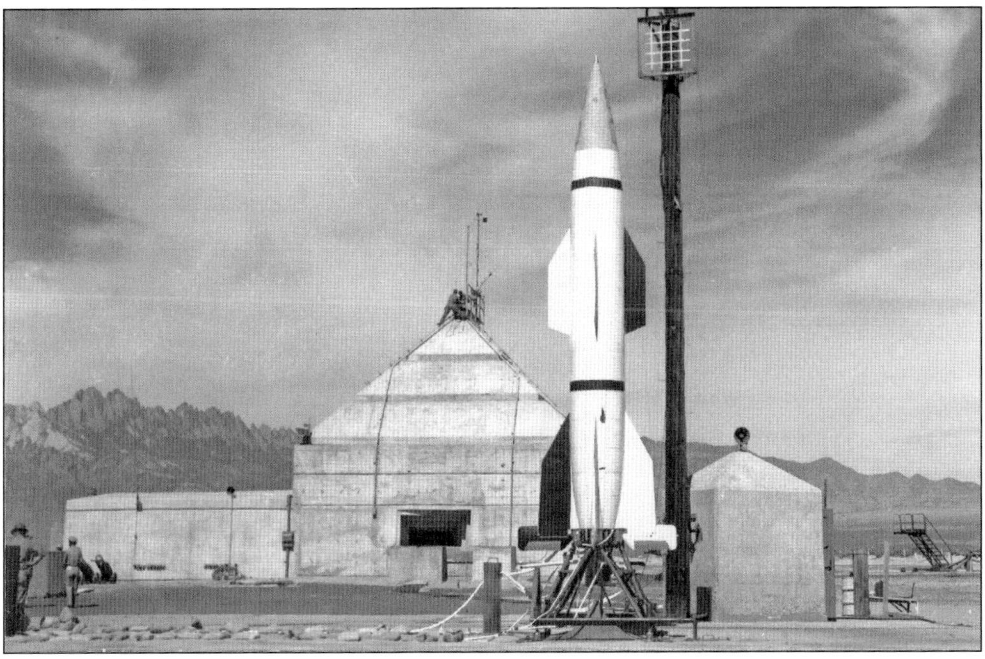

The General Electric WSPG Hermes project tested captured V-2s and began designing a U.S. version, the Hermes A-1, based on the German Wasserfall. All of these were fired from Army Launch Area No. 1 (now a National Historic Landmark, Launch Complex 33) observed from the army blockhouse in this 1950 portrait. (Courtesy of U.S. Army.)

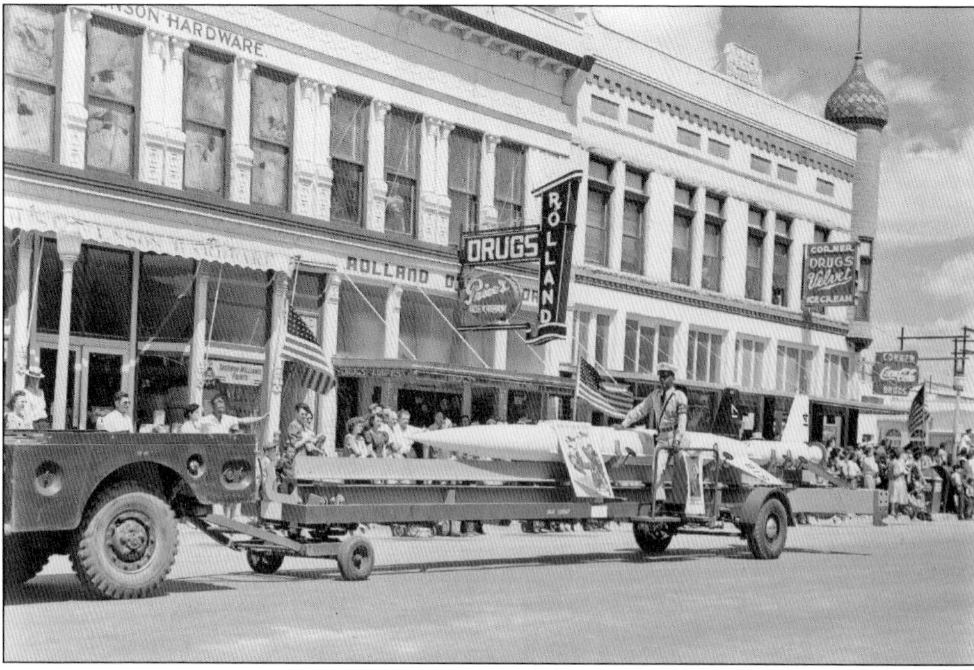

Missiles from WSPG and Holloman AFB became popular public relations items, participating in local celebrations, Play Days at White Sands National Monument, and in parades in Alamogordo beginning in the 1950s. Here an Aerobee promotes the Air Force in a parade along New York Avenue. (Courtesy of TBHS.)

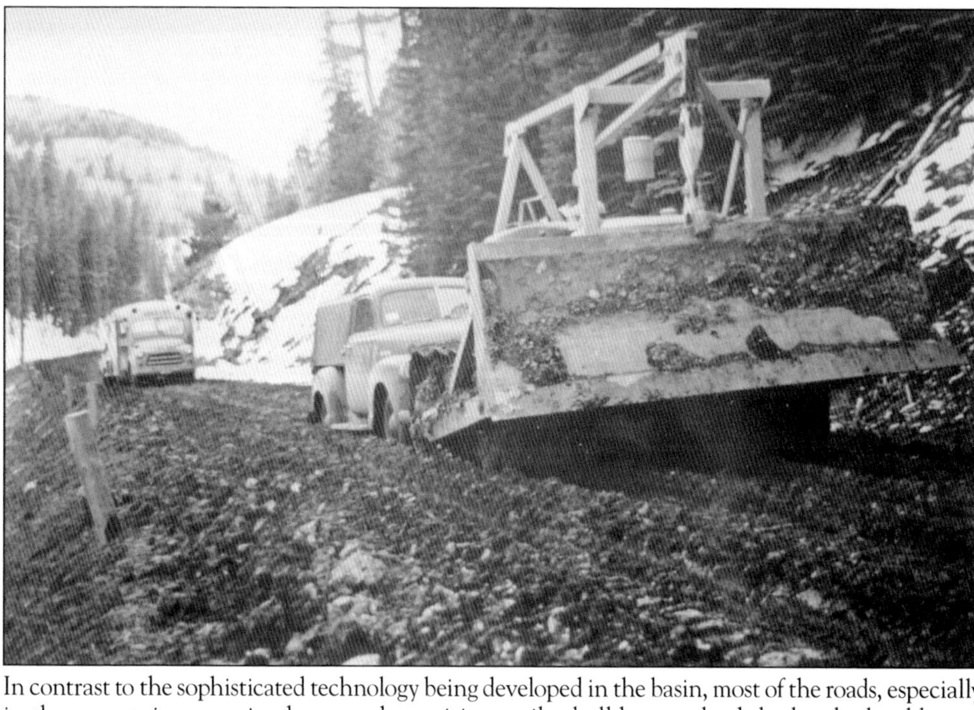

In contrast to the sophisticated technology being developed in the basin, most of the roads, especially in the mountains, remained unpaved, requiring a pilot bulldozer to lead the local school bus to Sacramento Peak Solar Observatory at Sunspot in the 1950s. (Courtesy of Emily Watson.)

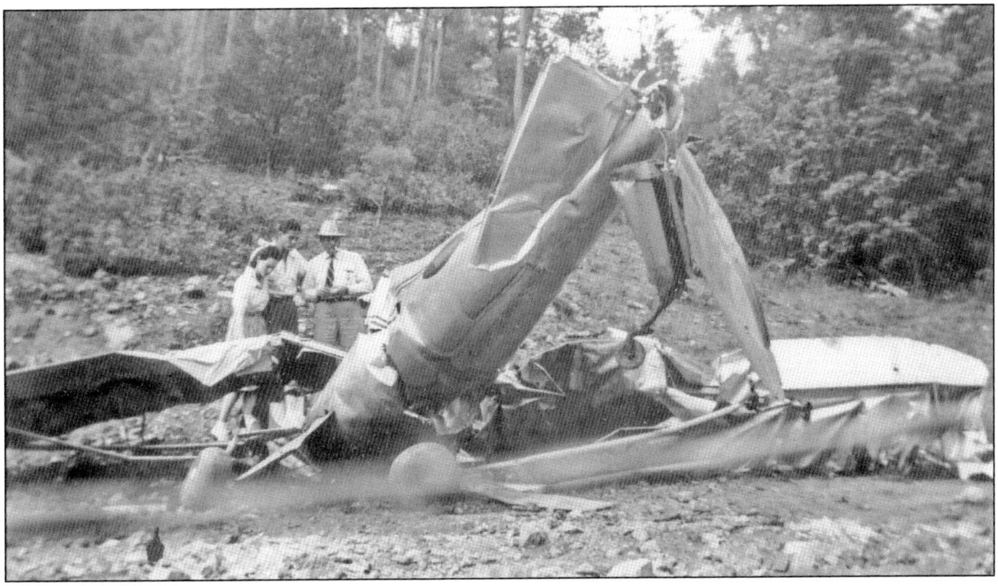

Private light aircraft were a popular and speedy means of travel in southern New Mexico since the late 1920s, but occasionally proved fatal when they crashed in the mountains, like this crash that killed Gerald Champion and Sheriff H. M. Denny in 1948. (Courtesy of Bellows family.)

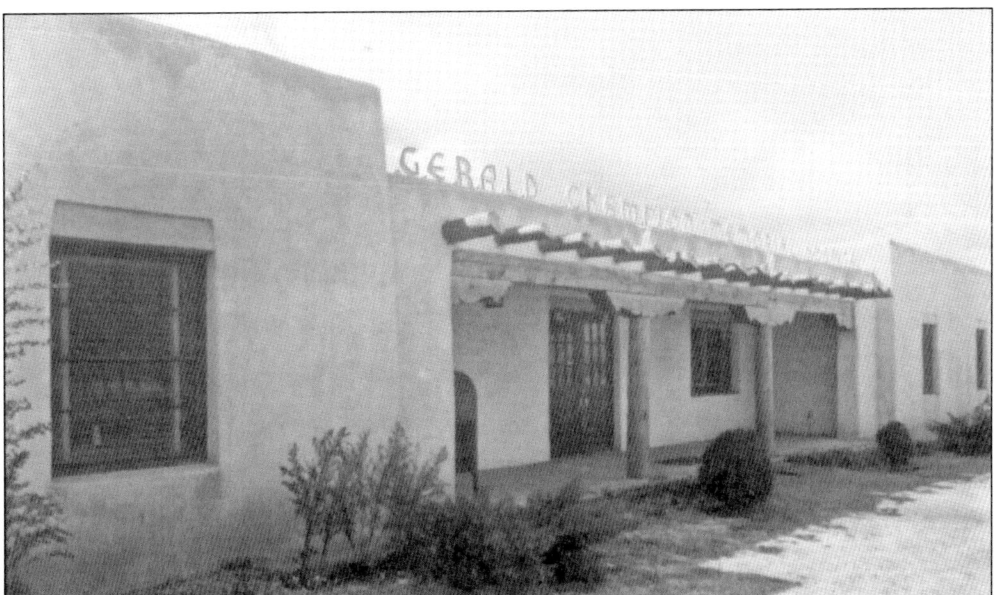

The original Gerald Champion Hospital was the first of several modern incarnations, which replaced the small railroad hospital from earlier days. (Courtesy of Millicent Shyne.)

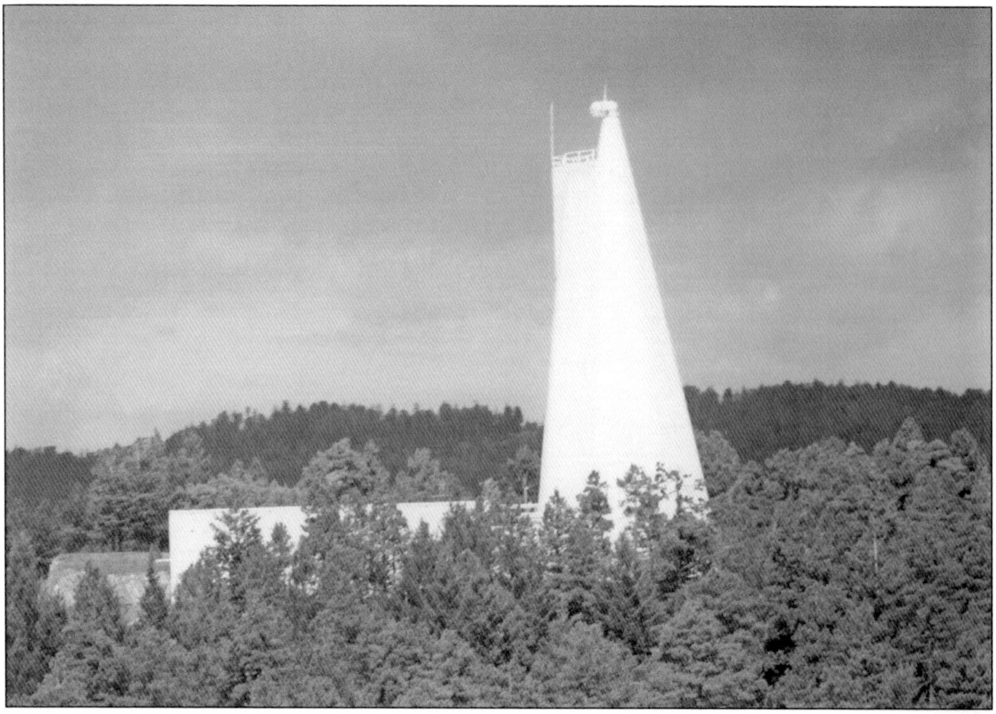

The monumental Dunn Tower Telescope at Sacramento Peak Observatory, started in 1958, stands 136 feet above the crest of the Sacramento Mountains, and extends 193 feet below ground, all floating on a bearing of mercury. (Courtesy of TBHS.)

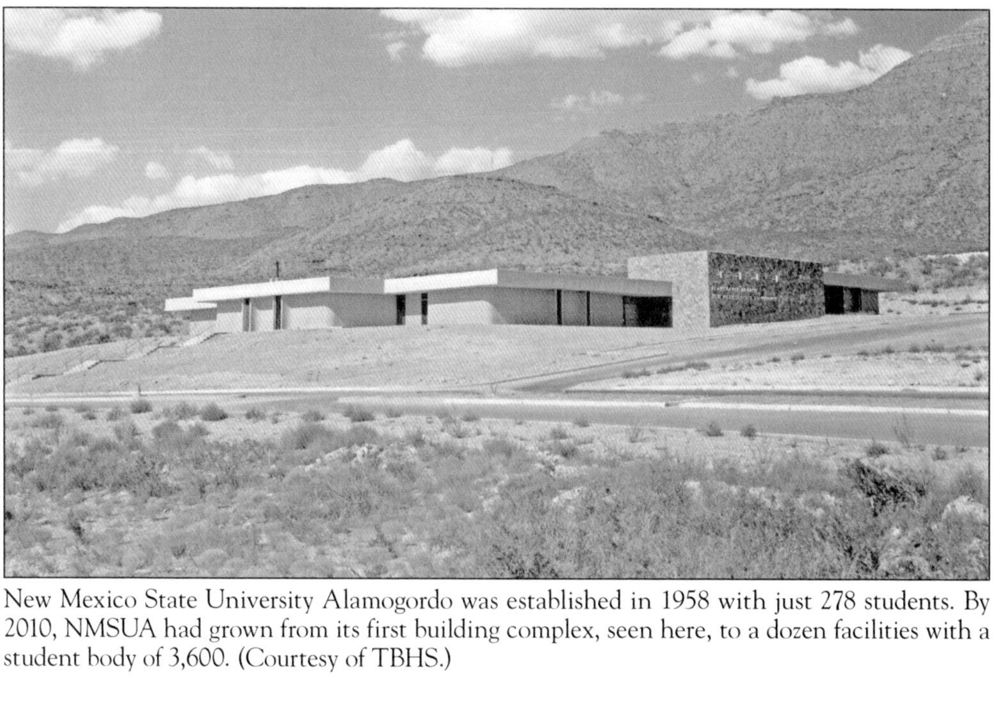

New Mexico State University Alamogordo was established in 1958 with just 278 students. By 2010, NMSUA had grown from its first building complex, seen here, to a dozen facilities with a student body of 3,600. (Courtesy of TBHS.)

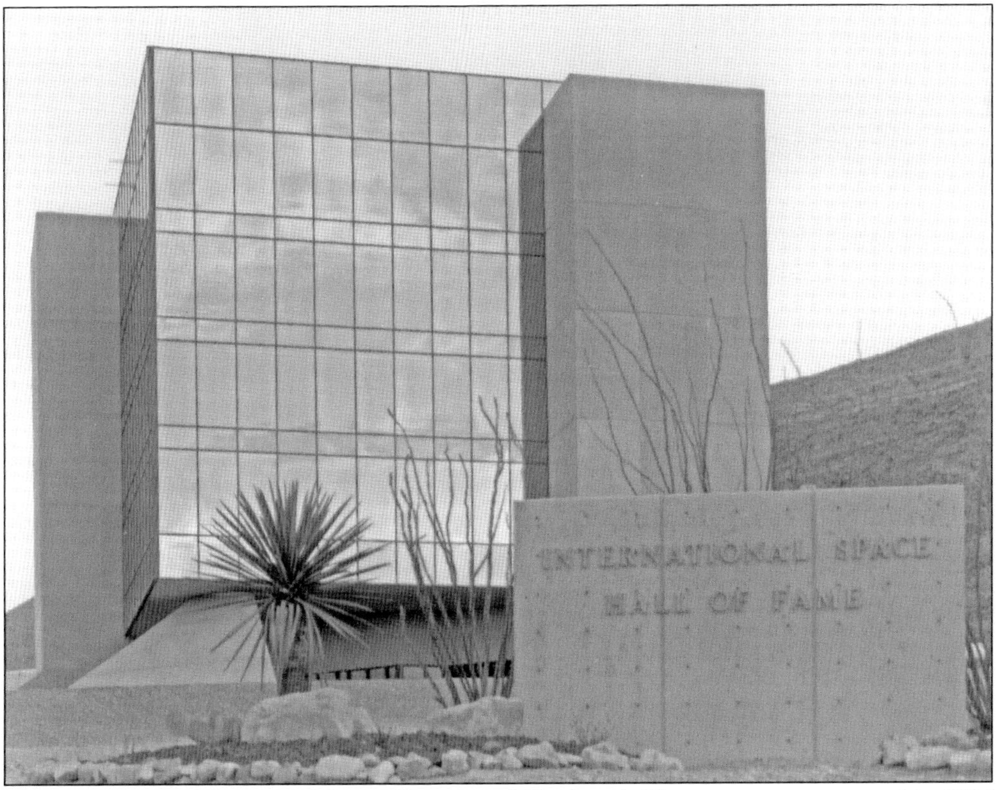

The New Mexico Museum of Space History and Tombaugh Planetarium were started in 1976 to document and preserve the region's unique contributions to the birth of space and missile technology. (Courtesy of TBHS.)

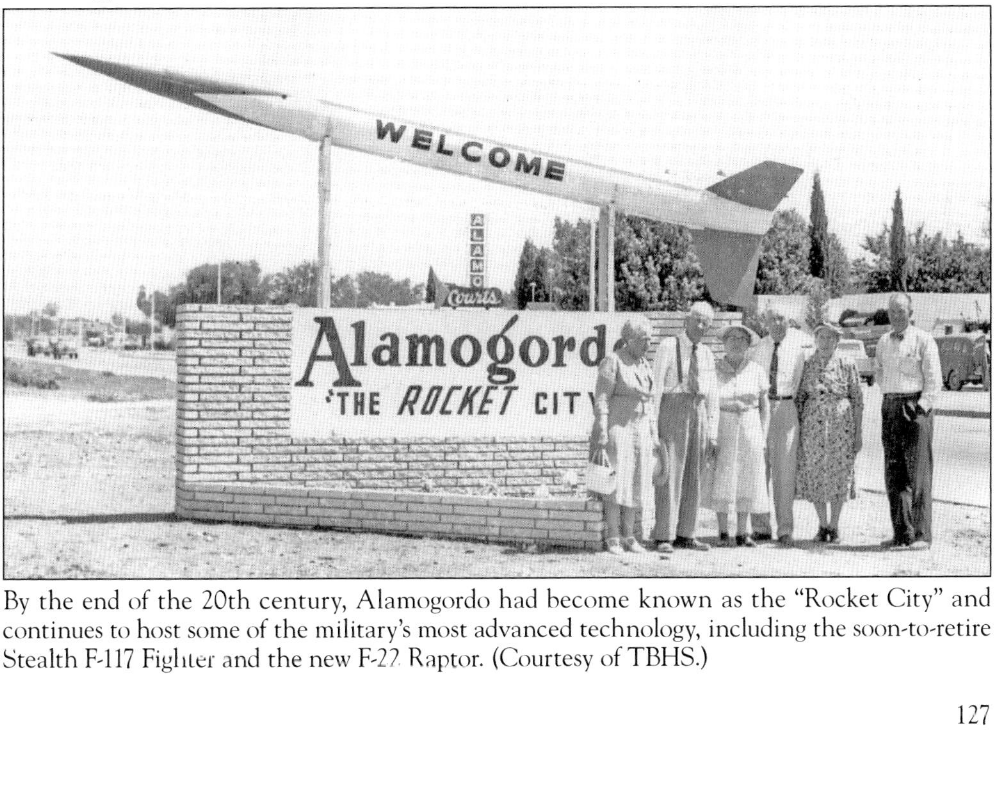

By the end of the 20th century, Alamogordo had become known as the "Rocket City" and continues to host some of the military's most advanced technology, including the soon-to-retire Stealth F-117 Fighter and the new F-22 Raptor. (Courtesy of TBHS.)